Waiting for Someone to Explain It

The Rise of Contempt and Decline of Sense

ROBERT HAGELSTEIN

LACUNAE MUSING

North Palm Beach, Florida

2019

Library of Congress Control Number: 2019903013

ISBN: 978-0-578-47672-8

Copyright © 2019 by Robert Hagelstein

First published in 2019
Lacunae Musing, North Palm Beach, FL
http://lacunaemusing.blogspot.com/

The Cover

The Photos on the cover were obtained from Wikimedia and licensed under Creative Commons. They have all been manipulated, resized or rearranged for artistic expression by Cover Designer S. M. Savoy.

- Obama and Putin, by Ranan Lurie
- Originally posted to Flickr by DonkeyHotey at https://flickr.com/photos/47422005@N04/22496487856. English: President Putin walking the media dog, Date 23 April 2008, Source Welleman
- Edited version of File: Yokozuna Trump vs. The RNC (23084608863).jpg and File: Cnn logo red background.png, Edited version of File:Yokozuna Trump vs. The RNC (23084608863).jpg and File: Cnn logo red background.png, 4 July 2017
- Rush Limbaugh Cartoon by Ian D. Marsden of marsdencartoons.com 6 March 2009, 17:39 Author Ian Marsden from Montpellier
- Cartoon of Ahmadinejad in New York, 17 April 2008, self-made, by Peter Welleman, also owner of the site www.funpx.com, where only Peter Welleman's work is published.
- The source image for this caricature of Congressman Todd Akin is a Creative Commons licensed photo from the <a href="https://www.flickr.com/photos/mobikefed/3350904282/">MoBikeFed's Flickr photostream. Todd Akin's co-sponsor Paul Ryan, DonkeyHotey
- Hillary Diane Rodham Clinton, aka Hillary Clinton, is a former Secretary of State, Senator from New York and First Lady of the United States. Clinton was a candidate for President of the United States in 2016. This caricature of Hillary Clinton was adapted from a Creative Commons licensed photo from Gage Skidmore's Flickr photostream.
- Black lives matter James Comey, odd AkinCaricatures of Paul RyanArt works by DonkeyHoteyPolitical cartoons from the United States presidential election, 2012United States Senate election in Missouri, 2012
- This caricature of Donald Trump was adapted from Creative Commons licensed images from Gage Skidmore's flickr photostream. 16 June 2016, 12:02, Donald Trump - Riding the Wrecking Ball Author DonkeyHotey

Printed in the United States of America

Digital books produced by Booknook.Biz

For my wife, Ann, my sons, Chris and Jonathan,
and daughter, Tracie

and

thanks to Ron and Bruce for their advice
and encouragement

CONTENTS

Introduction vii

Chronology 1

    09/11/2001 (2008 Entry) 1

    2007 4

    2008 7

    2009 30

    2010 73

    2011. 111

    2012 149

    2013 181

    2014 202

    2015 214

    2016 231

    2017 263

    2018 291

Appendix 309

    About the Author. 310

    A Special Day, A Special Woman 313

    Visiting the Past to See the Future 317

    Thoughts on Veterans Day. 326

    A Short Story 330

INTRODUCTION

How could a Donald Trump ascend to the Presidency of the United States? How can a $22 trillion national debt, steadily growing, be relegated to ho-hum news? Eugène Ionesco's program notes for his play *The Chairs* said "As the world is incomprehensible to me, <u>I am waiting for someone to explain it</u>." And while most of us have subliminally grappled with the anxiety of that broader existential statement, over the years I've speculated about the factors contributing to our growing political and economic turmoil, not to mention the polarization and dumbing-down of civil discourse.

In a way, it is the very methodology of history which compelled me to write this book. Histories are backward looking as they wrestle with the "facts," try to interpret them, and then build a thesis on them. This book is a history of sorts, or at least it touches some of the same data points that historians refer to. I don't have a problem with histories; they're very compelling reading. But, like Ionesco, I'm still waiting for the explanation!

There is nothing like the data points themselves—albeit anecdotal datum as they are selective in nature—and an immediate contemporaneous account (although written with a definite point of view). In effect this is a kaleidoscopic chronology of one person's (the ubiquitous "everyman") reaction to the political and economic developments of our times.

Most of the account of this 10 year plus time span is from my blog, *LacunaeMusing.com*. "La·cu·nae (-n) or la·cu·nas: An empty space or a missing part; a gap." I have been asked what

I meant by the blog's title and I credit a publisher I admired at McGraw Hill, Curtis Benjamin (who was also a former neighbor in Weston, CT). Benjamin labeled increasing specialization "the twigging phenomenon"—the tree of knowledge constantly developing new limbs as scholarship and scientific discoveries blaze forward. I wondered how Curtis Benjamin would see the Internet world, the ultimate in customized, personalized, specialized publishing. No doubt he would see it as an opportunity as I have to use the medium to muse about my life, interests and experiences over time.

If the audience is so specialized, why publish this book? Although so many of the entries in the blog itself pertain to my family and friends, boating, music, theatre, books, travels, and publishing, there are also those connected to broader issues of our world, politics, economics, and existential issues. The entries have been winnowed so the subjects discussed in this book are universal, the very ones impacting contemporary society.

Little did I know when I first posted on Wednesday, November 14, 2007 that we were at the beginning of an historic political and economic pivot point. Over time the content morphed into these broader areas, becoming a work of both a memoirist and an advocacy essayist.

The 1990s began with relatively low growth but federal spending cuts began to put the economy on course to declining federal deficits, turning a federal surplus beginning in 1998 and lasting until 2001. Imagine that. Seems to be unthinkable less than 20 years later the national debt is now $22 trillion and the deficit continues to grow.

A catalyst for this, but not the underlying systemic reason, is the horror of 9/11. The ensuing war on terrorism, particularly the Iraq War, has been a contributor to the deficit but our lifestyle and values are at the foundation. We are a society which must have it all, immediately. Living with debt, be it consumer, student, or real estate has become a way of life.

In addition, when the Supreme Court elected George W. Bush President of the United States the die was cast for the polarization of our political system and those internal wars reached new heights during the Obama administration and now are in hyper drive under Trump.

Little did we know the degree of financial engineering that was being devised at the time by an increasingly unregulated Wall Street or its consequences. How could we have foreseen that the fomenting unrest in the Middle East would literally explode into our lives, right here, on our homeland on 9/11/2001?

I was not writing my blog yet. Having just retired, my wife and I were enjoying the so called fruits of our labor, having bought a home in Florida while still maintaining our boat in Norwalk, Connecticut for the summers. It was while we were on our boat that the unimaginable thunderclap of the Twin Towers resounded. The very first entry in this book is the only one out of chronological order as it describes that unthinkable event, the one that put so much in motion.

Writing is essential to me, perhaps more for accountability than anything else. We've all borne witness to the turbulent times covered by the blog. Thoughtful writing, even if off the mark, is different than being a passive participant in the march of events.

Brenda Ueland, in her classic *If You Want to Write; A Book about Art, Independence and Spirit* said "At last I understood that writing was about this: an impulse to share with other people a feeling of truth that I myself had. Not to preach to them, but to give it to them if they cared to hear it. If they did not—fine. They did not need to listen. That was all right too.... You should work from now on until you die, with real love and imagination and intelligence, at your writing or whatever work it is that you care about. If you do that, out of the mountains that you write some mole hills will be published....But if nothing is ever published at all and you never make a cent, just the same it will be good that you have worked."

And so I work. And so there is accountability.

A word about the organization: I've tried to allow the entries to speak for themselves as a chronology although it was inevitable that some editing had to be done to minimize redundancies and also connective thoughts had to be introduced to make some sense of transitions of topics and the evolution of them. I thought about writing that connective prose at the beginning of each calendar year, and in some instances I did, but normally, the transitions are not that neat. Thus anytime you see narrative in *italics* that is connective text.

Also, I've included an Appendix which includes a few entries of a personal nature, as they explain a little more about me and whatever biases I may have brought to contemporary observations. To further elucidate those, there is also a brief biography in the Appendix.

Robert Hagelstein, March, 2019

CHRONOLOGY

Thursday, September 11, 2008
That Infamous Day
9/11. It has been seven years but it seems like yesterday. We all remember where we were at that moment. The only comparable moment in my life is remembering where I was when President Kennedy was assassinated.

On Sept. 11, 2001 we were on our boat in Norwalk, Ct., a clear somewhat breezy day with a deep blue sky. We had the TV on and, in complete disbelief, the tragedy unfolded before our eyes.

Although we were fifty miles away, we could see the smoke drifting south from the Twin Towers. To this day I still feel that sense of incredulity. Did this really happen here? My son, Jonathan, had been interviewed only a couple of weeks before by Cantor Fitzgerald, and offered a job to work on the 102nd floor of One WTC. They lost 685 employees on that fateful day. Jonathan decided to take another job. Is it merely coincidence and accident that governs life's outcomes? Or is it simply Shakespeare's more cynical line from King Lear: "As flies to wanton boys, are we to the gods. They kill us for their sport."

My older son is the poet of our family and this is what he wrote on that very day. One line in particular resonates: "If Hell opened up, and swallowed my life, it could not compete with what witnessed, I." May we never forget:

"9/11/2001
By Chris Hagelstein

Terrorist troops and bodies strewn
in Twin Tower screams, destruction loomed.
News stations on a journalistic mission
under our Flag's lost transmission:
America's Death.

Judgement of Religious Decree
driving Boeing bombs with air fuel
circulating vultures from above the sea,
smashing their prey
on this plain sun-filled day.

Television digital debris rained on video,
Looping the same sequence of carnage.
The surgery of media controlled the flow
but the State of Blood remained unknown.

Prayers beneath each citizen's eyes
were blessed wells now, for those who died.
No ceremony or speech could render a conclusion:
Those wired images played seemed like an illusion.

An Eye of some god was seeing us All
for each one's Blindness, was another's Call,
and in the skies above Manhattan, masked in smoke
exhumed old gods of hatred and hope.

If Hell opened up, and swallowed my life,
It could not compete with what witnessed, I:
Buildings falling and heroes crushed:

As day burned to night
and life—to dust.

Still, yet, in my hearts dismay,
Born here, I stand, no less bleeding
than those who survived this day:
For America is my body and my sea
executed on the stage of history."

His poem, which he wrote that day, is a first-hand emotional account of the horror and the hope. This is how we all felt and I remember our country briefly coming together. Unfortunately, Trump "remembers" it divisively, saying," Hey, I watched when the World Trade Center came tumbling down. And I watched in Jersey City, New Jersey, where thousands and thousands of people were cheering as that building was coming down. Thousands of people were cheering....It was on television. I saw it."

I give President Bush credit for going to the Islamic Center of Washington, D.C. less than a week after the tragedy to deliver a speech "Islam is Peace" to the American people and to reassure Muslim Americans. It is the easy path to foment racial hatred after such an event as Trump did and still does, but Bush had a different message: "America counts millions of Muslims amongst our citizens, and Muslims make an incredibly valuable contribution to our country. Muslims are doctors, lawyers, law professors, members of the military, entrepreneurs, shopkeepers, moms and dads. And they need to be treated with respect. In our anger and emotion, our fellow Americans must treat each other with respect." It made me feel proud to be an American, but that feeling eroded until President Obama was elected.

By then the economy was subliminally deteriorating and political divisiveness was beginning to build to a crescendo and that's about the time I innocently started my writing, more for personal reasons, but it quickly morphed into a mission to present the observations and views from the grassroots, an act of hubris thinking of it as a modern day Samuel Pepys' Diary which covered the turbulent events of his day such as the Great Plague, the Great Fire of London, as well as his day to day minutiae, like shaving. I've tried to leave out the shaving and although mine was not a daily blog, I've written it for more than ten years now. Pepys' Diary covers 1660-1669.

My earliest "political entry" was posted as the 2007 Presidential primaries were just heating up. It is laughable how naïve, although not altogether inaccurate, my main concerns were at the time. Bear in mind, the true state of the economy was yet an enormous iceberg under the surface and the Middle East (in the wake of the ill advised Iraq War) dominated thinking, making energy independence a key to both economic growth and addressing environmental concerns. We were not fully fracking for oil then, nor was our natural gas industry in full bloom. These subsequently have made us more energy independent but environmental concerns still abound, particularly those of global warming. So, my main argument, one for a "solar energy candidate" still has a ring of truth, simplistic though it seems in retrospect. Already, though, I was concerned about our most one-dimensional solution to all ills: borrow from tomorrow:

Sunday, December 2, 2007
Politics as Usual—Where is a Leader?
It is that time of the year—political demagoguery to seek the presidential nomination. No wonder it is easy to become inured to politics. Not one candidate exhibits the qualities of leadership but, instead, each is busy tearing down the other, trying to appease every voter. Politics as usual. Leadership as usual.

Whatever you might think of John F. Kennedy, he knew how to articulate an objective and rally the nation behind his viewpoint, albeit he was also a crafty politician—perhaps one of the best in my lifetime.

The Cold War was at its peak when he took office and behind the guise of exploring space and shortly after the Bay of Pigs fiasco in Cuba, Kennedy threw down the gauntlet on May 25, 1961: "I believe that this nation should commit itself to achieving the goal, before this decade is out, of landing a man on the moon and returning him safely to the Earth." It was a masterful stroke to rekindle American pride in the post Sputnik era and to establish a battleground in the Cold War (unfortunately, the other one being Viet Nam which was gradually being funded at the same time).

I remember how preposterous and unbelievable this objective seemed at the time, surely an impossible one to achieve. It was something more likely to come out of H. G. Wells or Jules Verne rather than the President of the United States. But I also remember sitting in an apartment on the upper west side of NYC with my future wife (Ann) on July 20, 1969 watching Neil Armstrong taking that "one small step for [a] man, one giant leap for mankind."

How does this relate to today's Presidential race? Where is the candidate who says, "If you elect me I will dedicate our country to achieving energy independence within a decade?" And this must be the central message of our future leader as all other issues, and in particular the economy and the environment, stem from our addiction to oil.

I remember the GE science fairs that were given at NYC high schools in the 1950's. The prototype of a solar power car was shown on stage and, then, when a spotlight was focused on its solar cells, the car slowly moved across the stage. It was proclaimed that this would be the car of the future in twenty-five years! The rudimentary technology existed even then, but as gas was 23 cents a gallon and we were able to produce the majority of our energy needs domestically, we did not need the backbone to commit our nation's resources to alternative energy. And at that time we were unaware of the long-term effect of fossil fuels on our environment.

While the goal of putting a man on the moon within the decade sounded impossible in 1961, energy independence indeed will be impossible without committing to it as a national goal. Failing to achieve that will leave our nation hostage to foreign interests. We think we are fighting the war on terrorism in Iraq. That war is stealthily brewing closer to home as our dollar declines, foreign interests are buying up assets, and we continue to mortgage our future by borrowing.

Not only do we have to create better incentives for conservation, but we have to use, further perfect, and expand our proven nuclear, solar, fuel cell, hydrogen, and wind technologies not to mention the newer tidal and wave technologies. Honda has already produced a hydrogen car that gets 68 miles to the gallon, the only "waste" product being water. Is anyone in Detroit or Washington listening?

If one of the presidential candidates ran solely on the platform of energy independence by 2017, he/she has my vote.

The dimensions of the crack in our economy began to become more readily visible, even to "everyman" and I began to focus on those issues (other entries at the time were dealing mostly with personal history and literature). This took a leap in fortifying my knowledge base and I sought out experts, an eclectic group including political analysts, economists, journalists, bloggers, and novelists, frequently quoting them when necessary. While financial markets were roiling, the depth of these problems became clearer and an existential threat to our political and economic system. These entries had a whiff of histrionics, but no wonder at the time. And no one foresaw what fracking and increased natural gas production would eventually mean for energy independence down the road, albeit not a permanent solution to energy demands promised by alternative energy.

Sunday, January 20, 2008
A Perfect Financial Storm?
The downgrade of AMBAC's financial-strength rating, and the possibility of downgrades of other bond insurers, including MBIA, could be the beginning of a perfect financial storm. These companies jumped onto the sub-prime lending train, along with major Wall Street financial institutions, to profit from the practice of providing credit to less than creditworthy customers, and with the encouragement of Washington to bring the American dream of homeownership to everyone. While the latter is a nice politically correct thought, greedy investors went along for the ride too, buying up "investment property" and homeowners indulged in the practice of using their homes as a piggy bank to buy luxury items. They used cheap money (thanks to the Federal Reserve) and exotic no money down, no interest payment loans, the repayment of which was dependent on future appreciated real estate values. This pot was mixed by mortgage brokers who could now sell off these loans in neat packages through Wall Street firms, with guarantees from the likes of AMBAC and MBIA. This brings us to the point of this post.

The bond insurers strayed from their main businesses in their greedy pursuit of a piece of the action, and that is their role insuring new municipal bonds. Cities and counties are dependent on reasonably priced debt to make investments in education and infrastructure. The bond insurers made it possible for many municipal bonds to attain AAA ratings, keeping their borrowing costs relatively low. Whether the bond insurers could actually cover a financial Armageddon, even without the CDO mess, is another issue, but so much of finance and investment is really about confidence, and this is what AMBAC and MBIA insurance conveyed.

Now, we are on the edge of a recession or we are already in one, and how deep it will be and how long, no one can tell, even by our Federal Reserve Chairman, Mr. Bernanke (who has not yet acknowledged we are in a recession). Municipal revenues are already under pressure due to falling property values. Add to that mix a severe recession, uncontrolled energy costs and their inability to raise capital, or at least at a reasonable cost without the bond insurers, and one has the perfect financial storm for dramatically decreased spending, loss of jobs, and lack of confidence in the financial system all of which just feeds upon itself in a deepening crisis.

Our chicken-little representatives on both sides of the isle are clucking an economic stimulus package such as throwing a few hundred dollars at everyone to spend immediately. Maybe we'll borrow the money from China or one of the other BRIC countries. Why not, we seem to be content to mortgage our future for immediate gratification.

It seems that a better thought out plan is needed to fix the present structural deficiencies of the financial system. It also wouldn't hurt to find sounder ways to fund this beginning with reducing the financial hemorrhaging of the Iraq war, not to mention getting our troops home. The "guns and butter" approach has failed us before.

Friday, February 8, 2008
Tautological Economics
After the Federal Reserve successfully contributed to a real estate bubble which has yet been allowed to completely unwind, Congress could not resist scoring political points, approving a $168 billion economic "rescue" package, the majority of which will be given to taxpayers as rebate checks. The political tag

team of President Bush and House Speaker Nancy Pelosi said the following:

Bush: "This plan is robust, broad based, timely, and it will be effective."

Pelosi: "We are making history. What has passed the Congress in record time is a gift to the middle class and those who aspire to it in our country."

While the part of the package that increases the level of expenses that businesses can immediately write off would seem to make sense, as this incentive is almost certain to guarantee investments in new capital equipment and is sure to stimulate job creation, the "gift" part is tantamount to handing a drunk a cheap bottle of wine.

True, it is in keeping with Keynesian economics, the theory being that this handout will be spent by the consumer and will reverberate throughout the economy. As noted in a footnote in a speech given by Ben Bernanke in 2002 before he was Chairman of the Federal Reserve, "Keynes once semi-seriously proposed, as an anti-deflationary measure, that the government fill bottles with currency and bury them in mine shafts to be dug up by the public." Of course, that was before helicopters so we now have a better method of distributing money to the masses without having to haul our sorry butts off to a mine shaft.

At least Keynes might have been referring to currency already earned, but where is this $168 billion coming from? We're going to print it or borrow it at the expense of future generations. We will simply increase the deficit. Where will the money go? Maybe we'll buy some plasma TVs or other electronics at our local Wal-Mart, most of which is made in China, the country that will be lending us the money so we can make those purchases. This would seem to be a form of tautological economics but if it works, why not borrow $1.68 trillion instead of a mere $168 billion? We can use the larger refund as down payments on new mortgages to buy some depressed real estate. Everybody wins!

But getting back to reality, most of the money will probably go to pay off debt, but given the extent of subprime and foreclosure issues, the rebates will only briefly push back the inevitable. In the 1980s we were able to deal with The Savings and Loan Crisis through the formation of the Resolution Trust Corporation. Shouldn't Congress be busy addressing our fragile economic system with a more permanent solution than just throwing money at the problem, a temporary fix at best?

It is hard to separate the people from the problem, problems whose tentacles reached into all aspects of our culture, society, our very democratic system. It increasingly became apparent how endemic the problem was in our culture. Borrow first, spend, and then worry about those loans in the future, while previous generations practiced saving first, not to mention most other cultures. As a moderate fiscal conservative (while being more socially liberal), this troubled me. Also personal indiscretions by our political leaders were becoming commonplace, or at least becoming more visible thanks to social media. The lack of moral leadership seemed to be more readily accepted by the public. And at this point the Presidential primaries were beginning and were turning into a spectacle, a form of entertainment for public amusement.

Monday, March 24, 2008
Silda, You Are Us
If you've seen the two brief news conferences where New York Governor Eliot Spitzer first admitted his appalling indiscretions and then when he announced his resignation, the image of the sad, shocked face of his wife, Silda, who stood by her man during the news conference, is indelibly etched in your mind's eye, as it is mine.

The microcosm of the event is bad enough, a man who over-zealously campaigned against the very thing he indulged in, one who was born into privilege and pursued power behind the veil of championing the public good. Perhaps self-loathing led him to become the Elmer Gantry of public prosecutors. His downfall might evoke the Aristotelian definition of tragedy, but it fails on the measure of not evoking pity. He got his just due. The only pity we can feel is for his wife and his children.

But as a metaphor, Silda's sad visage is emblematic of our own crisis, watching our country's cultural and economic decline. We stand by, helpless, shocked, bewildered.

American industry and values were once the envy of the world. The "arrogance of power," as the late Senator Fulbright put it ("the tendency of great nations to equate power with virtue and major responsibilities with a universal mission"), dragged us into Vietnam and now Iraq. We seem to be content following naïve or morally corrupt political leaders, damn future genera-tions. Rack up debt, abandon the environment, and watch our educational system become one of the least effective of all devel-oped nations. Our financial institutions are so unstable that Federal Reserve is now financing the excesses of this decade, with unknown consequences in the future.

Our energy policy is suicidal, a stake in the heart of the dollar, as we are content to massively export our dollars abroad to feed an insatiable appetite for fossil fuels. Greater reliance on alternative energy, within our technological reach, remains elusive thanks to the lack of leadership. And we now share oil and basic material resources with rapidly developing emerging economies, and there is no world solidarity about how to deal with the consequences to the environment.

With no incumbents running for the presidency, we might have had a chance to begin to expunge short-term thinking from the political agenda. But the Democratic primaries have dissipated into political demagoguery, with race rising to the surface. Republican and Democratic candidates alike claim to have a "plan" to deal with the economy, education, the environment, Iraq, terrorism, but these "plans" seem like nothing more than sound bites to get elected.

To be effective, our new President needs to be inspirational, someone who knows how to unite disparate voices, reach across congressional isles, and mobilize the best minds to reverse our spiraling decline. One has to wonder where we would be if the popular vote had determined the Presidency in 2000. We now need to be concerned about the consequences if Democratic "super delegates" ignore the Democratic primary popular vote.

Saturday, March 29, 2008
"He that goes a-borrowing goes a-sorrowing"
Here is another maligned minority ready to blame others for its own actions, and expecting the taxpayer to foot the bill: "FORE-CLOSURE VICTIMS INVADE BEAR STEARNS HQ, PICKET JP MORGAN." It's not that our hearts do not go out to those people, but why should those not in foreclosure pay for another person's poor judgment or even avarice?

Lost in the recent high stakes financial shenanigans are the savers, people who did not avail themselves of "easy money," to buy homes beyond their economic reach. Or those who refused to be seduced by home equity loans to buy into the American dream of vacations, new cars, and the easy, beautiful life which assaults us in a continuous loop on the media. Or those retirees who are dependent on their savings and social security to see them through. They are everything our government is not: responsible, truthful, balancing their budgets at all costs.

How can we punish savers? Let's start by giving them investment options based on chimerical ratings that are established by rating agencies paid by the very institutions they are rating.

2008 13

Then let's ratchet down their income from CDs as we try to bail out an economy of credit excesses. Let helicopter dollars rain down on all to encourage more spending! But, that's not enough; let their government take an unprecedented $29 billion dollar risk, ultimately at the taxpayer's expense, to bail out the bond and equity holders of Bear Stearns (an action rationalized as needed to save our entire financial system). Let's also talk about eliminating a more progressive graduated income tax in favor of a flat tax so, when savers spend their savings, which have already been taxed once when they were first earned, let's tax them again via a national sales tax. While we're at it, let's also undermine the dollar and introduce inflation so their savings buy less. Then, finally, as social security benefits are adjusted by inflation, let's artificially understate the real inflation rate to further erode their benefits!

What would Ben Franklin say today, "He that goes a-saving goes a-slaving?"

Thursday, May 1, 2008
Friedman for President
It is not surprising that the most emailed article from yesterday's *New York Times*, is Thomas Friedman's "Dumb as We Wanna Be"

I've missed reading Friedman who just completed a sabbatical book-writing project that expands an article he wrote for the magazine section a year ago. The book version, *Hot, Flat, and Crowded: Why We Need a Green Revolution—and How It Can Renew America,* will be published in August.

Why not start a write-in campaign to elect Friedman President? He always seems to have the right perspective on foreign policy and our economic and energy crisis. I also like his even-tempered demeanor. Someone once said you have to be crazy to want to be the President of the United States. Maybe that is the problem with a plan for his Presidency. Friedman is not crazy.

He calls Clinton and McCain's proposal for a summer gas tax "holiday" political pandering (Amen) and a form of money laundering, borrowing from China, moving it to the oil producing nations, leaving a little in our gas tanks as the broker for the transaction, but also leaving our children with the debt. The analogy would be funny if it were not so sadly true.

But the rest of the article goes to the core of the problem, not having a game plan to achieve energy independence, and helping to repair our decaying environment along the way.

The ongoing political shenanigans over this issue and the lack of a plan are glaring. I had thought our current administration was just too clueless to grasp the importance of leading our nation to energy independence through alternative solar, wind, and geo-thermal technologies. Imagine my shock at seeing Laura Bush recently conducting a TV tour of their home in Crawford, Texas, which is replete with geothermal heating and cooling and a system for capturing rainwater and household wastewater for irrigation. I would have expected this from Al Gore, but George Bush?

His public environmental policies are in direct contrast to what he has done in his own home. So it is not a question of not knowing better, it's knowing better but not leading our country to a better place, an immoral travesty of the public trust. Where would we be today if we had thrown down the gauntlet at the beginning of his Presidency? By delaying a commitment to energy independence, we have made the goal even more difficult as we must now start with massive debt, and a devalued dollar.

Instead, we pour resources into ethanol with the unintended consequences of food shortages and burgeoning food prices. Sounds like a good plan, subsidize the farmers to buy seeds and fertilizer (at triple the cost vs. last year), squeeze out food crops and tax our water resources, buy oil for the energy needed to convert crops to ethanol (be sure to take on more debt to get that oil), and continue to watch fuel prices escalate in spite of increasing ethanol additives, while paying much more for all food staples (hoarding rice along the way).

Yesterday the Federal Reserve laughably said, "readings on core inflation have improved somewhat" (which excludes food and energy). Maybe it's time we go back to the Consumer Price Index as a fairer measurement of inflation so government has to face the real facts.

One of the interesting consequences of writing a blog is not only to be alert to the shifting winds of history and my opinion of the same, but also to identify the very point in time I recognized something extraordinary. It was here I drank the Kool-Aid of thinking Barack Obama could lead us out of the wilderness. In some ways he did. As a man of integrity he brought some much needed dignity to the Office and respect around the world, but it took me years to realize he would be no panacea for many of the issues eating away at our nation. One could blame him, or simply our entire political system or the increasing impact of social media and its ability to give voice to hate-filled extremists, hastening the polarization of political discourse. Enter Senator Obama to whom I wrote an "open letter."

Tuesday, May 13, 2008
Open Letter to Senator Obama
Dear Senator Barack Obama:

Does history make the man or does man make history? Rarely is there a confluence of events which might help answer that question and, with your presumptive Democratic nomination for the Presidency, you have the opportunity to make the kind of difference our founding fathers did at the birth of our nation, or Lincoln did bringing our nation back from the brink of self destruction, or Roosevelt's seeing us through the most destructive war in history.

Although one could cite a litany of maladies our nation now suffers from, at the core is our loss of credibility abroad, our lack of a national plan for energy independence, and the ongoing irreconcilability of conservative and liberal values and its resultant impact on the social fabric of race relations, religious tolerance and educational opportunities.

Your life reads like a microcosm of the United Nations, born to a black, Kenyan father who was raised a Muslim, and a white mother who you described as being "detached from religion," who later divorced your father and married an Indonesian; thus you attended schools in Jakarta until you were ten years old. But you then lived with your white grandmother's family in Honolulu until you graduated high school. You met your wife Michelle, an African American, while you interned in a law office and you were married at the time you became a Christian.

I came of age during the tumultuous late 50's and 60's as the civil rights movement and the cold war raged, as we became mired in a senseless war in Viet Nam, and painfully endured the assassinations of beloved leaders, John F, Kennedy, his brother Robert, and Martin Luther King. Then, we succumbed to the national disgraces of the 70's, a wrecked economy, becoming hostages to countries that hate us in the Middle East, American prestige sinking to new lows, and the age of Watergate politics. The one thing we could point to with pride was our ability to set a national goal as John F. Kennedy did in 1961, to put a man on the moon by the end of that decade and actually doing the unthinkable, the impossible.

Today is not too far removed from then. Our economic difficulties of mounting national debt and a declining dollar, a decaying infrastructure, and the lack of better healthcare for our sick and better education for our young can be traced to a needless war, and to being hostage, once again, to oil producing nations. Racial and religious divisiveness still erode the fabric of our society. The view of America abroad has undermined our ability to effectively deal with terrorism and to address global environmental issues. Politics again slithers along a slippery Machiavellian slope.

It is extraordinary that we could be at the brink of electing you, our first African American President. If these problems were less extreme, this moment may not have arrived. Senator Obama, seize the day, and use this unique opportunity as a conciliator, to help bridge the abyss between races and religions, leading us away from Iraq and towards energy independence. We have the alternative energy technology, the clean natural gas resources, and nuclear capability to substantially decrease our dependence on fossil fuels if only we could develop the backbone to sacrifice short-term gratification for long-term gains, declaring it as a national objective. By achieving energy independence, our economic problems will diminish.

Your opponents have criticized your limited political experience, making it one of their main issues in attacking your candidacy. Lincoln too was relatively inexperienced, something he made to work to his advantage. Forge cooperation across the aisle in congress, creating your own "team of rivals" as Doris Kearns Goodwin described his cabinet in her marvelous civil war history.

Some people have pointed to 9/11 as a manifestation of the clash between the Muslim and Christian worlds. Given your personal background, you have what may be a unique opportunity to establish a dialogue between these two worlds and in so doing begin to restore our international standing. Just electing you will demonstrate to the world that we can put our ideals into action.

Until editing this book, and rereading entries, I did not realize how panic-stricken I and many other were becoming. The gathering economic storm can plainly be seen in the next entry. But soon it was back to pure politics and my shock at the time that

John McCain named Sarah Palin as his running mate. The primaries were now fully underway and I became increasingly obsessed by the circus like atmosphere and blatant lying, presaging our present day. The primaries became conflated with the economic crisis that was underway.

Tuesday, June 10, 2008
We are the Enemy
On that unspeakable day of September 11, 2001 we were in Connecticut, packing for an overseas trip. While the horror unfolded we could see the smoke from the Twin Towers more than fifty miles away across the Long Island Sound against the clear blue sky. I had thought we were confronting the worst of all possible enemies, one that cared not at all about its own life—in fact reveled in martyrdom—one that shared none of our moral values and would be content to wage war guerrilla style with no time constraints.

But, since then, we seem to be waging the battle for them. They no longer have to hijack planes to fly into our buildings as we have hijacked our own economy and can now be held hostage by any dictatorship du jour.

Here's what we've done since that horrific day:

*Wage an unnecessary war in Iraq that has cost more than one half trillion dollars to date or $341 million each day
*Consume more than 20 million barrels of oil each day of which we produce only about a quarter, meaning we have to send about $2 billion abroad each day a majority of which finds its way to the Middle East, Russia, and South America.
* Increase our unfunded Social Security and Medicare programs by $33 trillion (yes, trillion) since 2000 to a total of $53 trillion at the end of last year—a liability of about $455,000 for every American household

There is a litany of others that could be added to this list, but suffice it to say, our national debt is increasing at $1.59 billion per day. No wonder the dollar continues to sink which just increases the cost of our imported oil and leaves us even a greater debtor to other countries.

If we cannot even acknowledge these economic truths, there can be no national plan to deal with the dire consequences. Then we will not only lose the war, but also be the architect of our own defeat.

Saturday, August 30, 2008
President Palin?
I am not the first to make this observation—in fact it is the most obvious, knee jerk reaction to John McCain's pick of a VP running mate, but I might as well add my two cents. If, indeed, the VP selection is the most critical decision of a Presidential wannabe, McCain demonstrates how seriously deficient his judgment may be. Given his age and his prior health problems, I think we, the voters, have to consider Governor Palin's credentials as if she is running for the Presidency.

No doubt Sarah Palin is an attractive, hard-working person—she certainly seems to come across as such in the media, but to possibly cast her in the role of the President of the United States seems to be just downright irresponsible by Senator McCain and as politically calculated, and demonstrating bad judgment, as some of his television ads.

Friday, September 12, 2008
And the presidency goes to....
Why bother having elections? Seems like we could have a version of the Academy Awards decide the winner—the party which takes the most Oscars wins the election! This way we can

recognize what has become central to the election process: mass media persuasion. No longer will we have to bother with the real issues, which have become subordinated to personality and presentation.

"And the Oscar for the best sound bite goes to ..."

As Main Street's political belief is manipulated by the images created by Madison Avenue types, let the big award of the evening go to the slickest national convention, with the supporting awards going to the best TV ads that pander to the emotional issues du jour. Special categories can go to the bloggers and the most forwarded email. As a bonus evening of entertainment before the awards, let MSNBC square off against FOX News with Jerry Springer as the moderator—the candidates themselves would not even be needed!

The electorate's decision now resembles a consumer decision, not decided on the merits of the "product" but instead on brand image, carefully manipulated by focus groups and emotional advertising. It seems that the entire process has gotten out of hand. How about banning political advertising (and thereby also saving $millions) and solely determine national elections by a series of debates?

Monday, September 22, 2008
This "fundamental" is whining ...
After Senator McCain declared the fundamentals of the economy were strong last week, he first defended his comment by saying that by "fundamentals" he meant us workers (first time I've been referred to as a "fundamental"—sort of makes me feel important) and then, finally, after the heavens opened up and Bernanke and Paulson rained down reality on the economic picture he not only conceded that a crisis had begun, but he also said the following at the Green Bay Chamber of Commerce: "We've heard a lot of words from Senator Obama over

the course of this campaign ... But maybe just this once he could spare us the lectures, and admit to his own poor judgment in contributing to these problems. The crisis on Wall Street started in the Washington culture of lobbying and influence peddling, and he was right square in the middle of it."

Huh? The political rhetoric from both sides has sometimes made me sick, enough to make me wish that Michael Bloomberg was running on a third party ticket, but McCain's claim is so egregious I just can't be silent.

To blame Obama while McCain has been in Congress for 26 years and was one of five United States Senators comprising the so-called "Keating Five" scandal during the 1980s and a present member of the United States Senate Committee on Commerce (although this committee does not have responsibility for the financial services industry) and until just last week has been a staunch advocate of deregulating financial markets, particularly supporting Senator Phil Gramm's bill in 1999 which deregulated some restrictions on the financial services sector. Gramm has become a lead economic advisor for McCain's presidential run, the same person who called us "fundamentals" a bunch of whiners, and the only economic problem we have is a "mental recession" (which he naturally blamed on the media, a favorite tactic McCain et al are using). In 1999 Obama was in the Illinois Senate and a Senior Lecturer teaching constitutional law at the University of Chicago Law.

So how exactly is Obama responsible for the present economic crisis?

Friday, September 26, 2008
Political Cynicism
Here is one way to define the concept. Lead our country to the brink of economic disaster. Have the very administration which brought us there propose an emergency $700 billion "fix" to

provide liquidity so our economic circulatory system does not seize up, the plan proposed by the Secretary of the Treasury and the Chairman of the Federal Reserve, with our President finally making a speech to the nation in which he warns of the dire consequences of Congress not acting immediately. Congressional hearings immediately ensue, with the Democratic majority buying into the need for action. Both sides of the isle agree to the basic principles, including oversight protection, and we are told a deal is imminent. But wait, the Republican presidential candidate returns to Washington, on his white horse, his pearl handle pistol at his side and suddenly there is no agreement. A dangerous game of chicken unfolds: "If the Democrats and the President want the plan, let them pass it" the Republican choir sings. Heads we win, tails you lose. America or politics first?

PS Washington Mutual was just closed by the US Government, the largest failure of a US bank.

After all the debates, accusations, theatrics of the campaign, finally, election night. I expressed my feelings the morning after while subsequent entries began to reveal just how deeply we were at the abyss of economic Armageddon, which ironically years later, with the help of short term memory, Obama would be blamed.

Wednesday, November 5, 2008
President-Elect Obama
We were up most of the night watching the election returns, hoping on the one hand, but afraid of the "Bradley effect" on the other, and almost resigned to that possibility. When the election was called at 11 o'clock, we let our guard down and had a joyous celebration of hugs, high fives and kisses with our son Jonathan who is visiting. It was a time for some tears alongside our brimming happiness.

Ann said she wishes she were thirty years younger just to see what the real outcome of this election might be. But we've already lived through some of the most tumultuous years in American history with perhaps only the Revolutionary and the Civil War eras rivaling the events our lifetimes: WWII, the Cold War, the Civil Rights movement, Kennedy's New Frontier and his assassination, the Vietnam War and its aftermath, the assassinations of Martin Luther King and Robert Kennedy, the ignominious resignation of Richard M. Nixon, the tearing down of the Berlin Wall, 9/11 and its aftermath including the uncalled-for war in Iraq, and finally the decline of our reputation abroad and our near economic bankruptcy.

I have no illusions that much will change in the near term, but at least we've set a new direction and I believe that is the main responsibility of a President, to establish a moral compass, define objectives, and rally the nation to participate in achieving them. No doubt this will require sacrifices and I think we're finally prepared to make those.

What an historic night. It makes me think of how we felt when we watched Neil Armstrong walk on the moon—it was with complete wonderment. To think our country has come this far. I wonder what our founding fathers would think of this election, a real validation of the ideals of our constitution (although it specifically postponed any action on slavery for at least the first twenty years of our young nation). However, like the Declaration of Independence, this election is also a statement to the rest of the world, something all Americans can take pride in, even with all the problems we must begin to address.

So we pass the baton to another generation, a generation that waged an incredible campaign—with the liberating technology of the Internet—to achieve what I thought would not be possible in my lifetime, electing an African American to our nation's highest office. Last May I wrote an "open letter" to

Senator Obama, before he was officially designated the Democratic Party's nominee. I still feel the same way.

One of the reasons I write this blog is to provide a personal, grassroots perspective on some of the major events of my lifetime. Last night was one of those moments.

Thursday, November 20, 2008
It's Different This Time
Those are the famous words that have been used to explain any stock market anomaly. They were used in the dot.com era as the NASDAQ approached 5,000 to justify the heady prices at the time, or when oil was leaping towards $150 per barrel. But any parabolic rise or fall must regress to the mean. Or so it's been in my lifetime

I need not go into detail here concerning all the dominant economic undercurrents of today, the toxic assets the TARP program was thought to be resolving, the government's support of the Bear Stearns takeover, the collapse of Lehman Brothers, the bailouts of AIG, Freddie and Fannie, the discussions of bailing out Detroit's automakers, the reverberations in the financial markets throughout the globe. However, as a child of depression era parents, I guess subliminally I've always feared the unspeakable: a deflationary spiral with no bottom in sight. And somehow if does FEEL different this time.

Having lived through several economic cycles and piloting a business through them, the implosion of equity values in the 70's, the subsequent threat of hyperinflation, the high interest rates of the early 80's, the collapse of real estate in the 90's, the dot.com run-up on the heals of dire Y2K warnings, and finally the easy money that led to this decade's real estate run up and the interconnected toxic financial instruments engineered by financial institutions and hedge funds to make them rich, leaving someone else (us) to hold the proverbial bag. But as a society we were willing participants, eagerly spending what we didn't have; let future generations do the worrying! Our entire culture cried out buy, why postpone what you can have today, so we bought McMansions, Hummers, luxury goods, vacations, whatever our consumptive libidos desired, using our homes and credit cards as piggy banks.

And that is why this economic era does feel different than prior ones, at least to me, someone who has lived through these various cycles but only in the shadow of the Great Depression. We are just beginning to embark on the convulsive purging of these excesses. How it will end is anyone's guess. Even Secretary of the Treasury, Hank Paulson, looks like a deer in the headlights, changing his mind about using the $700 billion to buy bad mortgage debt securities (the very $$ Congress had to immediately authorize as financial Armageddon was imminent), probably because he knows it's not enough. And humbled Alan Greenspan, looking completely bewildered in his testimony to Congress in late October: "I made a mistake in presuming that the self-interests of organizations, specifically banks, were such as that they were best capable of protecting their own shareholders and their equity in the firms. Free markets did break down, and I think that, as I said, that shocked me. I still don't fully understand how it happened or why it happened."

We had long placed Mr. Greenspan on a pedestal, trying to decipher "Greenspeak," looking for little nuggets of wisdom to reassure ourselves that this time it was different as he ratcheted down interest rates for our borrowing pleasure. Now he is clearly admitting he has no clue why the present economic catastrophe has devolved. At least he can afford to admit his misjudgments, as he is no longer the Chairman of the Federal Reserve. But we now listen to Mr. Bernanke and Mr. Paulson, desperately clinging to the hope THEY know what they're talking about. The only certainty now is nothing is predictable. It's different this time.

One entry revealed the tip of an iceberg which would later be called "fake news" by Trump. This was quickly followed by real news about the depth of the coming crisis, and then Madoff reared his ugly head.

Wednesday, December 3, 2008
The Press is the Enemy
Amazing to read some of the latest Nixon tapes, particularly his comments on the media and academics, a leitmotif of the 2008 campaign as Republicans condemned the media and intellectual conservatives deserted the Party.

"Never forget," Nixon tells national security adviser Henry Kissinger in a taped 1972 Oval Office conversation, "The press is the enemy. The establishment is the enemy. The professors are the enemy. Professors are the enemy," he repeated. "Write that on a blackboard 100 times and never forget it."

Here is Sarah Palin's response to Katie Couric's question "Do you think the coverage of you has been sexist?"

"No, I don't. I mean, I know that there—it's obvious there's some double-standards here, you know, in terms of what the media has been doing, but I think that's more—I think more attributable to just the media elite, the Washington elite, not knowing who I am and just asking a whole lot of questions and not so much based on gender though, but based on just the fact that I'm not part of the Washington herd."

Wednesday, December 10, 2008
Anecdotal Headline Annotations
If I was handed a copy of today's *Wall Street Journal* only a couple of years ago, I would have thought the headlines were a forecast of an ethical and economic Armageddon.

How otherwise does one interpret the following captions, from just one day's newspaper?

"*Governor Jailed in Alleged Crime Spree
*AIG Faces $10 Billion in Losses on Trades
*Fannie, Freddie Executives Knew of Risks
*Restaurant Jobs, Like Tips, Shrink
*Panel to Criticize Handling of Bailout
*Specifics of Stimulus Take Shape
*Pressure Mounts on Merkel for Bigger Fiscal Boost
*Drop in Japan Tool Orders Exposes Global Spending Cutbacks
*Developing Countries Feel Slump
*Auto Bailout Moves Closer; Senate Battle Next Hurdle
*Sony to Cut 8,000 Jobs, Close Factories
*Resorts Feel Chill From Recession
*GM Sees Sales Plunge in Brazil
*NFL to Cut Jobs in Face of Recession
*New York Times Holds Talks With Lenders
*Safety Trumps Yield in Bill Sales. Investors Scoop Up 0%
    Short-Term Notes
*Fed Weighs Selling Own Line Of Debt
*Securities Firms Claw Back at Failed Bets
*Families Cut Back on Day Care As Costs—and Worries—Rise"

These headlines are pretty much in order as they appear and although they are selective, there are no offsetting, positive ones. Perhaps that is merely a tendency towards yellow journalism to sell papers. But no wonder we all live in a state of anxiety without any real explanation as to how we have arrived at this point (although many commentators are adept to spinning plausible stories with the advantage of hindsight) and, certainly, without understanding how the forces behind these stories might play out in the future.

Monday, December 15, 2008

Madoff Bailout?

Why not? Every other deserving group gets one. Too big to fail! And, according to the WSJ, maybe through the Securities Investor Protection Corporation (SIPC) there may be a back door in covering some of the losses, although the SIPC only has $1.5 billion left in its coffers and there will have to be congressional action to increase the kitty.

When the tide goes out the muck materializes. For years Madoff reported steady returns from the firm's "split-strike" conversion strategy, one of balancing puts and calls around a basket of large cap stocks and, presto, "steady" returns of some 7–9% no matter what the market does. Hint: when it's too good to be true. . . .

Midas Madoff sucked in his friends from the Palm Beach Country Club and Fund of Funds from around the world into the scheme (but, unfortunately many charitable and endowment funds as well). As one skeptical research firm, Aksia, reported to its clients concerning Madoff Securities, "We concluded that Friehling & Horowitz (Madoff's audit firm) had three employees, of which one was 78 years old and living in Florida, one was a secretary, and one was an active 47 year old accountant (and the office in Rockland County, NY was only 13ft x 18ft large). This operation appeared small given the scale and scope of Madoff's activities." The entire audit trail consisted of paper transaction confirmations, which Madoff, himself, closely controlled. It finally took a market downturn of the magnitude of this past year, with redemption requests from Madoff's clients, to finally expose the Ponzi scheme. The SEC couldn't see this?

According to the *Palm Beach Post*, "investors needed at least $1 million to approach Madoff [and] being a member of the [Palm Beach Country] Club also helped. But even with those prerequisites there was little guarantee that Madoff would take the client." Sort of the same deferential respect as demanded by the Soup Nazi in the Seinfeld series.

The incident is yet another regulatory failure and another corrupt Joker in our economic house of cards.

Friday, December 19, 2008
Another Ponzi Scheme
Tom Friedman made this observation but here's some more documentation from the *New York Times*:

While Bernie Madoff was "making off" with his illegal Ponzi scheme, ignored by the SEC in spite of sufficient smoking guns everywhere, Wall Street, the banking industry, and mortgage brokers, went blithely along with its own "legal" Ponzi scheme:

* Borrowing cheap money courtesy of the Fed
* Lending it out with exotic mortgage deals, including nothing down zero interest rate loans, the interest being added to the principal, to borrowers of little ability to pay back the loans, except if real estate values pyramid to infinity
* Packaging these subprime mortgages into CMOs to be sold to gullible investors throughout the world—emphasizing their safety because of "diversification" and AAA debt ratings conferred by rating agencies, based on chimerical insurance contracts issued by under-capitalized firms.

Everyone in the Wall Street food chain got rich. As the *Times* article pointed out, in 2008 "Merrill handed out $5 billion to $6 billion in bonuses that year. A 20-something analyst with a base salary of $130,000 collected a bonus of $250,000. And a 30-something trader with an $180,000 salary got $5 million." The head mortgage trader for Merrill, Dow Kim, had a salary of $350,000 but with his bonus he "earned" $35 million.

But these riches were based on income that really did not exist, the profits that we, as taxpayers are now trying to restore to our financial system via the bonanza bailout program. Meanwhile, Bernie Madoff is allowed to stay out of jail, putting up "his" Manhattan townhouse as bail, bought with funds from his clients, and Wall Street whiz kids walk around with what is really taxpayer money.

"As a result of the extraordinary growth at Merrill during my tenure as C.E.O., the board saw fit to increase my compensation each year."—E. Stanley O'Neal, the former chief executive of Merrill Lynch, March 2008

Monday, January 12, 2009
Bailout Math and Implications
In an effort to try to understand the more than $8 trillion guarantee our government has made to bailout our financial mess, I tried to assemble a spreadsheet and before long I was drowning in acronyms and conflicting information that was beginning to remind me of an elaborate shell game a Bernie Madoff might have constructed. How can we manage to make transparency so confusing?

To the rescue, though, is a magnificent, clear summary published by Bianco Research which came to my attention through the *From Behind the Headlines* blog by Michael Kahn. Here is a summary of Bianco's work (figures are in billions):

"Measuring the Size of the Bailouts

THE FEDERAL RESERVE (Net Portfolio Commercial Paper Funding,
Term Auction Facility, Other Assets, Money Market Investor Funding Facility, MBS/FHLB Agency in Reverse Auctions,

Term Securities Lending Facility, AIG Loan, Primary Credit Discount, Asset Backed Commercial Paper Liquidity, Primary Dealers and Others, Bear Stearns Assets, Securities Lending Overnight, Secondary Credit)
FEDERAL RESERVE TOTAL $5,065.0 Maximum / $1,839.5 Current

THE FDIC (FDIC Liquidity Guarantees, Loan Guarantee to GE)
FDIC TOTAL $1,539.0 Maximum / $139.0 Current

TREASURY DEPARTMENT (Fannie/Freddie Bailout, Spring 08 Stimulus Package, Treasury Exchange Stabilization Fund, Tax Break for Banks, Citibank Asset Backstop, Tem Asset-Backed Securities Loan Facility)
TREASURY DEPT TOTAL $1,803.0 Maximum / $597.0 Current

FHA (Hope for Homeowners) $300 Maximum / $300 Current

DEPT ENERGY (Auto Loans) $25 Maximum / $25 Current

GRAND TOTAL $8,707.0 Maximum / $2,875.5 Current

Here is a translation of how this looks in "real dollars:
$8,707,000,000,000/$2,875,500,000,000"

These staggering figures are before the Obama infrastructure / jobs programs get into full swing, so we can be talking about more than $9 trillion. To put this in perspective, according to the Congressional Budget Office GDP in 2009 will be $14.2 trillion, while outlays will be $3.5 trillion and total revenues $2.3, a deficit of some $1.2 trillion.

This assumes we can have confidence in government projections. Looking at the real world in a rear view mirror, this is how the budget deficits have been ramping up the National Debt since the Bush administration took office:

9/30/2000 $5,674,178,209,887
9/30/2001 $5,807,463,412,200
9/30/2002 $6,228,235,965,597
9/30/2003 $6,783,231,062,744
9/30/2004 $7,379,052,696,330
9/30/2005 $7,932,709,661,724
9/30/2006 $8,506,973,899,215
9/30/2007 $9,007,653,372,262
9/30/2008 $10,024,724,896,912
1/8/2009 $10,608,325,323,173

I include the latest figure (more than a $½ trillion increase in only 100 days) as it shows a parabolic trend. The extent to which the bailouts work is going to enormously impact the budget projections, both on the revenue and outlay sides of the ledger. Tweaking the former down because of the severity of the recession and the latter upwards because of more bailouts puts us on an irreversible course. It was not long ago that the main discussion concerning the long-term budget centered on the ticking time bombs of Social Security, Medicare, and Medicaid. These threats have not disappeared, but they become even more formidable as our precious resources have to be spent on surviving today to wage that war tomorrow.

Wednesday, January 14, 2009
The Bernie Reality Show
What a brave new financial world, one that can produce the confluence of a Bernie Madoff, his feeder funds, the regulatory (that is the lack of regulations) environment where such

a Ponzi scheme could thrive over decades, and the eager investors who convinced themselves that their steady "returns" in good and bad markets were an entitlement of their connections and station in life (as Jane Austen might have put it), not to be questioned by them. Now there is the endless media frenzy over Madoff, even including a camera trained on Madoff's apartment building in NYC. This is the perfect diversion from the more serious financial landscape of trillion dollar bailouts with consequences no one can foretell.

The same society that gave rise to Madoffian cupidity and deception is also addicted to reality shows such as *American Idol, Survivor*, etc. so here is the idea: give the man his own TV program, such as the one depicted in The Truman Show! That way, Bernie's every movement voyeuristically can be monitored with all advertising revenue going to the "BMVBF" (Bernie Madoff Victim Bailout Fund). What's the sense of sending him to prison only to make license plates? After the BMVBF is fully funded, sponsorship can then be diverted to TARP, TAF, TSLF, ABCP, HOPE and all the other bailout acronyms, present and future. Thanks Bernie!

With the financial disaster iceberg breaking through the sea of the political world, Barak Obama finally was inaugurated. What a world to inherit and what blame he would later shoulder, not always for its making but for its continuance. My later entries walk that line as well as the unreasonable expectation of his being a panacea for all the world's ills: relations with the Muslim world, racial discontent domestically, needed immigration solutions, and finally, reversing a ship that seemed to have struck that iceberg and was about to go down the same way that claimed the Titanic and the Great Depression. Nonetheless I greeted his inauguration with wonder and hope.

Monday, January 19, 2009
Early in the Morning
It is early in the morning on the eve of President-elect Obama's inauguration—in fact very early, another restless night. When it is so early and still outside, sound travels and I can hear the CSX freight train in the distance, its deep-throated rumbling and horn warning the few cars out on the road at the numerous crossings nearby.

Perhaps subconsciously my sleeplessness on this, the celebration of Martin Luther King's birthday, relates to the incongruous dreamlike images of the bookends of my political consciousness, from the Little Rock desegregation crisis of 1957, the freedom marches that culminated with the march on Washington in 1963 and Martin Luther King's historic "I Have a Dream" speech, to the inauguration tomorrow of our first Afro-American President. All this breathtaking demonstration of profound social change in just my lifetime.

Much has now been said comparing Obama to Lincoln. In my "open letter" to Obama that I published here last May I said "Your opponents have criticized your limited political experience, making it one of their main issues in attacking your candidacy. Lincoln too was relatively inexperienced, something he made to work to his advantage. Forge cooperation across the aisle in congress, creating your own 'team of rivals' as Doris Kearns Goodwin described his cabinet in her marvelous civil war history."

The Lincoln comparison is now omnipresent in the press, not to mention his cabinet selections indeed being a team of rivals. But I am restless because of what faces this, the very administration I had hoped for: a crisis of values as much as it is an economic one. The two are inextricably intertwined.

I am reading an unusual novel by one of my favorite authors, John Updike, *Terrorist*. One of the main characters, Jack Levy laments: "My grandfather thought capitalism was doomed, destined to get more and more oppressive until the proletariat stormed the barricades and set up the worker's paradise. But that didn't happen; the capitalists were too clever or the proletariat too dumb. To be on the safe side, they changed the label 'capitalism' to read 'free enterprise,' but it was still too much dog-eat-dog. Too many losers, and the winners winning too big. But if you don't let the dogs fight it out, they'll sleep all day in the kennel. The basic problem the way I see it is, society tries to be decent, and decency cuts no ice in the state of nature. No ice whatsoever. We should all go back to being hunter-gathers, with a hundred-percent employment rate, and a healthy amount of starvation."

The winners in this economy were not only the capitalists, the real creators of jobs due to hard work and innovation, but the even bigger winners: the financial masters of the universe who learned to leverage financial instruments with the blessings of a government that nurtured the thievery of the public good through deregulation, ineptitude, and political amorality. This gave rise to a whole generation of pseudo capitalists, people who "cashed in" on the system, bankers and brokers and "financial engineers" who dreamt up lethal structures based on leverage and then selling those instruments to an unsuspecting public, a public that entrusted the government to be vigilant so the likes of a Bernie Madoff could not prosper for untold years. Until we revere the real innovators of capitalism, the entrepreneurs who actually create things, ideas, jobs, our financial system will continue to seize up. That is the challenge for the Obama administration—a new economic morality.

Walt Whitman penned these words on the eve of another civil war in 1860:

"I hear America singing, the varied carols I hear,
Those of mechanics, each one singing his as it would be blithe
    and strong,

The carpenter singing his as he measures his plank or beam,

The mason singing his as he makes ready for work, or leaves off work,

The boatman singing what belongs to him in his boat, the deckhand singing on the steamboat deck,

The shoemaker singing as he sits on his bench, the hatter singing as he stands,

The woodcutter's song, the ploughboy's on his way in the morning, or at noon intermission or at sundown,

The delicious singing of the mother, or of the young wife at work, or of the girl sewing or washing,

Each singing what belongs to him or her and to none else,

The day what belongs to the day—at night the party of young fellows, robust, friendly,

Singing with open mouths their strong melodious songs."

It is still early in the morning as I finish this but the sun is rising and I'm going out for my morning walk. Another freight train is rumbling in the distance. I hear America singing.

But the financial agony went on and the reality sunk in like an anvil being pounded by a blacksmith. There was plenty of blame to share and politicians were scurrying to pin the tail on a donkey other than themselves.

Wednesday, February 4, 2009

Accountability

It's been called "draconian" by compensation "experts," the same ones that are employed by the financial services industry—a proposed cap of $500,000 for the "top executives" of companies receiving the TARP funds. Pass the collection hat for the CEOs of Bank of America, Citigroup, and General Motors who pocketed more than $37 million in total compensation in 2007, probably the peak year of the chimerical financial derivative.

But what about the rouges gallery of financial wizards who misrepresented risks to investors and yet cumulatively pulled down hundreds of $millions from an unsuspecting public and fled the scene, such as John Thain, Stan O'Neal, Robert Rubin, Chuck Prince, Dick Fuld, et al.?

To the rescue, a grass roots "claw-back" movement is underway, orchestrated by Nouriel Roubini, the NYU economist who warned about the current crisis years ago and Nassim Taleb, author of *The Black Swan: The Impact of the Highly Improbable.*

"Unless Rubin and others like him are made to mandatorily return their bonuses or are given some other punishment, the system that regrettably emerges is one in which it's the worst of capitalism and socialism, a situation in which profits were privatized and losses were socialized. We taxpayers have the worst."

Thursday, February 12, 2009
Our Financial Crucible
I was watching some of the House Financial Services Committee's hearings yesterday with the chief executives of Goldman Sachs, JPMorgan Chase, Bank of America, Citigroup, Morgan Stanley, State Street Bank, Wells Fargo Bank, and Bank of New York sitting there like a bunch of guilty school boys, being berated by their elders. These firms were the lucky recipients of the $700 billion banking bailout.

A number of questions were posed to score points for our lawmakers, questions that were expected to be answered by a show of the hands so we all can see the scarlet letter of guilt. Questions along the lines of "how many of you have received government money but have changed your credit card terms?"

The perplexed guilty parties sort of looked at each other (obviously wondering what is meant by the question), and as one would timidly raise his hand, the others would slowly follow. These questions went on and on, an embarrassment to those who posed them, those who were forced to answer, and those of us who are relying on this "system" to fix the problem. (Although they did manage to get John Mack of Morgan Stanley to say, "We are sorry.")

Most of these lawmakers are the very ones who once pressured financial institutions to make loans available to everyone no matter what their creditworthiness so they could boast their beneficence to their constituency. And the bankers are the same financial wizards who created leveraged products that passed off tremendous risk to investors, and, now, to us. We also had a Federal Reserve that fed the fire with practically free money, leaving Alan Greenspan recently wondering, "I still don't fully understand how it happened or why it happened."

One can empathize with the feelings of outrage, especially now that we learn that some seven hundred Merrill Lynch employees "earned" bonuses of more than one million dollars in 2008 as the firm lost $27 billion. Yesterday the apologists on CNBC generally defended Wall Street bonuses because even when a financial firm overall loses money there are individual "producers" who make pockets of money. The CNBC cheerleaders went on to say that these "producers" need to be "incentified"—otherwise they will be left only with their base salaries. Most people might be content with the latter and isn't this the kind of "incentive" which motivated "producers" to take excessive risk in the first place?

The questions posed at the witch-hunt hearings centered on why banks are not lending out all the money they received. What planet do our representatives live on? You can't force banks to lend money if people do not have jobs or are worried about losing jobs, and that is the central element in the crucible of today's financial times.

Monday, February 16, 2009
Another Shoe to Drop
Turn the bailout hose this way. Here is one waiting for a future of unknown proportions: "Government pension agency braces for recession"

The magnitude of the potential problem is best understood by going to The Pension Benefit Guaranty Corporation's description of its mission. The PBGC "is a federal corporation created by the Employee Retirement Income Security Act of 1974. It currently protects the pensions of nearly 44 million American workers....PBGC receives no funds from general tax revenues. Operations are financed by insurance premiums set by Congress and paid by sponsors of defined benefit plans, investment income, assets from pension plans trusteed by PBGC, and recoveries from the companies formerly responsible for the plans. PBGC pays monthly retirement benefits, up to a guaranteed maximum, to more than 631,000 retirees in 3,860 pension plans that ended. Including those who have not yet retired and participants in multiemployer plans receiving financial assistance, PBGC is responsible for the current and future pensions of about 1,274,000 people."

The PBGC already has an $11 billion deficit but the astounding part of the article cited above is the former Director, Charles Millard's contention that "a new investment strategy, which allows the PBGC to invest more aggressively in stocks and alternative investments, makes it less likely that it will need a multibillion-dollar congressional bailout."

That is the "strategy" to "protect" current and future pensions? Here is yet another government "safety net" that is not only vulnerable to the economic downturn but also has hitched its star to the future prospects of the stocks and alternative investments.

Friday, February 20, 2009
Moral Hazard of Loan Modification
One can empathize with Ric Santelli's widely heard rant and the reaction in the Blogosphere. No doubt the people who played by the book have the short stick in the $75 billion Homeowner Stability Initiative ("HSI"), but unless some way can be found to deal with the twin time bomb of mortgage foreclosures and more importantly, jobs and the threat of further job loss, the economy will continue to disintegrate.

There are people in homes who are employed but who borrowed too much or at terms that they can no longer afford, and who now may be motivated to simply walk away from their home and rent down the block and save a bundle. Hopefully, this group will be the plan's focus. Yes, if they walk their credit rating will become impaired, but outside of that it becomes a simple business decision. How the HSI deals with principal reduction has a weighty bearing on the moral hazard issue.

Proposals that involve reducing the mortgage principal balance have called for banks or the taxpayer (whoever takes the hit for the lowered principal) having a "call" on the appreciated value of the home (over the new principal amount) if the home is sold in the future. So, if the home's original mortgage was based on, say, a principal of $300k and the new principal is $200k, the bank/taxpayer would be entitled to the appreciated (assuming there is any) difference between $200k and the selling price in the future up to the original principal value. The problem with that approach is why would the seller bother to hold out for a price above $200k—there is no incentive (unless in the unlikely event the home can be sold for more than the original principal amount)—or would the bank then take it over as a foreclosure? Seems to me the bank/taxpayer needs a phased in participation in the selling price to avoid foreclosure down the road, or to provide incentive for the homeowner to get the best possible price, keeping government and/or the bank out of those logistics.

Thus, as far as principal reduction is concerned, the devil is in the detail, and it is here that the core moral hazard issue seems to lie. Other approaches of lowering the mortgage interest rate or converting adjustable rates to an affordable fixed rate or increasing the loan term are more straightforward and quantifiable and would seem to be easier to deal with—from a moral hazard perspective—than principal reduction. It certainly makes sense to find a way to help people who are employed and can afford a reasonable monthly payment to stay in their homes

Thursday, February 26, 2009
The Brave New World and the Economy Converge
Once in a while our local paper, *The Palm Beach Post*, gets a leg up on the rest of the newspaper media, covering a South Florida story that is probably gaining traction in other parts of the country. It is certainly a sign of our times, bioethical issues colliding with the consequences of financial hardship. The headline says it all: "More people choosing to turn their bodies into money-makers." Besides selling mundane body components such as blood, plasma or one's hair, eggs and 'womb rental' are in demand and pay big bucks. Donating eggs can fetch $5,000 while rent-a-womb surrogacy can "net from $18,000 to $70,000, whatever the couple and the carrier agree to."

Interestingly, there is a Catch 22: "not everyone qualifies as a donor, and women whose only reason to volunteer is that they're broke are often rejected." So, if you really need the money, don't bother to apply.

Furthermore, egg donors must be non-smokers, which is understandable, but they must also agree to take injections of fertility drugs, hopefully not to the degree to produce a litter as the Californian octuplet mother.

The Boca Fertility IVF Center "once had only one catalog of donors. Now there are two binders with a total of 100 donors. They include blondes, brunettes, whites, blacks, Asians, even Jewish women, who used to be difficult to find." As the economy deteriorates, genetic engineering or selective breeding could be on the rise.

"O wonder!
How many goodly creatures are there here!
How beauteous mankind is!
O brave new world!
That has such people in't!"
(Shakespeare's *The Tempest* from which Aldous Huxley derived
    the title of his famous novel).

Economists, meet the Bioethicists.

Saturday, March 7, 2009
The 177K
"I looked at my 401K and it's now a 201K ba-dum-bum-CHING!" So, the joke goes today, but, don't look now, it's a 177K based on the S&P 500. If you were able to buy the inverse of the change in the National Debt during the same period, your 401K would be a 485K. Interestingly, invested in gold it would be about the same, 498K, and with the 30 year Treasury bond you'd have a 544K for the same period. So much for hindsight, but much to be said about asset allocation.

The water torture nature of the decline in equity values, without the capitulation everyone has been waiting for, as well the disappearance of Bear Stearns, Lehman Brothers, Merrill Lynch, and the implosion of AIG, Bank of America, Citi, GM and, now, even GE, speaks worlds about the gravity of the situation. AIG has become a bottomless pit into which we have dumped $170 billion in taxpayer's money and now have 79.9% ownership of an asset that seems destined to become a black hole of unknown proportions. While President Obama's sincerity in following through on promises for health care reform and other social issues is applauded—and highly trumpeted on the government's new web site recovery.gov—if our financial institutions entirely fail, everything else becomes meaningless.

Paul Volcker gave one of the clearest explanations as to how we got to this point in a speech he gave in Canada a couple of weeks ago, saying "this phenomenon can be traced back at least five or six years. We had, at that time, a major underlying imbalance in the world economy. The American proclivity to consume was in full force. Our consumption rate was about 5% higher, relative to our GNP or what our production normally is. Our spending—consumption, investment, government—was running about 5% or more above our production, even though we were more or less at full employment. You had the opposite in China and Asia, generally, where the Chinese were consuming maybe 40% of their GNP—we consumed 70% of our GNP."

He argued, "in the future, we are going to need a financial system which is not going to be so prone to crisis and certainly will not be prone to the severity of a crisis of this sort." In effect the Glass-Steagall Act that had been enacted during Depression 1.0 separating commercial and investment banks— and had been repealed in 1999 thanks to Phil Gramm and other deregulation zealots—needs to be reinstated during this Depression 2.0. Where is Paul Volcker to lead the way back to the 401K?

Wednesday, March 11, 2009
Hope

Two stories today. This first one is from the *New York Times* "Timeless Lincoln Memento Is Revealed" describes the very careful opening of the back of Lincoln's first watch—by the National Museum of American History—as it was thought a secret message was inscribed therein. Indeed, there was "a message secretly engraved by a watchmaker who repaired it in 1861" which read as follows: "Jonathan Dillon April 13, 1861 Fort Sumter was attacked by the rebels on the above date. J Dillon April 13- 1861 Washington, thank God we have a government Jonth Dillon."

Here was an immigrant watchmaker who grasped the significance of the moment and felt compelled to inscribe his observations for some future generation, inside the watch of the President of the United States, which, as fate would have it, he happened to be repairing.

I juxtapose this story to a magnificent NASA photograph of the Shuttle that was taken last night with the full moon. It is scheduled to blast off tonight. We visited the Kennedy Space Center a couple of years ago with our friends Beny and Maria who live in Sicily. Another Shuttle was on the launching pad at the time, almost an incomprehensible sight because of the scale of the Shuttle and its supporting structure.

From the near dissolution of the United States to the technology that can achieve such a scientific feat, in less than 150 years. Any country that can accomplish that should be able to find the resolve and the means to end the present financial crisis. We would all like to say: "thank God we have a government."

Friday, March 13, 2009
Ambushed

Jim Cramer walked into Jon Stewart's studio last night and instead of his trademark rolled-up sleeves, he might as well have been dressed like a clown, ready to take a big cream pie in the face, intended for CNBC rather than Cramer personally, although he is emblematic of his "news" organization deserting its traditional 4th estate role for that of an "infotainmentmercial." Cramer at least is somewhat honest about his role. Some other CNBC "reporters" have become clandestine right-wing cheerleaders.

I deserted CNBC as a serious source for financial news the day that Lehman went under last fall as I was watching CNBC's "Squawk Box" and the show's Cheerleader-in-Chief, Joe Kernan, made some sort of a statement criticizing the critics of Lehman's leader, Dick Fuld, reminding them that poor Mr. Fuld had lost a fortune in the value of Lehman stock, conveniently neglecting he had extracted $484 million in salary, bonuses and stock options since 2000, failing to mention the equity value of Lehman had been built on spurious leverage. "Squawk Box" itself has turned into quick sound bites and chatty banter, and when they do have a serious interview, they superimpose sound effects, whooshing noises of charts, stock quotes, inundating the senses akin to watching a video game. Some of CNBCs confrontational interviews border on a financial version of the Jerry Springer show.

What a reversal of roles, the host of a comedy show becoming a spokesman for the questions the supposedly serious financial station failed to ask. Stewart was unrelenting in his probing and Cramer, to his credit, simply ate humble pie. I think he knows Stewart is right asking such questions as: Who is CNBCs audience, the Wall Street traders or us stooges trying to keep our 401ks afloat in a "fast trading" environment promoted by CNBCs endless litany of buy, sell, buy, etc.? How does this help us? Shouldn't CNBC be asking the tough questions of Wall Street instead of gaming our pensions? Wasn't CNBC, supposedly knowledgeable about financial matters, remiss in not recognizing that consequences of infinite leveraging would surely end in calamity? Isn't there a measure of responsibility that goes with reporting, and the freedom of the press, especially for a news platform that purports to be serious? "Let's face it, we're both snake oil salesman, but at least we [the Comedy Channel] label our product as such."

Monday, March 16, 2009
The View From Here
Although we are some 140 miles from Cape Canaveral, the view of yesterday's shuttle launch into the twilight sky was spectacular. The shuttle program is one of our nation's greatest accomplishments.

There were other developments over the weekend impacting another sort of "view from here." One story that grabbed some headlines, but then quietly went into the night was China's prime minister's concern about their holding some $1 trillion investment in American debt. Clearly there is some anxiety about the long-term safety of their investment, a remarkable public admission by such a large holder of US debt, one that is symbiotically attached to our hip—something akin to yelling fire in a theatre while sitting far from the exits. But in Barack We Trust, President Obama saying that our debt is safe in spite of our record deficits, bailouts, and our national debt about to pass the $11 trillion mark. I mentioned this "Black Swan" before, that is confidence in the ability of the US to meet its financial obligations, without hyper inflating its currency.

The other story that will not go quietly into the night, because of the measure of outrage, is the $165 million in bonuses that are being handed out to the same executives that had a hand in creating the alchemy of credit default swaps. We've heard this song before, when Congressional Hearings revealed the extent that bonuses were handed out to the banks.

Then there is also outrage that foreign counterparties profited by receiving some money through AIG's $170 billion bailout, but the main focus will continue to be the bonuses, although its size is but a pimple on the ass of the bailout vista.

The irony is the performance criterion of the bonuses is probably the very short-term thinking that encouraged leverage creation, AIG superimposing a hedge fund business on top of it, then, AAA rating. So why pay these bonuses? We're told they are "retention bonuses" to keep the "best and the brightest" in the AIG stable—as if there are not hundreds of unemployed qualified financial professionals who could immediately replace each of the AIG financial wizards. We are also told that these people will sue if they are not paid. Let them sue. Do they really want their names and reputations to go down in the annals of financial infamy?

But on to the happier news of the successful, although delayed, shuttle launch. The vapor trail appeared just three minutes after the launch over our home: beautiful and breathtaking.

Thursday, March 19, 2009
So we beat on ...
If the present financial crisis is the moral equivalent of war, it is appropriate that we have a "New-New Gettysburg Address" written by Jeff Mathews. It begins with "Four or five years ago our Investment Bankers helped bring forth on this continent, and around the world, a new banking system, conceived in Leverage, and dedicated to the proposition that all persons working for Investment Banks can create enormous Wealth for themselves with almost no Risk except to Taxpayers."

From *Naked Capitalism* an interesting, but rather technical explanation of the Federal Reserve's attempt to prop up housing prices through its "shock and awe" announcement yesterday of buying long term debt (created by the Treasury!). One has to wonder whether China's Prime Minister Wen Jiabao is now more than "a little worried" about their $1 trillion holdings of US debt and about being attached at the hip to US currency.

Finally, in the *Zerohedge* blog there is an insider's view of the day-to-day workings of AIG. As an outsider, it's like watching a car wreck in slow motion. Unfortunately, we're all in this collision.

Unless we have job creation, the Fed can drive mortgage rates to zero without much benefit. People borrow because of confidence, not merely because rates are low. Since the recent Fed move is acknowledged to be their weapon of last resort, one has to wonder what the Fed knows that we don't. But the last time we had artificially low rates and relatively strong employment we began the very leverage bubble that is now in the process of deflating. "So we beat on, boats against the current, borne back ceaselessly into the past." (From F. Scott Fitzgerald's *The Great Gatsby*)

Hindsight is insight. When I was writing "It's All a Mystery," little did I know—or anyone—that the Dow Jones average was bottoming out, and would be on a steady move up since. The market is a discounting mechanism, and it was perceived that an in-the-Federal- Reserve-we-trust attitude prevailed. Still that was about $10 trillion in national debt ago.

Tuesday, March 24, 2009
It's All a Mystery
We were away the last few days, while the economic scene continued to go from mildly inexplicable to downright unfathomable during the same short period of time.

The Federal Reserve is now buying up to $300 billion in Treasury securities, and $750 billion of mortgage-backed securities using the "Supplementary Financing Program" which in effect gives it the ability to raise its own debt: "The Treasury has in place a special financing mechanism called the Supplementary Financing Program, which helps the Federal Reserve manage its balance sheet. In addition, the Treasury and the Federal Reserve are seeking legislative action to provide additional tools the Federal Reserve can use to sterilize the effects of its lending or securities purchases on the supply of bank reserves."

Then, the Congressional Budget Office claims the national debt under the president's budget could be $2.3 trillion worse than the White House estimates. This could result in a $9.3 trillion dollar deficit over the next ten years, which would nearly double the present deficit. All this depends on so many variables that it really is impossible to forecast what they (the deficits) will be. (It is rumored that in the 1960's Senator Everett Dirksen once said "A billion here, a billion there, and pretty soon you're talking real money," something he later said he was misquoted on. Still this quote has persisted until recently when trillion has become the "new" billion. How long will it be before "quadrillion" becomes the new "trillion?")

On Monday, the Dow surged by almost 500 points, a Pavlovian response to the long-awaited Geithner "plan" of creating an auction mechanism for removing the toxic assets from banks' balance sheet "Essentially the Geithner plans creates a vehicle in which private equity accounts for 3%, public equity for 12%, and the rest is provided as debt by the public sector (through the Federal Deposit Insurance Corporation, FDIC)." The latter is from *Eurointelligence*, which also has a number of good links with views on this development as well as an explanation of the proposed auction formula. It seems like another excellent opportunity to privatize gains and socialize losses.

Wednesday, April 1, 2009
Waiting for someone to explain it
The global financial crisis: life imitating art? It's hard to see the connection, but as with any great work of music or literature, we could be smack in the development section, when themes

or characters, introduced in an earlier time, are permanently changed and emerge as something very different. This period in the financial crisis is being played out with the dissonance of a Shostakovich, or the absurdity of postmodern literature. As Eugene Ionesco wrote in the program notes for his play *The Chairs*, "as the world is incomprehensible to me, I am waiting for someone to explain it." Perhaps we all feel the same way about the global financial crisis. It would indeed be an absurdity to conclude that after these convulsions, it will be business as usual.

But the day-to-day machinations of the market, bailouts, and politics obfuscate the possible outcomes. Are the capitalistic underpinnings of the new world economy at an inflection point, to be changed for better or worse after this economic turmoil has passed? For some insight into a speculative, but well argued bigger picture I give a hat tip to my friend Bruce who put me onto the article "After Capitalism" written by Geoff Mulgan and published in the *UK Prospect Magazine*.

Capitalism, in spite of several boom and bust cycles has survived, although the US economy has changed drastically, abandoning some of its manufacturing capabilities to cheaper overseas labor, focusing on intellectual capital, and becoming more of a service oriented consumer economy. It is now just a part of a highly interconnected world economy dominated by multinational corporations. With an insatiable appetite for goods and energy, however, we've become a nation of borrowers, living on leverage and the largess of countries willing (still) to buy our debt.

At the same time the nature of capitalism has changed. The financial institutions that once existed to solely support industry are now an industry onto itself, trading derivatives and exotic financial instruments and, with this fundamental change, perhaps we've arrived at another precipice of "creative destruction," Joseph Schumpeter's term for the consequence of radical departures.

Mulgan argues that "capitalism is sure to change but will not disappear. Instead, it will not dominate in our culture as it did in the 'greed is good' era. Capitalism has been adaptable but in some ways has sown seeds of its own destruction". He cites the "collapse of the savings rate—to around zero by 2007 in the US when it needs to be closer to 30 per cent to cope with ageing ... a stark symptom of a capitalism that has lost the ability to protect its own future."

Then, in retrospect, the Great Depression can be seen as both "a disaster and an accelerator of reform. One implication of [Carlota] Perez's work, and of Joseph Schumpeter's before her, is that some of the old has to be swept away before the new can find its most successful forms. Propping up failing industries is in this light a risky policy. Perez suggests that we may be on the verge of another great period of institutional innovation and experiment that will lead to new compromises between the claims of capital and the claims of society and of nature."

Mulgan postulates, "If another great accommodation is on its way, this one will be shaped by the triple pressures of ecology, globalisation and demographics." This will lead to changes away from consumption to savings and will underscore capitalism's need to come closer in balance with nature rather than its destruction. Capitalism, in effect will become the servant rather than the master. But "it remains to be seen what political visionary will seize upon 'servant capitalism.' (Obama should be ideally suited to offering a new vision, yet has surrounded himself with champions of the very system that now appears to be crumbling.)"

Where today's seismic financial activity will settle is still a black hole of the unknowable, but for an interesting macro view on the future of capitalism, check out Mulgan's piece.

It is impossible to completely disentangle some of my personal life with views of the politics and the economics of the era I'm covering in this book. My life in publishing included frequent trips to London and close associations with Brits who are still friends today. Obama's first trip abroad was there.

Sunday, April 5, 2009
When a man is tired of London ...
... he is tired of life. Samuel Johnson uttered those famous words to his biographer James Bosewell some two hundred and thirty years ago. I'm still basking in the glow of President Obama's and First Lady Michelle's London visit to attend the G-20, replaying in my mind the images of London, our President's news conference and Michelle's moving visit to a girls school in Islington, north London.

If I could live in any place other than where we have, I would choose London. I often visited there during my career usually to confer with our distributor, Eurospan, run by my late dear friend, the charismatic Peter Geelan. I would also see numerous UK publishers with whom we traded copublications, or go to the London Bookfair, or stop by London on my way to the Frankfurt Bookfair.

Frequently Ann would accompany me for the London part of the trip so we managed some vacation time there as well. After staying at several London hotels, including the Dorchester where we had to nearly pole vault into our bed at night, we sort of settled at The Cavendish, which in the Edwardian era was run by Rosa Lewis, the infamous "Duchess of Duke St." Located across from Fortnum and Mason on the corner of Duke and Jermyn Streets, it is ideally situated near Trafalgar Square, St. James and Piccadilly Circus, the heart of London's great theatre district where we went as often as our schedule allowed. So it was at this hotel where I would meet Ann during my business travels, and later, we brought Jonathan as well, the first time as young as 14 months old.

We were at the Cavendish when a young British policewoman was killed in 1984, shot by someone from the nearby Libyan Embassy on St. James Place. Between the Irish Republican Army threats and other clouds of terrorism, traveling in London was sometimes filled with anxiety, but the British people take such adversity in stride. The Cavendish became an armed camp during the standoff with the Libyan Embassy and right outside our window, which had a view to the Embassy, there were police sharpshooters. We slept on a mattress on the floor that evening, along with 8-year-old Jonathan, all of us anxious to stay out of the line of fire. We were leaving the following morning and that standoff lasted at least a week longer.

I treasured going to Eurospan's offices at 3 Henrietta Street facing the venerable Covent Garden. This area is rich in literary tradition. Number 3 had housed the publishing home of Gerald Duckworth, Virginia Woolf's stepbrother and no doubt Henry James and John Galsworthy had visited as well, as Duckworth published both. Jane Austen's brother Henry, a banker, lived at 10 Henrietta Street and she had stayed there when in London, saying the house was "all dirt and confusion, but in a very interesting way."

The scenes from *My Fair Lady* that were filmed in Covent Garden were right outside the door of 3 Henrietta Street and, according to Peter, a scene from Alfred Hitchcock's 1972 film *Frenzy* was made in the building itself. As per Wikipedia, "much of the location filming was done in and around Covent Garden and was homage to the London of Hitchcock's childhood. The son of a Covent Garden merchant, Hitchcock filmed several key scenes showing the area as the working produce market that it was. Aware that the area's days as a market were numbered, Hitchcock wanted to record the area as he remembered it....The buildings seen in the film are now occupied by restaurants and nightclubs, and the laneways where merchants and workers once carried their produce are now occupied by tourists and street performers."

Of course, I remember when Covent Garden was a public square mainly devoted to the fruit and vegetable market, but in its transformation to today's tourist attraction, its character was mostly retained. Eliza Doolittle might still recognize it while selling flowers from the portico of St Paul's.

While meetings with Eurospan would easily last the entire day, there was always time for fun in the evenings, sometimes a party at the offices itself, or at Peter's flat, typically ending in a crowd moving on to dinner at a nearby favorite restaurant. And in those days, and since, London has some of the best food in the world if you're the guest of someone in the know. When I retired, Peter's son, Michael who took over the business with his partner, Danny, who was in charge of finance, presented me with a montage of photos of those years, which I proudly display on my bookshelf next to my desk.

When Jonathan was along, Ann and I made it a point to journey by underground to Pinner in west London to visit Danny and his family. Over the years we became close to them and they visited us in the US as well. When my older son Chris, who was a superb high school soccer player, was invited to play in Europe, he stayed with their family and visited English football clubs with Danny, who played competitive amateur football.

I can still see Mum (Danny's mother), his wife, Pat, Danny in my mind's eye, and their two beautiful daughters, Claire and Lisa skipping down the streets of Pinner with our young son Jonathan, so reminiscent of the streets of Kew Gardens near where I grew up, obviously modeled after these London environs. One year I hand carried Cabbage Patch dolls for his girls so they would be the first in the UK to have the "prestigious" dolls. When they were introduced in the early 1980's around Christmas time in the US, there were long lines and even fistfights to get one. Ann was not to be messed with though when she waited on line for them at a local toy store before we journeyed to London.

So I watched the Obama news coverage with a mix of nostalgia and pride, reminded not only of the special kinship the United States has with the United Kingdom but also of my own close personal ties. It was my fervent hope that as President, because of his political views, his multicultural background, and his leadership abilities, Obama would help repair what, by any objective measure, was diminished respect for the United States abroad.

What better place to start than London town? I had not anticipated what First Lady Michelle would bring to the table. Her speech to the Elizabeth Garrett Anderson School, her genuine, heartfelt emotion, and the outpouring of love to her resonates with reciprocal devotion. And who could not be impressed by the arm in arm embrace with the Queen?

Repairing a tarnished reputation takes time, it takes mutual respect; and if the G-20 accomplished nothing else, it seems to have established the right direction. Perhaps a new sense of confidence begins to percolate the world economy as well because of agreements made at the G-20. So much remains to be seen on that score and I have been pessimistic by the accelerating debt that is being incurred. But as economics relates to trust, in the system, and between nations, this may be a start to break the vicious cycle of gloom and doom.

I was struck by President Obama's news conference, where he seems so much at ease, affable, and his responses clearly belie the attacks by some of his critics as his being teleprompter dependent (as if his predecessor was not). I conclude with the question that was posed by Jonathan Weisman, the *Washington Post* Congressional reporter, about America's standing in the world and our President's reply. It's the kind of truth that does inspire the "hope" that became a campaign mantra.

"Q: Thank you, Mr. President. During the campaign you often spoke of a diminished power and authority of the United States over the last decade. This is your first time in an international summit like this, and I'm wondering what evidence you saw of what you spoke of during the campaign. And specifically, is the declaration of the end of the Washington consensus evidence of the diminished authority that you feared was out there?

OBAMA: Well, first of all, during the campaign I did not say that some of that loss of authority was inevitable. I said it was traced to very specific decisions that the previous administration had made that I believed had lowered our standing in the world. And that wasn't simply my opinion; that was, it turns out, the opinion of many people around the world.

I would like to think that with my election and the early decisions that we've made, that you're starting to see some restoration of America's standing in the world. And although, as you know, I always mistrust polls, international polls seem to indicate that you're seeing people more hopeful about America's leadership.

Now, we remain the largest economy in the world by a pretty significant margin. We remain the most powerful military on Earth. Our production of culture, our politics, our media still have—I didn't mean to say that with such scorn, guys ... you know I'm teasing—still has enormous influence. And so I do not buy into the notion that America can't lead in the world. I wouldn't be here if I didn't think that we had important things to contribute.

I just think in a world that is as complex as it is that it is very important for us to be able to forge partnerships as opposed to simply dictating solutions. Just a—just to try to crystallize the example, there's been a lot of comparison here about Bretton Woods. 'Oh, well, last time you saw the entire international architecture being remade.' Well, if there's just Roosevelt and Churchill sitting in a room with a brandy, that's a—that's an easier negotiation. But that's not the world we live in, and it shouldn't be the world that we live in.

And so that's not a loss for America; it's an appreciation that Europe is now rebuilt and a powerhouse. Japan is rebuilt, is a powerhouse. China, India—these are all countries on the move. And that's good. That means there are millions of people—billions of people—who are working their way out of poverty. And over time, that potentially makes this a much more peaceful world."

And that's the kind of leadership we need to show—one that helps guide that process of orderly integration without taking our eyes off the fact that it's only as good as the benefits of individual families, individual children: Is it giving them more opportunity; is it giving them a better life? If we judge ourselves by those standards, then I think America can continue to show leadership for a very long time.

Just rereading the foregoing in the age of Trump magnifies the difference a President can make. Recent trips abroad revealed how mystified those overseas are about how we could have elected such a person. One can blame the entire election process, and our celebrity culture, something I deal with later in these pages. Meanwhile, getting back to the economic crisis which was underway ...

Thursday, April 16, 2009
Swimming against the deflationary tide
There was a small, unobtrusive article in today's *Wall Street Journal*: "A Deflated Fed Battles to Keep Prices Up"

Here are the bullet points:

* "In March the consumer-price index slipped 0.4% below its year-earlier level, the first decline in over 50 years"

* "It is hard to imagine [consumers] returning to their spend-thrift ways anytime soon"
* "Falling prices would make it tougher for borrowers to pay off debt, leading to even more defaults and even tougher lending standards"
* To fight back ... "the Fed could buy the Treasuries issued to finance such moves. In practice, that is like printing money and handing it out to households, and it is pretty much what is happening now."
* "When the fight is between falling prices and the Fed, it is hard to predict which will prevail."

Add to this mix, 30-day T-Bills now yield nearly zero (0.02%). Soon, one may have to pay the Treasury to hold short-term deposits, but nonetheless if deflation persists or worsens equities and bonds will not be able to compete with cash. Everyone is expecting inflation as a consequence of government spending, but prolonged deflation would be a Black Swan with potentially serious consequences. Gold fell more than $13 an ounce today, below a technical support level, another indication that inflation may not be the main worry.

Friday, April 24, 2009
Bank Stress Test Obfuscation
The highly anticipated "bank stress test results" were announced a few minutes ago, a non-announcement that had so little detail about the health of the banking system it left me wondering the same way I did when I received the following letter from my bank a while ago. The names have been changed to protect the guilty. Why can't the taxpayer and the consumer have some straight talk?

"Gobbledygook National Bank
123 Main Street
Everywhere, USA 99999

Dear Gobbledygook Customer:

We are writing to advise you of important changes to the recurring automatic payment program in which are currently enrolled.

Through the end of the year, your scheduled automatic payment will not be processed if, up to three days prior to your payment due date, you make other payments which satisfy the total minimum payment due. If we cancel any scheduled payment-in-full of your new balance we will automatically adjust any finance charges that accrue as a result of the cancellation.

Effective with your automatic payment schedule to be processed at the beginning of the year, the monthly automatic payment amount you have authorized will be processed even if you have made additional payment(s) satisfying the total minimum payment due for that month. However, the automatic payment will not be processed during any month in which your account does not have an outstanding balance on the payment due date.

If you would like to make any changes to your automatic payment plan, please contact us.

If you prefer, you can call Customer Service at the phone number indicated on the back of your Gobbledygook credit card.

Thank you for your business. We look forward to serving you now and in the future.

Sincerely,

Oliver Obfuscation
Senior VP, Gobbledygook National Bank"

Monday, May 11, 2009
Slowly Letting Out the Bad News
Among all the talk of green shoots, the recession bottoming, and the hope that the spending will produce growth, a new

headline from Reuters: "White House forecasts higher U.S. budget deficit."

One gets the feeling that the Obama administration has little choice but to let this kind of bad news out slowly, hoping the market and the psyche of the country can absorb it without disrupting the tenuous nature of the recovery, particularly in the credit and stock markets. Until REAL unemployment recedes deficits will inevitably grow beyond forecasts. The recent unemployment figures include some "gains" because of recently hired government census workers and fails to count workers who have just given up or are working part-time, and does not yet include the 1.6 million college seniors graduating this year.

Sunday, May 24, 2009
Bombshell
"We are out of money."

This is the "news" we've feared, although expected, but not so soon: the admission that the US economic system (not necessarily the stock market which lives in its own fantasy land before it adjusts to reality) is insolvent. President Obama, responding to a question about the cost of health care in an interview on C-SPAN yesterday, said, "Well, we are out of money now."

Obama's admission seems to be a continuation of the letting-the-news-out-slowly "strategy" the consequences of which are staggering, not only for holders of US Treasuries, but just about every world currency because of the symbiotic relationships between the lending economies and the consuming economies. For some time I've been concerned about this, particularly because of the mathematical confluence of rising healthcare costs and rising unemployment. "Are T-Bills "risk free," especially as the US seems to be on a course to guarantee every debt and every major corporate shortfall, not to mention the twin time bombs of Social Security and Medicare/Medicaid as the baby boomers retire and unemployment rises? Now there is a Black Swan." So, today's headline "Fix is hard for Medicare, Social Security finances" does not come as a surprise, but it is disturbing that we have so long delayed the inevitability of facing up to this hydra headed conundrum. "If we cannot even acknowledge these economic truths, there can be no national plan to deal with the dire consequences."

Maybe President Obama's statement was more of a Freudian slip, but it is now out there, to be "pondered" by the markets, and, hopefully, to be finally faced up to by Congress

Saturday, May 30, 2009
Prelude to Panic
That's the headline from today's *Palm Beach Post*:" Prelude to panic: Tax rolls plummet."

Surprise, surprise? More anecdotal evidence that the recession is indeed the "Great Recession" and local government is out to lunch "with countywide values lower than feared." Where have they been during the past year while the clock was ticking towards the end of their June 30 fiscal year and the beginning of the new one? Foreclosures and rising unemployment should have spelled out reality. All one needs to do is to drive through many of the neighborhoods in Palm Beach County where "For Sale" signs are interspersed with euphemistic "For Rent" signs.

Here are some bullet points:

*" Property Appraiser Gary Nikolits had been expecting 'the quickest free fall since the Great Depression' but his estimate of a 12% decline has now been revised to 13.5%
* Taxable countywide property has declined to $138 billion from $159.6 billion last year with 38 cities, towns, and villages having larger percentage declines

* Given the 13.5% decline in values, county administrators pro-
    posed a 13.5% tax rate increase (as well as laying off 175
    workers, an undisclosed percentage of total employees)."

When times were "good" (fictitiously good, that is), our town
in PBC was eager to spend. $Millions went into the "beautifica-
tion" of a street which might have been more beautiful if some
of the homes were updated, but as the municipality cannot just
hand out money to homeowners (only the federal government
can do that), they constructed little islands in the middle of the
road and planted vegetation. Much of this beautification is now
gone but the islands remain, constricting traffic and leading to a
reduction in the speed limit: so much for handing municipalities
the "benefits" of inflation. Now, faced, with deflation, and rising
unemployment, no problem, presto, a proposed tax increase.

Thursday, June 4, 2009
Inspirational Diplomacy
I am an early riser so was able to see President Obama's entire
speech today as he delivered it at Cairo University. If a main
criterion of being a successful President is to be inspirational,
Obama passed that test.

It was not a speech of diplomacy per se but its prelude, setting a tone and putting forth ideals. I fear progress on the broad
objectives President Obama set out in the speech will be delayed,
another victim of our economic malaise. This dilutes the energy
that can be focused on international goals and until domestic
issues such as the deficit and unemployment are under control,
the ability to make significant progress abroad will be impaired.

Nonetheless, the speech is one that realizes the hope I
expressed more than a year ago in an open letter to then Senator
Obama: "Some people have pointed to 9/11 as a manifestation
of the clash between the Muslim and Christian worlds. Given
your personal background, you have what may be a unique

opportunity to establish a dialogue between these two worlds and in so doing begin to restore our international standing. Just electing you will demonstrate to the world that we can put our ideals into action."

President Obama made several references to the need for honesty, putting forth some very sensitive key issues to his Egyptian audience, such as the future security of Israel and the need for Palestinian statehood, and Iran's place in a nuclear world.

And if I am to be honest, during my lifetime the American Presidency sometimes has been a source of embarrassment, culminating in President George W. Bush having to duck shoes thrown at him. When I traveled the world I would occasionally feel the undercurrent of anti-Americanism, the stereotype of the "ugly American" that President Obama has asked the Muslim world to renounce as he has said we must "fight against negative stereotypes of Islam wherever they appear."

During my adult lifetime I can think of only two comparable speeches as noteworthy as Obama's: President Kennedy's "Ich bin ein Berliner" June 26, 1963 speech in West Berlin and President Reagan's June 12, 1987 speech at the Brandenburg Gate, proclaiming "Tear down this wall!" a challenge to Soviet leader Mikhail Gorbachev to destroy the Berlin Wall. I was in Frankfurt Germany on October 3, 1990 when Berlin was united into a single city-state and East/West German unity was achieved, the words of Kennedy and Reagan resonating in history.

Hopefully President Obama's Cairo speech similarly will be recognized as an inspirational turning point sometime in the future. Words and leadership make a difference

Wednesday, June 24, 2009
Citigroup Raises Pay as Unemployment Rises
It is a tired old argument in the financial service sector, raising salaries "to retain the best talent." Today the *New York Times* reports Citigroup Has a Plan to Fatten Salaries.

It goes on to note "industrywide, total compensation is expected to rise 20 to 30 percent this year, approximately to the levels of 2005, before the crisis, according to Johnson Associates, a compensation consulting firm." It was during that time the instruments of financial destruction began to flourish, so why not roll back the clock to then?

Having run a business in both good times and bad times, we all benefited from the former and we all had to tighten our belts during the latter. Why should the financial services industry be exempt from the financial laws of gravity and why does the Board of Directors approve such policies while their shareholders suffer and their businesses take government funds? Bank of America and Morgan Stanley are also raising base salaries. Guess they too are concerned about "retaining the best talent." All of this as unemployment rises—where does this logic end? It almost seems like a back door form of price-fixing, as isn't it inevitable that the expense of these coordinated salary increases find their way into the cost of financial products?

Juxtapose that to an article in the same edition of the *Times*: "Despite Recession, High Demand for Skilled Labor." Some jobs such as registered nurses, geological engineers, and welders are going unfilled, even during the recession. These are jobs that actually produce something and are critical to our society. One might as well work in the financial services industry where compensation is immune to supply and demand

Friday, July 17, 2009
Goldman Insatiable Sachs
While Citigroup, Bank of America, and Morgan Stanley, Troubled Asset Relief Program recipients are finding ways to circumvent TARP compensation restrictions, Goldman Sachs, having "paid back," those funds may brazenly pay out some $773,000 per employee as total compensation in 2009. This

comes on its reported net earnings of $1.81 billion and reve-
nues of $9.43 billion for the quarter ending March, 2009, a
nifty operating profit of almost 20% in the depths of the "Great
Recession." Don't get me wrong, I'm all for profit and the capitalist system, but Goldman had taken TARP funds, and was the
largest recipient of AIG TARP money due to collateral calls on
mortgage related Collateralized Debt Obligations, and presumably AIG (we, the taxpayer) may be on the hook for more. The
herd of financial firms has thinned and we have handed them
monopoly-like power.

While I recognize that the financial mess was primarily
an inherited one by the Obama administration, we are not
addressing the toxic assets that are still haunting the books
of many financial institutions. Bad mortgages and a weak real
estate market persist, and unemployment continues to grow.
We may have forestalled the complete seizure of the financial
system, but the structural weaknesses remain, and taxpayers are
underwriting a postponement of a solution, benefiting financial
institutions such as Goldman.

Paul Krugman at the *New York Times* makes these key points
about GS' earnings and compensation plans in his column, "The
Joy of Sachs:"

"First, it tells us that Goldman is very good at what it does.
Unfortunately, what it does is bad for America.

Second, it shows that Wall Street's bad habits—above all, the
system of compensation that helped cause the financial crisis—
have not gone away.

Third, it shows that by rescuing the financial system without
reforming it, Washington has done nothing to protect us from
a new crisis, and, in fact, has made another crisis more likely."

His conclusions are must reading. Wall Street seems to
be calling the shots in Washington, all of this while reported
unemployment flirts with 10% and with real unemployment
substantially higher as dispirited workers who have given up

looking for a job, or part-timers who want a full-time job, are not even counted. Sounds like a good time for record payouts at Goldman Sachs.

As Mary Elizabeth Lease wrote in the early 1890's, "It is no longer a government of the people, by the people, and for the people, but a government of Wall Street, by Wall Street, and for Wall Street."

Monday, August 3, 2009
Headline Tedium
Bailouts, bonuses and Madoff. Are we getting tired yet of the endless litany of related headlines such as the *Wall Street Journal*'s recent "Bank Bonus Tab: $33 Billion; Nine Lenders That Got U.S. Aid Paid at Least $1 Million Each to 5,000 Employees"?

The rock star of these "fab" financial "leaders" is Andrew Hall who makes a bundle for himself trading energy contracts for Citigroup's energy-trading unit Phibro LLC, with compensation approaching $100 million for 2008. It is interesting to read Sunday's *New York Times* front page article on his activities and compensation. No doubt he is a talented individual and I suppose if Citigroup didn't want his operation's expertise in "taking advantage of unusual spreads between the spot price of oil and the price of an oil futures contract," other firms would be lining up to pay his price. That is the American way. We know how to lavish money on our superstars, whether from the media or sports, or in this case, dice-rolling trading moguls.

The *Times* refers to his compensation as "his cut of profits from a characteristically aggressive year of bets in the oil market." It also says "the company, for example, often *wagers* that the price of oil will rise so fast during a particular period, say six months, that it can make money by storing oil in super-tankers and floating it until the price goes up. ' Finally, 'right before the first Gulf War, Phibro placed an elaborate *bet* that the price of oil would spike and then go down faster than others were anticipating. The company earned more than $300 million from the *gamble*."

I emphasize *bets, wagers*, and *gamble*, as these words cut to the heart of the matter. Arbitrage and hedging can be a means of controlling risk or it can magnify risk to the point of endangering the entire financial system. Is this what our banks should be doing: betting, gambling and waging? Heads they win, tails the taxpayer loses? I have to wonder what the consequences would have been if Mr. Hall's trades had gone disastrously against Citigroup. Would he have been personally at risk for the same $100 million he "earned" being on the right side? Do we want our banks, the bedrock of our financial system engaging in such activities—aren't these the domain of the individual entrepreneur and private capital? To what extent does such "trading" create spikes such as $147 for a barrel of crude oil while there is a glut of the commodity?

Then there is the continuing rhetoric about having to reward the financial superstars that got us into this mess in the first place, or they will "walk." I like Warren Buffet's homey comments on this topic so I quote from his 2006 letter to his Berkshire Hathaway shareholders. Although this is aimed at CEO pay in general, which is also absurdly high in many (but not all) corporations, it applies to our banks and other financial service firms as well:

"CEO perks at one company are quickly copied elsewhere. 'All the other kids have one' may seem a thought too juvenile to use as a rationale in the boardroom. But consultants employ precisely this argument, phrased more elegantly of course, when they make recommendations to comp committees. Irrational and excessive comp practices will not be materially changed by disclosure or by 'independent' comp committee members.... Compensation reform will only occur if the largest institutional shareholders—it would only take a few—demand a fresh look at the whole system. The consultants' present drill of deftly selecting 'peer' companies to compare with their clients will only perpetuate present excesses."

Another mind-boggling headline "Picowers Rebut Suit Tied to Madoff Fraud" is from Saturday's *Wall Street Journal*. And The *New York Times* version of the same "Big Investor Counters Charges in Madoff Case." According to the Madoff bankruptcy trustee, Irving Picard, Picower's accounts posted gains of more than 100 percent a dozen times between 1996 and 2007, with one gaining 950 percent, but this counter suit contends the latter was "only" 37.6 percent and none of his accounts earned more than 100 percent "in any single year."

But the $5.1 billion Picower withdrew over the years may have represented a return greatly exceeding any reasonable return during the same period. How a knowledgeable investor (presumably Picower qualifies) could believe that Madoff can "guarantee" steady returns of 10 to 12 percent a year and be satisfied by the statements received from Madoff to bear out those returns is beyond me. I still think the "idea" of creating a new reality TV show, something we seem to be better at than regulating financial Ponzi schemes (either private or government sponsored) might be just the ticket to fund the innocent victims of Madoff.

I fear that while we bail out banks, insurance companies and their like, leaving present compensation practices in place, we just continue to perpetuate financial risk taking, swinging for the fences, making "bets and wagers" that will just dig us into a deeper future hole. As the headlines attest, the "challenge" remains. A true recovery requires jobs, jobs, jobs—and how are they going to be created—by banks trading energy futures? What happened to the commitment to the infrastructure? Our roads, utilities, and public transportation are falling apart. Alternative energy seems DOA. Aren't these the areas our financial recourses should be focused on, ones that will create jobs, in construction,

69

technology, and finance, and can lead a true economic recovery we can pass on with pride to future generations?

Thursday, September 3, 2009
The Vanishing Work Ethic
Hat tip to my former colleague, Jim Wright, who put me on to Steven Malanga's interesting and well-researched article in the *City Journal*, "Whatever Happened to the Work Ethic?" which strikes at the heart of our economic crisis. Things have changed in America where we used to work hard to make things and where borrowing and bailouts were eschewed.

As Malanga states: "What would Tocqueville or Weber think of America today? In place of thrift, they would find a nation of debtors, staggering beneath loans obtained under false pretenses. In place of a steady, patient accumulation of wealth, they would find bankers and financiers with such a short-term perspective that they never pause to consider the consequences or risks of selling securities they don't understand. In place of a country where all a man asks of government is "not to be disturbed in his toil," as Tocqueville put it, they would find a nation of rent-seekers demanding government subsidies to purchase homes, start new ventures, or bail out old ones. They would find what Tocqueville described as the 'fatal circle' of materialism— the cycle of acquisition and gratification that drives people back to ever more frenetic acquisition and that ultimately undermines prosperous democracies."

On the eve of President Obama's inauguration I wrote that the challenge for the Obama administration is a new economic morality. I still await that new economic morality.

Meanwhile, since the National Debt passed $11 trillion in March, the markets have moved strongly on the upside, led by the financials, anticipating a recovery from the Great Recession. I see little difference in the general shape of our financial institutions other than the federal government (uh, we the taxpayers) standing ready to bail out any deemed to pose a systemic risk to the system. As of the end of August the National Debt now stands at $11.8 trillion, so over the next several weeks that will undoubtedly pass the $12 trillion mark. That's $1 trillion in additional debt in only 6 months. I make this observation in advance as this blog will go silent for several weeks while are traveling overseas.

By this point in time "the market" had recovered, the Dow surpassing 10,000. Meanwhile interest rates were driven down to zero, an essential ingredient in that advance. There was no competition from the traditional investments of bonds or cash. In effect, the Federal Reserve was "forcing" investors to take risk, to borrow. It seems at this point we abandoned any concerns about the deficit, as long as we could get our investment "fix."

Tuesday, October 27, 2009
Awash in Liquidity
I defer to another insightful analysis about the economy and why we might be at an investment inflection point, this time turning to the world's leading bond manager, Bill Gross at PIMCO. His monthly investment outlook, "Midnight Candles," details why the investment "bubble" is a long standing one, that as a nation which once relied on the production of real things, we became focused on "paper asset" appreciation by the 1980's. Governments have artificially influenced those prices since then. Gross distills this in an interesting observation: "How many TV shots have you seen of people on the Times Square Jumbotron applauding the announcement of the latest GDP growth numbers or job creation? None, of course, but we see daily opening and closing market crescendos of jubilant capitalists on the

NYSE and NASDAQ cheering the movement of markets—either up or down."

That sets the macroeconomic scene, which has compounded the crisis of the last couple years. More recently investors have flocked to riskier assets as the Fed has flooded the markets with liquidity and driven interest rates to nothing. Unless the real economy grows substantially, this has to end badly when the Fed reverses course. For this reason, Gross believes asset prices might be peaking.

Gross is certainly one of the more literate, philosophical money managers around, and his prefatory remarks set the stage in that venue. As one who is about Gross' age, I identify with his feelings about being "Everyman." I suspect he has read Philip Roth's novel of the same title, but that's another matter.

Finally, and it had to happen, almost a year after President Obama was inaugurated, I began to express some disappointment. I had expected so much. I concluded the year with a very brief, despondent entry which hinted at a moral and political problem which would soon populate my blog and will be subsumed within these pages, gun control and the kind of society that would tolerate the NRA's interpretation of the 2nd amendment to include military style weapons. And so we end the first decade of the new millennium, setting the stage for the rise of Trump.

Sunday, December 6, 2009
Pull Up! Pull Up!
Like many people, I feel disillusioned by the first year of Obama's Presidency. This is probably more my problem as he is a mere mortal and inherited so many crises, long time in the making, deeply ingrained, that he would have to be Superman, flying around the world to turn back the clock of time, to undo

faulty foreign policies, reconnect the dollar to some form of the gold standard, change the unrealistic long term promises of Medicare and Social Security, roll back the deregulation of our financial institutions, and I could go on and on, but you get the picture of, perhaps, a society in a spiraling decline. Despite our cries of "Pull up! Pull up!" the ground closes in.

I still think the President could have devoted more of his first year to policies addressing what I called a "new economic morality." Instead, he had focused more on healthcare, not that that is not also important. But Main Street seems to have been sacrificed at the altar of Wall Street and we are angry. Who truly believes the economic crisis is solved rather than being merely postponed? Let another generation deal with it, the same response of previous administrations. How long can we kick the proverbial can down the road? What kind of healthcare can this nation have if it is bankrupt?

So, I confess, I got caught up in "the dream," the fantasy that one man, Mr. Obama, could make such a huge difference and in such a short time. I've been chastened by disillusion.

Wednesday, December 30, 2009
Ghost of New Year's Future?
If you read only one forecast for 2010, let it be this one by James Howard Kunstler who writes a blog, *Clusterfuck Nation*. While I hope things will not evolve as badly as he speculates, he may have the direction right, the ephemerality of the "recovery" from our duct-taped economy, government's complicity, and our lack of moral fiber as a nation to do the right thing. "We're a nation of thugs and louts with flames tattooed on our necks, who call each other 'motherfucker' and are skilled only in playing video games based on mass murder."

Amen to that.

A new year begins and the tug of war between fiscal stimulus and austerity continues. It seems at this point, before the midterm elections, the economy dominated thinking. This was also the moment when the Tea Party populism was rising.

Tuesday, January 5, 2010
Well Worth Noting ...
Two interesting articles, one an interview with Richard Koo, a former economist with the Federal Reserve Bank of New York and now chief economist of Nomura Research Institute, which appeared in this week's *Barron's Magazine*, "A Japanese Rx for the West: Keep Spending" and the weekly commentary of the economist and mutual fund manager John Hussman, "Timothy Geithner Meets Vladimir Lenin."

Koo's views might seem to be counterintuitive—government needs to increase deficit spending on a three to five year plan while the private sector is repairing its balance sheet. Japan failed to recognize the dangers of "a balance sheet recession" and the USA could make the same mistake. I would agree, provided spending is focused on our infrastructure or alternative energy, or on myriad other public projects that resonate in our economy, creating jobs while fixing our roads and public transportation, encouraging energy independence, reducing greenhouse gases, and improving our educational system. Such investments are aimed at Main Street, not Wall Street. I would imagine Koo would be the first to note that bailouts of irresponsible investment bankers do not constitute the kind of government borrowing he means.

Koo contends that while the private sector repairs its balance sheet, writing down debt on devalued assets, it is imperative for the Federal government to borrow because even if interest rates are zero, the public sector cannot be induced to borrow: "The only way the government can turn this economy around is to do the opposite of the private sector—borrow the money the private sector saved and spend it, which means fiscal stimulus. That's what saved Japan from entering a Great Depression."

In effect we can't make businesses borrow by giving capital to the banking system which only encourages more reckless economic behavior—it has to be spent elsewhere, and what better place than our infrastructure and energy independence?

John Hussman, meanwhile, writes about the very kind of borrowing we must eschew, especially as it is being done without our elected constituency's input: the Treasury's recent announcement that it would provide Fannie Mae and Freddie Mac UNLIMITED financial support for the next three years, reminding us that it was Vladimir Lenin who said: "The best way to destroy the capitalist system is to debauch the currency."

As Hussman notes, "in a single, coordinated stroke, the Treasury and the Federal Reserve have encroached on spending powers that are enumerated for the Congress alone." And perhaps worse, "... homeowners who have been diligently making their payments will keep their homes, and homeowners who took out mortgages they couldn't afford will keep their homes as well with no adverse consequence to the lenders—since the underlying loans are now owned largely by the Fed, and the Treasury has pledged its unlimited support. Why pay one's debts if it becomes optional, and the Treasury stands to absorb unlimited losses at public expense?"

Friday, January 15, 2010
The More things Change....
... the more they stay the same. It's as if we did a Rip Van Winkle during the past six months, awakening to the Sturm und Drang of the banker's bonus controversy, listening to the same blather

from CNBC about our stalwart bankers' right to riches as they have paid back their TARP money, the consequences of a capitalist system at work. Six months ago I noted the absurdity of Citibank's salary increases, their logic being they were "needed" to retain the best talent. Today's news is record bank bonuses, even surpassing those paid out in 2007 at the top of the market: "top 38 firms on pace to award $145 billion for '09, up 18%" per the *Wall Street Journal*.

We've become a Corporatocracy—this is not capitalism, which is supposed to reward success, not underwrite failure—and the bonuses are just another piece of evidence that the Obama administration, while talking up change, has been conned. TARP repayments is a smoke screen, masking the myriad other ways the taxpayer is subsidizing bank profits, be it AIG back door payments, federal government guarantees, or the zero interest rate environment which gives banks access to free money (buy a 6 month CD today and see what YOU get as lender). $145 billion in bonuses while unemployment is well over 10% (if you count people who are no longer part of the labor force as they've given up looking for jobs)? One would think banks would grasp the PR downside of the issue, or do they live in their own amoral world?

And as brilliantly noted in a piece in *Naked Capitalism*, "Obama's 'Get Tough on Banks' Again Tries to Play the Public for Fools," Obama's proposed tax on banks is merely a slap on the wrist, nice political fodder to appease the masses, but it clearly falls short of the reforms that are needed in the industry. *Naked Capitalism* contrasts Obama's weak stance to the soaring rhetoric of FDR when he took office: "....the rulers of the exchange of mankind's goods have failed, through their own stubbornness and their own incompetence, have admitted their failure, and abdicated. Practices of the unscrupulous money changers stand indicted in the court of public opinion, rejected by the hearts and minds of men."

Thursday, January 21, 2010
Obama's First Year
Yesterday's *Palm Beach Post* carried an outstanding editorial, putting Obama's first year into perspective, and I sent a letter to the editor yesterday as well. The timing of each was particularly apt as the editorial appeared the day after Brown's victory in Massachusetts, a clear wake up call, and my letter pointed out the need to listen more to Paul Volcker if we are going to achieve some real financial reforms and, eureka, today Obama is going to finally back some of Volcker's ideas. At long last!

The *Post* editorial, A clear-eyed look at Obama's first year in office makes many excellent points:

"* [He faced] not just an economy on the verge of the deepest recession in 70 years but unrealistically high expectations
* [Although he has had varying degrees of success,] he has stuck to the agenda he touted as a candidate
* The GOP strategy from the start has been to oppose and deceive ... Given recent poll numbers Republicans seem to be succeeding with their strategy of opposition and an appeal to ignorance or short memories.....
* The worst aspect of the last year has been the spillover of illegitimate criticism from the campaign. It is the criticism ... that attacks Barack Obama as less of a person, less of a patriot and thus undeserving of the presidency....Out of this rage comes the bizarre call to 'take back our country' from where it supposedly has drifted in just 365 days.
* We'd like to take back the country, too, but we'd like to take it back from a media/political culture that lives only in the moment
* The problems that Mr. Obama inherited were caused by Democrats and Republicans, Wall Streeters and Main Streeters.....We are back from the brink of one disaster but far from real economic recovery.

* Mr. Obama deserves decent marks, but he can do a lot better. That's what new presidents have the rest of their term to accomplish. An impatient America must wait longer to truly judge Barack Obama."

My January 20 letter in response follows. If it appears in the newspaper, it will be in a truncated form, so here is the full-blown version ...

"To the Editor:

How appropriate that your excellent editorial should appear the day after Scott Brown's victory in Massachusetts. How sadly ironic, and ominous, that Ted Kennedy's seat should go to one who opposes the very programs his predecessor would have supported.

Your editorial sprinkles some reality dust on the whole matter, reminding us that even though we, and especially the Republicans, have deified Reagan, he too had first year short-comings not unlike President Obama. And how quickly we forget (or the media helps us forget) that today's economic and foreign policy problems are ones the present administration mostly inherited. And as you say, we are all complicit in the matter. Only a few years ago many Americans thought they were living the good life, using their homes as piggy banks to finance excess. We were once a nation which once relied on the production of real things, but became focused on 'paper asset' appreciation.

Nonetheless, the clarion call of the Massachusetts election does underscore some serious weaknesses of the Obama admin-istration, most notably, in my opinion, the failure to achieve real banking reform. Yes, we needed first to rescue the entire finan-cial system, but we continue to sacrifice Main Street at the altar of Wall Street and people are angry. Who truly believes the eco-nomic crisis is solved rather than being merely postponed? This issue becomes conflated with others like healthcare, the anger simply spilling over from one to the other.

Interestingly, Obama had enlisted Paul Volcker, who helped rescue our financial system in the early 1980's, in his campaign and once elected exiled him to the minor post of chairman of the newly formed Economic Recovery Advisory Board. He has been calling for sweeping banking reform measures such as bringing back some of the best points of the Glass-Steagall Act separating investment and commercial banking, arguing that the best way to avoid 'too big to fail' is make them so they are not too big and consigning riskier financial activities to hedge funds to which society could say: 'If you fail, fail. I'm not going to help you. Your stock is gone, creditors are at risk, but no one else is affected.'

Instead, the Obama administration has engaged in political rhetoric on this issue, like taxing banks and criticizing bank bonuses (although indeed they are outrageous). We need a new economic morality and that is what the Obama administration has failed to address, certainly deserving as high a priority as healthcare, and has failed to heed Paul Volcker's sage-like advice."

Monday, January 25, 2010
Volcker, Stiglitz, Hussman....
Here's some positive news from or about people who can help point us in the right direction. First there was the big news that Paul Volcker will finally take a key role in addressing economic reform, particularly with the reinstatement of some of the key features from the Glass-Steagall Act. Joseph Stiglitz touches upon that need as well as other issues in an extract from his new book, *Freefall; Free Markets and the Sinking of the Global Economy* in a piece entitled "Why we have to change capitalism"

We now know the true source of recent bank bonuses: "free money" profits: According to Stiglitz, "the alacrity with which all the major investment banks decided to become 'commercial banks' in the fall of 2008 was alarming—they saw the gifts coming from the federal government, and evidently, they believed that their risk-taking behaviour would not be much circumscribed. They now had access to the Fed window, so they could borrow at almost a zero interest rate; they knew that they were protected by a new safety net; but they could continue their high-stakes trading unabated. This should be viewed as totally unacceptable." Also, Stiglitz puts the bailouts in the context of the bigger picture: "the failures in our financial system are emblematic of broader failures in our economic system, and the failures of our economic system reflect deeper problems in our society. We began the bailouts without a clear sense of what kind of financial system we wanted at the end, and the result has been shaped by the same political forces that got us into the mess. And yet, there was hope that change was possible. Not only possible, but necessary." As a consequence he argues for "a new financial system that will do what human beings need a financial system to do."

Meanwhile, the *Financial Times* carried an excellent piece on Paul Volcker now that he is again front-and-center, "Man in the News: Paul Volcker." For too long now Volcker inexplicably had been pushed off the center stage. Last March, as the market was in complete free fall, my tongue-in-cheek piece about "the new era of the 177K" asked, "Where is Paul Volcker to lead the way back to the 401K?" Per the *Financial Times*: "this week the towering former Fed chief stood by Barack Obama's side as the president embraced what he dubbed the 'Volcker rule' banning proprietary trading—over the reservations of some of his most senior economic advisers."

Then, John Hussman, the economist who runs his own mutual funds, and each Monday blogs about his views, published, today, a lengthy, carefully reasoned "Blueprint for Financial Reform." This is an extraordinarily detailed eight point plan/proposal; it deserves careful consideration by our elected officials. Needless to say, he sides with Volcker. Hussman for Chairman of the Federal Reserve or bring back Volcker?

I've argued that in addition to financial reform, the main economic focus must be job creation.

Monday, March 1, 2010
Bill Gross Redux
As I've noted in some prior blog entries, Bill Gross, the world's preeminent bond manager from PIMCO, also happens to be an excellent writer. I read his monthly comments as much for their style and wit, as I do for their content. His piece this month "Don't Care," although primarily about the sovereign debt crisis, segues into the topic using the experience we've all had, the vapidity of cocktail conversation, the inherent disinterest of people in other people, coming to the conclusion that "the careful discrimination between sovereign credits is becoming more than casual cocktail conversation. A deficiency of global aggregate demand and the potential impotency of policymakers to close the gap are evolving into a life or death outcome for the weakest sovereigns, with consequences for credit and asset markets worldwide."

But I am not going to discuss sovereign debt here (perhaps the most serious one ultimately being our own) but, instead, the experience he so eloquently and hilariously describes as the blather of the social gathering. He even incorporates a graph entitled the "Cocktail Party Empathy Chart," the X-axis being "Seconds Into The Conversation" and the Y-axis being "How Much I Really Care About What You Are Saying." As one might imagine, there is a diagonally dropping line from ten to zero in about ninety seconds.

Although Gross covers the five topics such conversations normally wander off to, I'll use his general observation as my own segue into a very recent experience relating to another entry, in which I said I was happy to see the preview performance of *American Buffalo* as it gave me an opportunity to form my own opinion of the production. Since then, three professionally written reviews have appeared, one in the *Palm Beach Post* which was positive but, I thought, could have been more enthusiastic and two unconditionally excellent reviews, one in *The New Times*, Broward/Palm Beach and the other from *Skip Sheffield's* blog.

We were at a social gathering recently and someone asked whether anyone had seen this new production of *American Buffalo* so I began to glowingly describe the production and was interrupted by the comment that the *Palm Beach Post* didn't seem to be overly enthusiastic. Exactly my point I began to say, and before I could expand upon that it was pretty clear to me this person was more interested in talking about something else relating to one of those five "unbearable minute-and-a-half" topics, not really wanting a thoughtful reply. On Bill Gross' X/Y graph, I hardly lasted the 90 seconds!

But why should this be a surprise? We don't even listen to each other on the bigger issues. Look at the recent hyped meeting on healthcare between the President and leaders of Congress, each party pushing its own agenda, preening for their constituents in the all-day televised meeting. Hey, it makes no difference whether we will bankrupt the nation, as long as I look good! Who cares what the other has to say?

But I digress. Thanks, Bill Gross, for reminding us that we need to listen to each other, although I guess he might agree it all seems pretty hopeless.

Friday, April 9, 2010
Anecdotal Headlines
I haven't done this in awhile, in fact not since December 2008 as the Dow was rushing towards its low during this recession—

that is to highlight some of the headlines from the *Wall Street Journal*, anecdotal evidence of where the economy and the market might be heading. Back then we were in the thick of it, virtually every headline pointing to fraud, bailouts, bankruptcies, and rising unemployment.

Today, while the Dow basks in the glow of massive liquidity injections in a low interest rate environment, approaching 11,000 as I write this, and investment bankers are rewarding themselves with record bonuses, the economy swims on against the tide of high unemployment (much higher than reported), kicking the state/municipal finance crisis down the road, and rising foreclosures. (We still wait on the consequences of future resets of adjustable rate mortgages.) No one really has an idea of how this will resolve. The CNBC cheerleaders are on the side of a continuing rising market, while there is no shortage of Armageddon forecasters who advise buying gold and farmland and head for cover. No forecaster I, but we seem to be moving from headlining the symptoms, and are getting more to the heart of the matter. It's interesting that "Fed Chiefs Hint at Low Rates Possibly Into 2011" can be juxtaposed to "Mortgage Rates Hit 8-Month High of 5.21%," perhaps an indication that the government has less control over the outcome than it did when this crisis began. From today's *Wall Street Journal*:

"*Foreclosures Hit Rich and Famous
Houses with loans of $5 million or more will likely see a sharp
    rise in foreclosures this year, according to a RealtyTrac study.
*Greek Bond Crisis Spreads
Concern over a potential liquidity shortage at Greece's private-
    sector banks fueled a sharp selloff in Greek debt and equity
    markets
*States Skip Pension Payments, Delay Day of Reckoning
The deferrals come as pension experts say the funds need the
    money more than ever

*Jobless Claims Rise Unexpectedly
*Cash Crunch Will Force Governments to Do Less
*Fed Chiefs Hint at Low Rates Possibly Into 2011
*Los Angeles Faces Threat of Insolvency
Dispute Between Municipal Utility and City Council Over Electricity Rates Deepens Fiscal Crisis; Bond Rating Cut
*Big Banks Move to Mask Risk Levels
Quarter-End Loan Figures Sit 42% Below Peak, Then Rise as New Period Progresses; SEC Review
*Mortgage Rates Hit 8-Month High of 5.21%"

Environmental issues are inextricably linked to our future and therefore is part of the big picture I am endeavoring to cover in these pages. It was at this point in time that the disaster of The Deepwater Horizon oil spill was underway. The subject populated my blog in a visceral way.

Tuesday, May 4, 2010
(Lack of) Contingency Planning
It is sickening to watch the unfolding environmental and economic tragedy in the Gulf. I know nothing about the business of drilling for oil, but even in the modest publishing business I ran for decades, contingency planning had to be formalized and a high priority on an ongoing basis. One needs to be prepared for the unthinkable. In our business, we built safeguards and redundancies in case our business data was wiped out or there was a natural disaster such as a flood. Of course, if such a disaster did occur and if all our planning failed, it would have affected little more than our business and our authors and customers. One would think that disaster planning for companies in the business of drilling for oil along our fragile coast would be of a magnitude and comprehensiveness befitting the potential consequences, to not only their own business, but to the environment as well.

BP's (and presumably the oil industry's) singular reliance on a device known as a blowout preventer to circumvent such a disaster seems to be a plan without any backup plan. Isn't this where the federal government should have had an active role—overseeing any drilling of this nature, requiring not only a first line of safeguards, but a disaster plan that can be immediately implemented in the event the first line fails? Much more, so much more, is at stake here.

Now we are told that BP has contracted to have three huge rectangular concrete and steel chambers built that can be lowered onto each of the three leaks. Apparently, this, too, is not without risk, but it may be the best chance at stemming the flow. These will be ready in about a week! Meanwhile, oil continues to gush. Why, why, are not such chambers ready for immediate deployment around the Gulf? It seems that, like with Hurricane Katrina, we are doomed to "plan" using a rear view mirror, drilling, baby, drilling our planet into oblivion.

Monday, May 24, 2010
Potpourri
Towards the end of the week I am going into the hospital for "a procedure" (a minor one to the medical community, a major one to me) so I attribute this posting to some free floating anxiety and an attempt to get some thoughts down on several topics, all suitable for their own entries. I think of them as a bunch of tweets, albeit more than 140 characters.

The first thing on my mind, other than "the procedure" is how quickly we've become inured to the major catastrophic saga of the last month: the oil "spill" in the Gulf of Mexico. I present as anecdotal evidence Sunday's *New York Times.* "All the News That's Fit to Print" fails to mention anything on the topic until more than halfway into the first section, although the front page did carry an article on premium prices for a Jon Bon Jovi "concert" in Hershey, Pa.

Why, I wonder, are we not pressing with all the public opinion power at our disposal for some resolution to this disaster? To watch BP, Transocean, and Halliburton in the brief Congressional Hearings was sickening, each pointing to the other to blame in a see no evil, hear no evil, speak no evil routine, finally all pointing to the Minerals Management Service which "oversees" drilling activity. BP says it will pay "all legitimate claims," the operative word being their interpretation of "legitimate," but that is far from the main issues: why were there no contingency plans in place and how, with all this country's resources, is there no way to stop this fire hose of black destruction on the pristine waters of the Gulf? Every single one of us should be holding these companies and the federal government responsible and let our justifiable anger be heard.

Maybe I take this personally as we live in Florida and appreciate the natural beauty of its waterways and beaches. But I felt the same way after the Exxon Valdez and it is absolutely stunning that we have failed to learn the sad lessons of drilling in fragile environments.

Then, I shift to another aspect of living in Florida, particularly south Florida that is blessed with some of the finest theatre talent. I've written before on the incredible productions at Dramaworks, the West Palm Beach theatre dedicated "to theatre to think about." Yesterday we saw a concert version of Sondheim's classic *Into the Woods* performed by the Caldwell Theatre Company. There we discovered that some of the actors we've seen repeatedly at Dramaworks and Florida Stage not only can also sing, but do so at professional levels befitting Broadway. In particular I mention Jim Ballard (who we saw only a few nights before in a Noel Coward reading at Dramaworks), Elizabeth Dimon, Wayne LeGette, and Margery Lowe, and I apologize if I am overlooking others. Also, as a pianist myself, I found Michael O'Dell's keyboard accompaniment remarkable—almost three hours of Sondheim's intricate melodies played flawlessly and lovingly. All in all it was a great performance of one of Sondheim's best works, the lyrics of "Children Will Listen" reverberating in memory:

"Careful the things you say
Children will listen
Careful the things you do
Children will see and learn
Children may not obey, but children will listen
Children will look to you for which way to turn
So learn what to be
Careful before you say 'Listen to me'
Children will listen"

We saw Stephen Sondheim last year in West Palm Beach on the eve of his 80th birthday. He is a national treasure, our last remaining tie to the greats of Broadway.

Finally, and I'm not sure about the appropriate transition to this topic, but I continue to be mesmerized by Raymond Carver's writings, including his essay "On Writing."

From that essay, here is classic Carver as it is exactly what he does: "It's possible, in a poem or a short story, to write about commonplace things and objects using commonplace but precise language, and to endow those things—a chair, a window curtain, a fork, a stone, a woman's earring—with immense, even startling power. It is possible to write a line of seemingly innocuous dialogue and have it send a chill along the reader's spine."

Thinking about a friend who admitted he wrote something just to make a deadline and make a buck, knowing he could have written something better if he took the time, Carver writes, "If writing can't be made as good as it is within us to make it, then why do it? In the end, the satisfaction of having done our best, and the proof of that labor, is the one thing we can take into the grave. I wanted to say to my friend, for heaven's sake go do something else. There have to be easier and maybe more honest ways to try and earn a living. Or else just do it to the best of your abilities, your talents, and then don't justify or make excuses. Don't complain, don't explain."

It seems this advice is applicable to everything as we journey into the woods.

Sunday, May 30, 2010
Perfect Storm
It is Memorial Day weekend, one of profound sadness, for the service men and women who gave their lives for our country, and now what seems like a deathwatch for the fragile ecology of the Gulf of Mexico.

The latest failure on the part of BP to stop the oil leak in the Gulf via a "top kill," one that was said to have a 60-70% probability of succeeding, now seems like just another attempt to string along an anxious nation until the "permanent fix" of drilling an intercept relief well is supposed to be concluded in August.

Now there is a new stop gap "plan," which involves cutting off the damaged riser and capping it with a containment valve. Per BP: "We're confident the job will work but obviously we can't guarantee success," pretty much what was said of the top kill method. So we can all hope that this is not just more media hype and cutting the damaged riser does not just release more oil. One cynically gets the sense, watching all of these improvised attempts, that we've seen this movie before, Mickey Rooney and Judy Garland (the Government and BP) saying "Hey kids, let's put on a show!"

Here's the "perfect storm" scenario: NOAA's forecast that the impending hurricane season being nearly as active as the one in 2005 and the possible impact on the rescue and cleanup activity by the armada of ships and platforms and miles and miles of containment booms in the Gulf.

It is speculation as to how a Katrina might further spread oil inland or even suck up and deposit surface oil in its torrential rain-making machine, but one thing is clear: cleanup efforts and relief well drilling would be profoundly affected. The combination of the spill and an active hurricane season is an environmental catastrophe of even more untold proportions. And it bears noting that early season named storms are more likely to form nearby, particularly in the Gulf and the Caribbean.

The only potential "good" to come from this might be our country's willingness to make the sacrifices we made in fighting wars, pulling together as a nation and declaring energy independence via alternative energy. I am not some Pollyanna thinking that we can suddenly drive our energy needs via alternative means. We need better technology, an improved infrastructure, and be willing to pay a steep tax on fossil fuels to support such efforts.

But that is what it is all about: the national willpower to achieve this objective and to save our environment as well. Since we seemed doomed to forever plan using a rear view mirror, this might be the only good that can come from this disaster.

Friday, June 4, 2010
Spill, Baby, Kill
The first heartbreaking images of oil-soaked, dying wildlife are now reaching the media, a reminder of the Exxon Alaska disaster. When will we ever learn that technology is not a failsafe solution and we have no business drilling in 5,000 feet of water without ironclad contingency plans? And, now, this is in our own backyard. Indeed, we might as well have set off a nuclear bomb in the Gulf of Mexico, as the long-term effects will be

similar. Barring a quick capping of the "spill" a wasteland waits, destroying the delicate ecosystem along our very borders, and inevitably to the promised economic recovery as well.

New supercomputer studies suggest it is "very likely" ocean currents will carry oil from the Deepwater Horizon spill in the Gulf of Mexico around the tip of Florida and thousands of miles up the U.S. East Coast this summer. Perhaps Washington will finally get the message when the Gulf Stream delivers some of this oil to the Potomac River.

Monday, June 7, 2010
Long-Term Thinking
Until we clear out bad loans, requiring those who made them to take losses, we are doing nothing more than applying band-aids to wounds that need major suturing.

It is amazing to watch the markets since late 2007 as governments around the world have gone into hock, writing blank checks to the financial sector. This has reengaged investors, driving up markets, and leaving risk-adverse investors with the option of getting no return or being forced into riskier investments. It is as if governments are introducing the same problem as a solution. We all get a sense that there will be serious long-term consequences and perhaps recent developments in Europe are indicative. In the U.S. we have time bombs of Fannie, Freddie, deteriorating state and municipal government finances, Medicare and, now, the economic consequences of an ecological disaster in the Gulf, which will linger for generations. How much longer can difficult, lasting solutions be deferred?

Meanwhile, investors can always follow Dilbert's Scott Adams' investment "advice" bearing in mind that in humor there is much truth, although he does carry the disclaimer "not to make investment decisions based on the wisdom of cartoonists."

Thursday, June 10, 2010
"Legitimate" Claims

By now we've all seen the $50 million media blitz by BP in which Tony Hayward articulates that all "legitimate" claims will be honored, as well as the recent news story that it will pay these claims for "as long as it takes." There is a world of meaning in the word "legitimate" and in a first step to define it before BP's legal army begins to mobilize, BP announced it would appoint an "Independent Mediator to review and assist in the claims process," that person apparently yet to be appointed (again, by BP, not an independent authority). This "Independent Mediator" will make advisory decisions" on claims, with those decisions subject to the following:

"* If the claimant feels the advisory decision is unreasonable, he or she retains all rights under OPA either to seek reimbursement from the Oil Spill Liability Trust Fund or to file a claim in court.

* If BP feels the advisory decision is unreasonable, the company may choose not to accept it, but the claimant then may use the Independent Mediator's decision in claiming against the Oil Spill Liability Trust Fund or in a subsequent court action."

Note the reference to the Oil Spill Liability Trust Fund as the first line of defense for BP. Congress created this Fund in 1986 to pay the claims of "any person or organization that has incurred removal costs or suffered damages due to an oil spill may submit a claim." Supposedly it is funded at $2.7 billion. However, the Fund site says: "British Petroleum is now accepting claims for the Gulf Coast oil spill. Please call them at 1-800-440-0858." So, back to you BP!

According to BP, "90 percent of the damages or income loss claims paid out so far had gone to individuals—primarily fishermen, shrimpers, oyster fishermen and crabbers. The rest had gone to smaller businesses, and the company was also moving to respond to claims by medium- and large-sized businesses."

No mention is made of the elephant in the room: state and local governments along the Gulf that depend on their revenue from property tax and sales tax. These are under stress to begin with and, now, with tourism disappearing, and properties along the Gulf going unsold (anyone want to buy a home near a beach with tar balls for an unknown period of time?), home valuations are plummeting, along with the associated property tax. Florida, which has no state income tax, is dependent on sales tax revenue, a large portion of which comes from tourism with its beaches and water being the major attraction. And, with the Gulf Stream, no part of Florida is immune to the threat of oil contamination.

The ripple effects of lost revenue to small and large businesses, increased unemployment, plummeting home values and increased foreclosures, and finally to tax revenue, are large and long lasting. So, BP, what about the "legitimacy" of claims of state and local governments for the lost tax revenue, this year and perhaps years to come? Thus far BP's track record, on promptly paying claims, truthfully reporting the scope of the spillage, going all out to save the precious wildlife and shorelines of the Gulf, is poor. This does not bode well for how BP's legal team will finally attempt to define "legitimate."

Wednesday, June 23, 2010
Lack of Contingency Planning Redux
It is a sickening feeling, helplessly watching the slow motion catastrophe in the Gulf of Mexico, which is rapidly becoming a dead sea. Now we are told that the pipe that was sending warm water to eliminate the formation of hydrates was damaged by one of the remote subs and it had to be withdrawn for inspection

and perhaps repair, sending tens of thousands more barrels of oil into the Gulf daily. Given the incredibly high stakes, how could there not be another such pipe ready for immediate deployment? Or an entire lower marine riser package cap? Where is the contingency planning and who is responsible, the government, BP, or is it Larry, Curley and Moe?

Tuesday, June 29, 2010
Market Report
The S&P was down 3.1% today as the market reacted to slowing growth in China, continuing high unemployment, and signs that deflation, not inflation, is the problem de jour. The 10-year Treasury Note now yields less than 3% reflecting that belief. *New York Times'* Paul Krugman characterizes this as "The Third Depression." John Hussman, the economist turned mutual fund manager, more mildly states that this is a resumption of the recession. Pain management stocks were up 2.4% in today's down market.

Wednesday, July 21, 2010
Top Kill Redux
As much as I would prefer to write just about anything else, I seem to be helplessly drawn into the vortex of what has become part of a national Zeitgeist of failure, our (industry and government) inept attempts, first, on a macro scale—not having the proper guidelines and oversight for off shore drilling—and then the resulting disaster at hand, BP's poisoning of the Gulf of Mexico. Three months into this catastrophe and we are now playing a dangerous game again, pondering a new "top kill" AKA "static kill" which, who knows (no confidence they do), might carry the danger of erupting the sea bed, the final straw in finishing off the Gulf of Mexico. If, on the other hand it is

successful, or if at least the latest BP cap on its errant well holds without such an attempt, it proves only one thing: there are technical solutions that could have been part of a non fabricated contingency plan, one that would have cost BP (as well as other oil companies) a bunch of money to have standing by, but would have spared the Gulf of Mexico a fate that is still unknown in its gravity. The lack of oversight that accepted the BP's original plan as the only shield for the ecosystem of the Gulf and the livelihood of its inhabitants is appalling. Future deep water drilling without a credible contingency plan, which should also include the concurrent drilling of a potential relief well, is unthinkable.

The midterm electioneering was now underway as well as the debate over the long term impact of zero interest rates on the economy and indirectly on income inequality. This became an increasing focus of mine. As I said in these pages, I am a fiscal conservative and social liberal, not necessarily mutually exclusive. It's all about the means to the end. The rise of the Tea Party—one could argue the very grass roots from which Trumpism could grow—gave voice to tax cut rhetoric and thus my commenting on that development. And increasingly encroaching on my writing are entries on the impact of the mass media and the Internet on polarization and plain brain washing, more foreshadowing of Trumpism.

Wednesday, August 11, 2010
Inflation or Deflation?
I remember watching *Wall Street Week* with the late Louis Rukeyser in the late 1970s and early 1980s during another alarming economic period, with talk of South American style inflation reaching the U.S. and the mindset that goes along with that fear, people buying gold, eschewing long term US Treasuries which were yielding around 15%. It seemed each and every week

investors were waiting for reports on the "money supply" with any large increase reinforcing the then prevailing view. In retrospect, how much simpler and more benign economic matters seemed then.

Now money supply measurements are not even discussed. Instead, we wait with baited breath for the Fed's latest interest rate decision, endeavoring to parse the Federal Open Market Committee's statements, comparing them with prior statements for clues as to what the future holds.

Today seems to be the inverse of those days with US Treasuries yielding nearly nothing, and the fear of deflation driving investor psychology, leaving few alternatives to us average folk not of CNBC's fast money crowd. By the Fed's decision to reinvest its portfolio of maturing mortgages in U.S. Treasury debt, rather than shrinking its balance sheet, it has embarked on a method of monetizing debt. Normally this would ring the inflation bells but not in this economic environment where spending is a higher priority than reducing debt or saving. Deflation is a state of mind that once it takes hold becomes a self fulfilling prophecy, particularly in the wake of the economic turmoil and bailouts of the financial sector of the last few years, with high unemployment and state and local government fiscal problems, leaving the Fed with few remaining options. And, unlike inflation, we have little experience with it other than the 1930s and Japan's ongoing battle with it since the early 1990's.

As reflected by CD rates of nearly zero, it is an investment environment where one has two choices, take risk (which is being encouraged by the government's actions) or put your savings under a mattress (which, in a deflationary environment produces a positive return without risk). Inflation or deflation? One has to wonder what the Fed knows that we don't. It is a conundrum for the saver. Bring back the good old days of *Wall Street Week*

Friday, September 17, 2010
The More Things Change....
Welcome to the twilight zone. When I read stories such as Microsoft possibly borrowing to increase its dividend and use the money for stock buybacks, I see it as just another sign of the American economic system gone wild. There was once a day when companies borrowed money to finance expansion for the production of goods. Now we borrow to pay shareholders or make titanic bonuses to executives. Or we finance our deficit by borrowing from China to keep the American consumer, AKA Hamster on a Wheel, buying at the local official distributor of goods made in China (and other emerging countries), Wal-Mart. But even with interest rates at all time lows, we cannot create borrowing demand in housing, or small business so unemployment remains intolerably high.

In the past I've written about the economic conundrum we've created for ourselves, the problem of job creation, the local government crisis, the underfunded pension guarantees, entitlements, banking bailouts, the inflation/deflation tug of war, and in general our consumption oriented society. In fact, while everyone feels a little better as we have thrown so much $$ at the economy to keep it afloat, repair some damage to everyone's 401Ks, the really major challenges lie ahead, and in one of the more divisive political environments as the midterm elections loom. The more things change, the more they stay the same.

Monday, October 18, 2010
Tale of Two Economists
In an ironic twist, an economist turned entrepreneur writes a rigidly academic critique, "The Recklessness of Quantitative Easing," and an academic pens an anecdotal piece of writing on a different but related subject, "I Can Afford Higher Taxes. But They'll Make Me Work Less."

"Recklessness" by John Hussman argues that the Federal Reserve's announced intention to pursue a second round of QE is to drive "interest rates to negative levels in hopes of stimulating loan demand and discouraging saving" and to "increase the supply of lendable reserves in the banking system." But will this increase output and employment?

Hussman thinks not as "interest rates are already low enough that variations in their level are not the primary drivers of loan demand." There is simply a lack of confidence—both for the consumer and businesses—that they will have the income in the future to pay off loans. So low or even negative interest rates is not a barrier and "removing a barrier allows you to move forward only if that particular barrier is the one that is holding you back (the economic term being "constrained optimization" as he explains.)

"Instead, businesses and consumers now see their debt burdens as too high in relation to their prospective income. The result is a continuing effort to deleverage, in order to improve their long-term financial stability. This is rational behavior. Does the Fed actually believe that the act of reducing interest rates from already low levels, or driving real interest rates to negative levels, will provoke consumers and businesses from acting in their best interests to improve their balance sheets?"

The effect of all the talk about QE2 has been to propel gold to new highs and to further erode the value of the US dollar as the Fed dramatically expands its balance sheet. "But once the Fed has quadrupled or quintupled the U.S. monetary base from its level of three years ago, how will it reverse its position?" Hussman's answer is that many years down the road it will be forced to sell off the instruments it is buying, driving interest rates much higher as foreign buyers might be absent from such auctions, and undermining whatever recovery might have begun of its own accord, just further accentuating the boom bust cycle.

He has constructive suggestions, fiscal responses that might include "extending unemployment benefits, ensuring multi-year predictability of tax policy, expanding productive forms of spending such as public infrastructure, supporting public research activity through mechanisms such as the National Institute of Health, increasing administrative efforts to restructure debt through write downs and debt-equity swaps, abandoning policies that protect reckless lenders from taking losses, and expanding incentives and tax credits for private capital investment, research and development." Of course many of these require the cooperation of Congress and watching the mudslinging of the midterm elections, one has to wonder.

But Hussman's article is must reading in its entirety, especially if you are an individual investor and wondering how to position a portfolio in this strange new economic world. The net effect of the Fed's actions, besides the obvious nearly zero return on any CD you might buy, is to "force" the investor to move into riskier assets commodities in particular and equities as well. One could also "play" the decline of the dollar by investing overseas or in US multinational companies, which derive a majority of their income abroad. But to what extent QE2 is already baked into the prices of these riskier assets is anyone's guess. There is also the possibility of a more protracted deflationary period than anyone can imagine right now, with the ongoing real estate crisis and high unemployment having a continuing impact. There seems to be a heavy reliance on the Fed's future actions leading to an idyllic outcome. I think Hussman would disagree.

One of his suggestions as noted is "ensuring multi-year predictability of tax policy" which leads me to the other economist, Professor Mankiw who is professor of economics at Harvard and was an adviser to President George W. Bush, whose administration has to share some if not a majority of the responsibility for our present economic morass.

Professor Mankiw's op-ed piece in the October 9th *New York Times*, through a convoluted and highly subjective mathematical exercise, argues the proposed tax increase on the 2% wealthiest Americans—some attempt at least to close the budget abyss—will lead to such people not working much, including, alas, movie and rock stars and even novelists! Outraged, and disappointed that I might not see another Harrison Ford movie, or see my first Lady Gaga concert or that Jonathan Franzen will put down his pen, denying us his next novel in protest, I immediately shot off a letter to the editor of the *NY Times* business section, in which Mankiw's article appeared. Some very good letters were published in response, but not mine. The nice thing about a blog is I can publish my own rejections! So here is what I wrote:

"While it is hard to argue with Professor Mankiw's math ("I Can Afford Higher Taxes. But They'll Make Me Work Less") of what his incremental income might become thirty years in the future in a halcyon tax-free world, his conclusion that movie stars, novelists, rock stars, and surgeons might work less if taxes are increased is based more on his own anecdotal view of working. By his own admission: 'I don't aspire for much more than a typical upper-middle-class lifestyle,' and that's fine, but don't blame the tax code for declining his next free lance opportunity. If he should climb down from his Ivy tower and look at the real world with real unemployment around 15%, people trying to work to simply support their families and hold onto their homes rather than handing down wealth to succeeding generations, he might have a little more empathy for a progressive tax code that did not seem to destroy incentives during the Clinton years, the last years in which our country actually had a surplus. And even Warren Buffett and Bill Gates see the fairness in having some sort of an inheritance tax."

Maybe the *Times* found it too preachy or politically oriented. Perhaps I should have concentrated on the nature of work itself.

Remember Hussman's comment about constrained optimization, that removing a particular barrier only has a beneficial impact if indeed it was that particular barrier holding you back? If Mankiw is entitled to personalize his argument, so can I. I worked as hard when in a higher incremental tax bracket as I did when they were lowered. Why? I loved work, simple as that. And, that is what is missing not only from Mankiw's formula but how our society looks at work and values workers.

I remember my first visit on business to Japan in the 1970's, the taxi cab drivers waiting at the hotel for a fare, their cabs gleaming as between fares they would polish and clean their cars. The refuse collector doing his job well was as highly valued by society as a company executive. Japan today, of course, suffers some of the same maladies as ours, with a twenty-year head start on the phenomenon of deflation, so perhaps that has taken its toll on their workers. Somehow, as a society, we need to value all workers and restore work as something to be embraced.

Of course we don't always have an idyllic choice of the work we do in our lifetimes, but we do have a choice of doing it well or not and by choosing the former, we open a path to finding it meaningful. I'm sorry Prof. Mankiw chooses whether he will write an article or accept an invitation for a speech merely based on what his incremental income bracket might be, although I think most people would envy that he actually has a choice.

Friday, October 29, 2010
Telling It the Way It Is
You have to admire Bill Gross, the eponymous bond king who runs PIMCO's portfolio. His latest monthly Investment Outlook in part takes on the silly season of the midterm elections and its outrageous campaign tactics. The election nearly neatly coincides with Halloween and the ghoulish nightmare of the endless direct mailings and automated phone calls insult the intelligence

of the American voter. The negativity is overwhelming. Being on the National Do Not Call list is irrelevant as apparently the people who make the laws can easily bend them for their own benefit so night after night negative recorded messages besiege our land line. If you do not answer, the recording ends up on your answering machine—some of them can last minutes. When we're home, call recognition winnows most so we can easily answer and hang up almost simultaneously.

The mailbox is stuffed with dire warnings, black and white photos of the opponent which makes him/her look like a ghost and then a nice colorful photo of whomever the mailing supports. Fill in any politician's name you want "[Blank] Is Sucking the Life Out of the Economy." Or another one we received today: "[Blank] Has a Secret She Doesn't Want You to Know." Some are sent by a major party while others are sponsored by "organizations" that sound mighty impressive but are totally unknown such as "Citizens for Lower Taxes and a Stronger Economy, Inc." Hey, I want a stronger economy and lower taxes—I should be for what they're for!

Just imagine a political system with campaigning that relies totally on televised public debates and published position papers (on the Web, in newspapers) but NO PAID ADVERTISEMENTS or CALLS. Imagine saving all those wasted resources and putting them to better use, especially in these dire economic times.

I'm sick of it and so is Bill Gross. As I said, you have to admire his stance, a risk he takes as he is not a politician, but represents a major financial institution. He's also a damn good writer. Good riddance to the midterm elections. When will we ever learn? He argues that the two party system no longer works. Here is some of what he said, just too good to be left out of this entry:

"... Was it relevant in 2004 that John Kerry was or was not an admirable 'swift boat' commander? Will the absence of a mosque within several hundred yards of Ground Zero solve our deficit crisis? Is Christine O'Donnell really a witch? Did Meg Whitman employ an illegal maid? Who cares! We are being conned, folks; Democrats and Republicans alike. What have you really heard from either party that addresses America's future instead of its prurient overnight fascination with scandal? Shame on them and of course, shame on us. We're getting what we deserve. Vote NO in November—no to both parties. Vote NO to a two-party system that trades promises for dollars and hope for power, and leaves the American people high and dry."

Thursday, November 4, 2010
Take Tea and See
The electorate has spoken and so has the Federal Reserve. The Party of No will now be in a position to speak words of more than that one syllable.

Meanwhile, Mr. Bernanke's monetary gift to the markets of quantitative easing is propelling them to new highs, especially assets benefitting from a weak dollar. Like sheep investors are being herded into a pen of commodities, export-focused stocks, and corporate bonds, anything but prosaic government bonds and CDs. QE2 is to stem deflationary forces and to stimulate the economy but the Fed is entering uncharted waters with its actions and will it create jobs? Beware of Federal Reserve economists bearing gifts to stimulate inflation and then be careful of getting more than what we wish for. The markets might party while Bernanke plays out QE2, and maybe even QE3, but what is the end game and don't markets ultimately discount what IT perceives as the end? I refer again to John Hussman's important observations on the subject.

As to the election, the results were no surprise. I remember being "amused" by the rhetoric heard immediately after Obama's victory into his first few months in office, the Dow dropping almost two thousand points in that short period of time as being "evidence" of his "dangerous" economic agenda. It was immaterial that the markets had already been in a swoon for a year before by even a greater percentage. As the Dow recovered, up more than four thousand points since the "Obama low" not a peep about his policies being responsible.

Of course, neither the decline shortly after his taking power nor the Dow turnaround has much to do with his policies. The Federal Reserve can take responsibility for markets on steroids. A year ago I said "I still think the President could have devoted more of his first year to policies addressing what I called a 'new economic morality.' But Main Street seems to have been sacrificed at the altar of Wall Street and we are angry. Who truly believes the economic crisis is solved rather than being merely postponed?" That anger has spilled over into the midterm elections and, now, we will have the help of the Party of No—and, who knows, perhaps they will have something positive to say and do. Time to take some tea and see?

Wednesday, November 10, 2010
A Taxing Question
How rich is too rich? Actually, I published a book by that title almost twenty years ago and some of its ideas are as relevant today as it was then (*How Rich Is Too Rich; Income and Wealth in America* by Herbert Inhaber and Sidney Carroll: Praeger, 1992). Two points from that book stuck with me. First, there is the very descriptive opening chapter of looking at income distribution as an imaginary "sixty minute grand parade," tax payers being the marchers, grouped by their height which would be representative of their incomes, the first marchers having the lowest income and the last the highest, with "height" determined by the "average" taxable income being equal to the "average" height of an individual American. The "parade" in effect is an X/Y graph, the Y axis being the income (height), and the X axis being the minutes of the "parade." The first few minutes one

sees no marchers even though we can hear some noise. These are people with negative height, those who report the loss of money in that taxable year. It isn't until about ten minutes into the parade that we see marchers between 10 and 24 inches in height and it isn't until 36 minutes we see the so called "average height" taxpayer march by. With about only 20 minutes left, heights begin to rise dramatically. With the last five minutes giants appear, people whose heads are so high we can hardly make out their faces without binoculars. The marchers in the very last minute of the parade are so tall we can only see their feet. These are people of accumulated, sometimes inherited, wealth and in the last few seconds the marchers are the size of sky scrapers. In effect, the parade shows a slowly rising gradient until the far right of the curve when it begins a parabolic rise and then shoots straight up off the graph.

While the numbers might have changed over the last twenty years, the concept has not. Probably, if anything, the "parade" has become even more dramatic, more parabolic, with a steeper rise at the end. And, those at the end of the parade pay now less as a percentage of their income to the government than at any time before.

To listen to the Tea Partiers, a roll back of taxes of the very wealthiest to pre-Bush rates is an evil, evil thing. Just think of the trickle-down effect that would be lost to the little folk who stand in line for the crumbs falling from the tables of the fabulously wealthy. It is ironic that these dire warnings of the effects of a tax increase on the wealthy are carried into battle on banners hoisted by "Joe the Plumbers"—it shows the power of the conservative media and the most virulent impact of the Internet. It just makes no sense that the people near the middle of the parade should become pawns for the people at the very end.

Actually, I think the converse is true: it is an evil thing for people who have benefitted from being able to accumulate wealth in the greatest of all capitalist democracies, not to give back more for that opportunity. The argument goes that asking these people to pay more will remove the incentive for them to work, and maybe if we're talking about 70 percent of one's income that might be true. But in 2000, people reporting AGIs of more than $1 million paid 28% of their income as taxes vs. 23% five years later. In 2005 there were 304,000 households reporting income of more than $1 million, more than a trillion dollars of income or $3.375 million per household. And mind you of those, there are a few at the very end of the "parade" with incomes that have so many zeros they would be hard to read. The latter are sports stars, entertainers, and, of course, very, very successful entrepreneurs.

Are they going to work "less hard" by paying an additional five percent overall? That five percent would mean another $50 billion going to the US Treasury, at least a beginning to address the ongoing deficit. And, of course, if you look at the $250,000 level as the cut off as suggested by President Obama, there is much more to be gleaned, but given the midterm elections, that level is probably going to be raised if it is not eliminated altogether.

The alternatives that are occasionally pushed by the Tea crowd, such as a flat tax, is, in effect, a regressive tax, with the lower income people having to pay the same taxes on necessities as the wealthy, which just further splits the great economic divide in this country. A national sales tax does the same thing and as we are now so dependent on consumer spending, that could be the death knell for the economy. No, a progressive tax structure has been this country's basis for supporting its national programs and we have been able to grow in spite of these supposed "disincentives" of higher taxes at a higher bracket.

No doubt the current tax structure is hopelessly and needlessly complicated and THAT is where the discussion should also be focused. There are so many loopholes, that a revised graduated tax structure would not have much teeth without addressing those as well. And then there is the issue of capital gains and dividends. We certainly want to encourage taxpayers to reinvest in our equity markets.

The other point I never forgot from that book was its commentary on the estate tax, arguing against the estate tax altogether, provided there was an alternative system of "estate dispersion." Rather than taxing one's estate at death, it suggested a tax-free disbursement up to a certain level per recipient (rather than per estate). For argument's sake, call that $1 million per recipient. Amounts exceeding that would begin to be taxed on some kind of graduated basis. Those would be life time totals, so if an individual receives money from different inheritances, they would be accumulated and taxed on that scale. "No longer would the estate tax system generate an American royalty—those freed from the need ever to be economically productive. This alternative system would generate for all the incentive that most of us have in the outcome of our own economic lives. No longer would a large part of our national wealth be beyond responsive use."

Now, the incredibly wealthy could give a million dollars each to a thousand different people, all tax free (if those recipients also received no other inheritances in their lifetimes). The point is that those thousand people would put that capital to work, rather than vesting a billion dollars in one's immediate family who might decide to simply live off the income and pass it on to the next generation, and the next. Or he/she could still leave more to the immediate family, but it would be subject to taxation, perhaps substantial taxation on a graduated basis.

"Wealth great enough to entitle one to membership in the elite comes from two sources—enormous earnings or inheritance. Prudent public policy should allow those, who, through individual ingenuity, talent, or luck, gain a fortune to use and enjoy it for life ... but if these individuals have the power to transmit immense wealth to others after death ... they can write the rules controlling this wealth, possibly many generations into the future. This breaks the chain of personal effort that is tightly bound, for most of us, to personal reward. Economic resources, controlled by rules set up by the dead, are denied to those who might well be more productive."

If the Republicans and Tea Partiers interpret their gains to mean they now have carte blanche to keep the Bush tax cuts for the highest wealth tier—people who would be hurt by some roll back to pre-Bush tax levels—the result will only increase the deficit further. There would seem to be no upside to such an action; in effect it is deficit increasing initiative they claim to condemn. Failure to make tax reforms that lead to a more graduated income tax and closing loopholes, and not having a sensible inheritance tax also just further drives a stake between the haves and the have-nots.

On a related subject, the so called "wealth effect" the Federal Reserve is trying to engineer with its QE2, is still another factor favoring the haves.

Tuesday, November 23, 2010
All the News That's Feigned to Print
The Rupert Murdoch-owned *Wall Street Journal* reported yesterday that the Rupert Murdoch-owned HarperCollins Publishers will sponsor a 10-day book tour by their author, Sarah Palin, who is a contributor to the Rupert Murdoch-owned Fox News.

The occasion is the publication of her book *America by Heart: Reflections on Family, Faith, and Flag*, a follow-up to her best-selling *Going Rogue*. In addition to those credentials for her inevitable run for the Presidency, Ms. Palin is also the star of her own reality TV show, "Sarah Palin's Alaska." Her daughter Bristol is indirectly campaigning by her appearance on "Dancing with the Stars," another prime time "reality" media production.

In addition to those qualifications, Ms. Palin has a bachelor's degree in communications, having attended a number of colleges in the pursuit of that degree, was a TV newscaster, and served as a mayor of a town of some five thousand people and for a couple of years as governor of Alaska with a population about the size of El Paso, Texas. She resigned her governorship to pursue her interests in self-promotion.

Besides having Rupert Murdoch's News Corp empire as a backer, she owes her political career to John McCain who brought her to the national stage in a desperate act to carry the 2008 presidential election.

Can this "rogue" politician continue to skillfully manipulate public opinion by charisma alone and a friend in high places? And will she continue to supply News Corp with all the fodder necessary for higher ratings, greater circulation and therefore more advertising and sales? A nice symbiotic partnership? You Betcha.

Wednesday, December 1, 2010
Cheery Tidings from the Social Security Administration

For the second year in a row, this happy news from the SSA, received in the mail yesterday: "Your Social Security benefits are protected against inflation. By law, they increase when there is a rise in the cost of living. The government measure changes in the cost of living through the Department of Labor's Consumer Price Index (CPI). The CPI has not risen since the last cost-of-living adjustment was determined in 2008. As a result, your benefits will not increase in 2011."

What a country, retirees are protected from the ravages of inflation, and, better news, yet, there is no inflation! Hooray! There is certainly no inflation in interest rates from CDs, that's well documented. Thank you, The Federal Reserve!

Of course the SSA's Cola adjustments are made through the most bizarre calculation. Sounds like a lot of sleight of hand.

It is interesting to review how the CPI gets measured and how such measurements might distort what inflation seniors really face. According to Bureau of Labor Statistics Consumer Price Index the prices of certain items have actually declined over the last year, specifically Window Drapes (8.00%), Peanut Butter (5.10%), Bedroom Furniture (5.00%), Dishes (4.40%), and Sports Equipment (4.00%). But, with the notable exception of Peanut Butter which many seniors may have resorted to consuming, these items are probably not frequently among their purchases. On the other hand, let's look at some of the offsetting increases: Funerals +2.20%, Dental Services +2.80%, Nursing Homes +3.50%, Physicians Services +3.50%, Prescription Drugs +3.90% and Hospital Services +9.30%

No inflation for seniors? Ha. Also, for a quick peek into the future, let's review the past: According to the Bureau of Labor Statistics, the purchasing power of a 1984 dollar is now $.458 while a 1967 dollar is only $ .153.

No doubt entitlement programs need to be looked at along with taxes to get our fiscal house under control, but inflating away the dollar and playing shell games with Social Security is what happens when Congress cannot agree on anything and political posturing is all our representatives seem to be able to do. We've become a sound bite democracy

Wednesday, December 1, 2010
Dueling Headlines
No sooner after writing the last entry of this same date, these two headlines from AP accosted my in box:

"AP Extended unemployment benefits for nearly 2 million Americans begin to run out Wednesday, cutting off a steady stream of income and guaranteeing a dismal holiday season for people already struggling with bills they cannot pay. Unless Congress changes its mind, benefits that had been extended up to 99 weeks will end this month

AP GOP says it'll block bills until tax cuts extended. "'While there are other items that might ultimately be worthy of the Senate's attention, we cannot agree to prioritize any matters above the critical issues of funding the government and preventing a job-killing tax hike.'"

Translation: if the peasants have no bread, let them eat cake! Translation for "job-killing tax hikes" for those in the highest income bracket: trickle-down economics with no basis in fact.

This was exactly my fear after the midterm elections: If the Republicans and Tea Partiers interpret their gains to mean they now have carte blanche to keep the Bush tax cuts for the highest wealth tier—people who would not be hurt by some roll back to pre-Bush tax levels—the result will only increase the deficit further.

Tuesday, December 7, 2010
Rebels Without a Cause?
It was a "chicken-run" by the Republicans and the Democrats, drag-racing to the edge of the Bush Tax Cliff as the sun was setting, but who really bailed out of the car and who remained will be revealed in two years. In the movie, the adversaries, Jim (played by James Dean) and Buzz, check out the abyss of the cliff before climbing into their cars:

"Buzz: This is the edge. That's the end.
Jim: Yeah. It certainly is.
Buzz: You know something? I like you. You know that?

Jim: Why do we do this?

Buzz: You got to do something, now don't you?"

And that seems to be the nature of the "deal" between the two parties: "You got to do something, now don't you?" On the surface, President Obama caved in. Someone had to and it was pretty clear the Republicans were prepared to fly off the cliff to preserve the precious Bush tax cuts for "everyone," especially for the wealthiest, the old Razzle Dazzle 'em of trickle-down economics.

We now continue the drag race to the same cliff in two years but this one also includes the Presidential election. If the "compromise" just further expands the deficit without creating meaningful jobs, the Democrats will blame the Republicans who will be left in the car. Of course the American people will be in the passenger's seat. "This is the edge. That's the end."

Friday, December 10, 2010

She's Quick on the Trigger

With targets not much bigger than the president's deficit commission. I don't think I've ever actually READ anything by Sarah Palin, although I've seen her paraded before TV cameras, so it was with some interest that I noted "her" opinion column in the *Wall Street Journal*, "Why I Support the Ryan Roadmap; Let's not settle for the big-government status quo, which is what the president's deficit commission offers."

I had expected a folksy take on the topic in keeping with her TV persona, perhaps sprinkled with homey references to Alaska wildlife, or more aptly the disappearing wildlife when Sarah Oakley has her high-powered rifle with telescopic sight at her side, but instead was greeted by a more or less professionally written piece of journalism, quite possibly with the help of the people at News Corp which owns the *WSJ* and also owns Fox which in turn employs Ms. Palin. She or her ghost writer is "disappointed" in the deficit commission's recommendations but commends the commission for exposing "the large and unsustainable deficits that the Obama administration has created through its reckless 'spend now, tax later' policies." I go speechless when reading such an accusation, feeling like Melville's Billy Budd confronting the evil Claggett. Sarah, do you really believe what "you" wrote? Not only are the deficits at least partially shared by your Party (not to mention the National Debt most of which could be pinned on the Bush era), but Congress now has the opportunity to roll back some of the tax forgiveness for the super wealthy, both in terms of incremental tax rates and the inheritance tax, and your Party is stonewalling that prospect. However, pardon my impertinence, "a man never trifles / with gals who carry rifles ... *Annie Get Your Gun*

2011 opens with an entry on home owning, the prices of which had been reeling because of the financial crisis. And now that the midterms were out of the way, thoughts of the Presidential election of 2012 were beginning to fill the media. The conservative press and its pundits were turning viciously against Obama and I was bewildered by it, a naiveté in retrospect. With hindsight, its roots were and are a form of racism, the American original sin which permeates today's political and social discourse.

Wednesday, January 12, 2011
American Dream Diminished
Owning a home was once a cornerstone of the American Dream. Go to school, work hard, get married, buy a home with a mortgage, have children, try to give them better opportunities than you had, work hard some more to pay off the mortgage, retire and do the things you couldn't do while you were working. It all

sounds prosaic now, even old fashioned, but I suppose if I had to describe my life in a few words, that description would be a rough outline. Lucky for me, I loved my work so I never thought a moment about following just about the same blueprint as did my parents.

They were children of the Great Depression and after the war, the urge to own a home was overwhelming, a symbol of financial security and success. Levittown became the poster child for postwar suburbs throughout the country, and upon my father's return from WWII, they immediately bought their first house, around the corner from my grandparents' home, and blocks from my other grandparents, in Richmond Hill (borough of Queens in NYC). I think they paid less than $5,000 (this is 1946 mind you) and we lived there until I was 13 when we moved to a larger home, in a "better section" of the same community. Both homes still stand today, remarkably unchanged. Those were the only homes they owned during their entire lifetimes.

By comparison, our home-owning has been more prolific (and equally remarkable, our past homes have been renovated to such a degree they are now nearly unrecognizable). After renting apartments in Brooklyn and then the upper West Side of Manhattan with my soon-to-be-wife, we ultimately moved to Connecticut where I was then working, first renting a small house in Westport, and then finally buying our first home which was almost across the street from where we were renting. It was 1971, the beginning of a steady increase in real estate prices and by 1974 we sold that first home and moved into a larger one in neighboring Weston where we lived for the next 22 years and raised our family.

The 1990s saw a moderation of real estate prices—even a decline in some areas. It was the time of the savings and loan crisis, but with our children out on their own or off to college, our two acre home in Weston seemed unnecessary and we wanted a home in a "neighborhood" and by the water, so we sold and bought a 100 year old cape on the Norwalk River in East Norwalk. We thought that might be our home for the rest of our lives but, unexpectedly, my working life was at its end four years later and that is when we decided to move to Florida, the fourth home we've owned and, who knows, perhaps our last.

But, someplace along the way, the American Dream of home owning has become an American Nightmare. Fore-closures and the federal takeover of Fannie Mae and Freddie Mac are just ongoing symptoms of the developing crisis that has stemmed from the housing bubble of 2000-2007, mort-gages being eagerly issued by banks with zero down to less than credit-worthy buyers, or to those in the "business" of flipping homes for profit, these loans condoned or even mandated by government. This activity and Wall Street's eagerness to cash in by taking inappropriate subprime loans and rolling them into exotic collateralized mortgage obligations, "rated" AAA by another accomplice in this crime against the American Dream, the rating agencies, conning investors into thinking they were getting a "guaranteed" return on a "riskless" investment, fueled the fire.

Also complicit is the Federal Reserve. By addressing the crisis with "Quantitative Easing" the Federal Reserve has post-poned the day of reckoning. By Federal Reserve Chairman Ben Bernanke's own admission in a November 2010 *Washington Post* opinion piece, it is the "wealth effect" of past QE's that has contributed to the stock market's recovery, saying "higher stock prices will boost consumer wealth and help increase confidence, which can also spur spending." This Fed induced bubble simply accelerates the "boom bust cycle," one that may end ugly when 'the can' can no longer be kicked down the road.

We all see the macro effects of QE, the rise in speculative investments, animal spirits being drawn out by low interest rates, a surge in commodity prices (of which there are relatively fixed amounts in relation to monetary creation out of thin air) but the gorilla in the room is our state and local governments. There has been a sudden flood of articles about their failing finances; a Google search will unleash an avalanche of them and I've written about this before as well.

In a nutshell, our state and local governments have promised too much in their pension obligations and now that the revenue tide is running against them with lower property tax revenues from falling real estate prices and foreclosures, not to mention their poor fiscal habit of financing certain projects with the assumption there will always be the opportunity to roll over debt with more debt in the future, the homeowner finds himself in the crosshairs. The cavalry of the Federal Reserve which rode to the rescue of banks and AIG has decided to leave municipalities and homeowners to their own devices, Bernanke saying "we have no expectation or intention to get involved in state and local finance. [States] should not expect loans from the Fed."

Consequently, it is now a vicious cycle, lower property values begetting a smaller pie for municipalities, which results in millage increases being levied by local taxing authorities, which in turn results in still lower property values. Being a homeowner today leaves one obligated to share in the past profligacy and poor planning of one's local government. Many would have difficulty selling their homes at any price to escape this obligation, turning the American dream of home owning into a nightmare.

Tuesday, February 15, 2011
Conservative Media Goes Rogue
Recently I was trapped in traffic in my car, channel surfing for news on the Egyptian revolution, and came across a Fox funny person, Glenn Beck. I should have surfed on by, but was fascinated by his off the wall comments—which admittedly I am probably taking out of context as I only listened to him for a

couple of minutes—but if I understood the thesis correctly, Obama's secret agenda (as a "community organizer") is to organize the youth of the world (evidence: Obama appealing to "the youth of Egypt" during the crisis) in an attempt to encourage some sort of a new Industrial Workers of the World? Did I hear that correctly? And what does Beck have against youth?

Between Beck, Sarah Palin and Rush Limbaugh (BP&R), a flood of bizarre assertions have been made about Obama's motivations, and the conservative media is drowning in their spewed sewage. It is one thing to call Obama incompetent, or having the wrong priorities (neither true for the most part, at least in my opinion), but to foster these conspiracy theories is quite another. No American president has been so reviled by conservatives and, frankly, I can't figure out why and how the conservative movement thinks it can benefit from this kind of extremism, other than selling more newspapers, books, and media time.

No doubt, there is a buck to be made by BP&R and conservative leaning media, particularly Rupert Murdoch's News Corporation which now owns Fox, the *Wall Street Journal*, and the book publisher HarperCollins, just to name a few. This media giant can now create persuasive circular arguments, hiring Sarah Palin as a Fox News Contributor, having HarperCollins publish "her" book, the *Wall Street Journal* and other media quoting the wacky output of this celebrity politician, and, then have Fox News quote the *WSJ*. Murdoch began turning the UK's newspaper industry into sensational tabloids at the end of the 1960s and some of the same methodology seems to be migrating to more recent ventures.

However, to my surprise, I read Michael Medved's opinion column in yesterday's *Wall Street Journal* discussing this very issue of the demonization of Obama—and a "fair and balanced" one as well (maybe I'll keep my subscription after all)—"Obama Isn't Trying to 'Weaken America'".

Of course, as a conservative commentator, Medved fears that the BP&R's fixation on Obama as an evil-doer will ultimately be the ruination of Republican chances in the 2012 election. He rightfully points out that while the history of the presidency is fraught with mistakes, essentially the office has been occupied by people of good intentions. I could argue that although Nixon's presidency might have begun there, it ended in the office's worst betrayal, but I agree with Medved that the presidency's history "makes some of the current charges about Barack Obama especially distasteful—and destructive to the conservative cause."

Tuesday, March 1, 2011
Inflation Takes a Haircut
Jon Hilsenrath, normally a straight forward journalist who is the chief economics correspondent for *The Wall Street Journal* covering the Federal Reserve, made an argument on CNBC today essentially basing the real inflation rate on the price of his haircut. He was interviewed by Joe Kernen, who is enamored by his hair as well, in regard to today's testimony before Congress by Ben Bernanke.

According to Hilsenrath, the Commodity Research Bureau's (CRB) indexes "do not hit American households ... we do a lot of other things with our money, like haircuts, which is one of the benchmarks I use, and [they] are not rising....The people who look at food and energy ignore those other things."

While the CRB puts commodity inflation well into the double digits, the CPI reports nearly no inflation (1%) excluding food and energy. Surely, between the two is the REAL inflation rate that is taking its toll on most Americans, particularly retirees.

Jon (and Joe), instead of preening your haircuts as anecdotal evidence of there being little inflation, you should walk in the shoes of a balding retiree. I just happened to have reconciled our 2010 expenses, and have accurate data going back eight years. Comparing that data our income was up only marginally as, even though social security kicked in during the period, investment income declined substantially due mostly to bonds and CDs maturing and having to be replaced by lower yielding investments (the Fed's attempt to force investors into riskier investments, the very issue that almost started a depression). Indeed, fuel and groceries were among the most significant inflationary items over the eight year period, up almost an identical 68% in our case. But what I found interesting there were also large increases in items that are not only essentially non-discretionary, but they are nearly monopolies as well, the consumer having only marginal choices, such as health care, insurance (car, home and health), water and sewage, communications (cable, telephones, Internet), and, most lately, real estate taxes. These take their toll on retirees.

But as I now generally buzz cut my remaining locks, haircut expenses were de minimis so there must be little inflation. Thanks for the fine journalism, Jon and Joe.

Friday, March 18, 2011
Engineering Failures and World-Wide Consequences
The similarities between the BP oil spill disaster in the Gulf of Mexico and the ongoing nuclear Fukushima Daiichi crisis in Japan are striking.

Both were unimaginable before they happened. Both the nuclear facility and the oil rig had what was thought to be containment and shut down protection, as well as redundancy features, in the event of a serious accident. In each case, these systems failed. The response to each event was similar, a series of improvisational Hail Mary attempts to mitigate the damage, resembling a disaster movie in slow motion. Each catastrophe has long term consequences to the earth's ecosystem and human health, way beyond the immediate geographic area of its origin. The lack of contingency planning in the Gulf crisis is evident again in the Japan disaster.

Surely, given the facts of Chernobyl and Three Mile Island there are commonalities with Fukushima Daiichi. No doubt the first line of defense in the construction of a nuclear facility or a deep water drilling rig has to be containment and redundancy features and bulletproof regulatory oversight, first at the national level, but perhaps with international participation as well. Too bad the UN is not a more effective institution. It needs to be in this area.

Any country that constructs these engineering marvels, for drilling oil in the deepest of oceans, or generating nuclear power, facilities that have world-wide consequences when they fail, should be required by the world community to maintain a national task force with readily available and deployable equipment to deal with catastrophic failure (rather than totally relying on the company responsible such as Tokyo Electric Power or BP). How much time was lost in dealing with Fukushima Daiichi when the tsunami destroyed its redundant pumps and power generating equipment?

Perhaps this may be oversimplification, but if we have the technology to create these engineering leviathans, we should also have the resources for a nuclear (and deep water drilling rig) immediate response task force, a small army trained for this once in a generation disaster, with the necessary deployable equipment (such as generators that could have been airlifted immediately to the Fukushima Daiichi site allowing the resumption of core cooling systems). We only need the universal will. Meanwhile, we all helplessly watch this terrible disaster unfolding in Japan.

This next entry is a 180 degree diversion from the topics I'm covering in this book. Its relevancy is clear. The book could

have easily ended with the last entry. In fact there would be
no book, just a discontinued blog. Here you are going nicely
along with your life and suddenly....Well I'll let the entry tell
the story ...

Thursday, April 21, 2011
Widow Maker Redux
Last fall I unknowingly had a 99% blockage in the infamous
Widow Maker's artery, the LAD. If it were not for the fact that I
regularly exercise, the problem would have gone unnoticed, and
indeed my case would have resulted in another widow.

At that time, a cardiac catheterization revealed the blockage
and I was given the option of less invasive three kissing stents
vs. open heart surgery. Naturally, given the choice between
the intrusive bypass, the possible complications, and the long
recovery, I choose the path of least resistance. After all, couldn't
I undergo the more invasive option if the stents didn't work?

Following that procedure, I began a cardiovascular rehab
program, which consisted of 36 sessions. Once again exercise
saved my life. I was on my 33rd session when I started to feel
some burning sensation in my chest after about 15 minutes on
the treadmill (I was doing 30 minutes at 3.8 mph). It would generally pass and I rationalized it was gas, but, here is the value
of such programs (one that may become vulnerable to cuts in
Medicare): the extraordinarily caring cardio nurses on duty
reported it to my cardiologist who called me in for a nuclear
stress test. I got through the test, so I went about my business
again waiting for results the following week.

In fact, immediately afterwards, boating friends of ours
from Connecticut, Cathy and John, visited us and over the next
four days we took our small boat out to watch the moonrise
over Singer Island, ran the boat up to Jupiter the next day to
the funky, fun, Guanabanas Tiki Bar and Restaurant where we

could tie up at their splintery old docks and enjoy a little bit of the Caribbean right here in Palm Beach County.

The following day we went to Peanut Island, our favorite destination on our boat, watching Tiger Wood's yacht, 'Privacy' (Tiger put the boat up for sale recently if you have a spare $20 million or so and can afford the crew and maintenance) glide by as Ann and company played Scrabble on the beach. We enjoyed lunch al fresco and later barbecued dinner and left as the sun slowly set.

A possible negative report on the stress test was the farthest thing from my mind, and I went about my normal activities as usual. In retrospect, our friends' visit could not have come at a better time.........the calm before the storm. Life as usual.

My follow up appointment with my cardiologist was the day after they left. Apparently, the stress test, combined with the burning symptoms when exercising, called for another catheterization and, as was explained to me, the sooner the better. The following Monday, March 28, I went into the hospital and had the catheterization expecting, at worst, Restenosis, which usually happens within 3-6 months after stent placement and I was still in that time frame from my previous procedure. I thought I would wake up to still another stent or a treatment of intra-coronary radiation (brachytherapy).

Wishful thinking. I was told my Widow Maker was now more than 90% blocked again (turned out later to be 100%) with another artery 50% and I would need dual bypass open heart surgery. There is a delightful acronym for this surgery as it is sometimes called: CABG ("cabbage"). I was to become a cabbage patient. Luckily for me, one of the gifted thoracic surgeons in the area, Dr. Arthur Katz, was available for the task, and also I was at the Palm Beach Gardens hospital which is a leading heart hospital.

First order of business was to get as much as possible of the blood thinning Plavix out of my system before surgery. I had been on the drug since my first stent more than six years ago. However, knowing that I had such extensive blockage in the LAD (the LAD coronary artery supplies a very large part of the heart muscle) made it a judgment call of how long we could wait. The surgery was scheduled for March 31 but after a blood test, it was delayed one more day (April Fool's day). Our younger son flew in from Tokyo (where he had been during the earthquake, but that is another story) to be with me and my wife. His presence made all the difference to Ann who bore the brunt of seeing my struggle and trying to communicate status reports to friends and family via email and phone. My older son, Chris, could not be here but Ann kept in constant touch with him.

Dr. Katz specializes in surgery without the use of a heart lung machine (off-pump, it's called), something I was grateful for as I have heard about cognitive recovery and other issues resulting from that. But as it turned out, my operation was anything but routine. First, endotracheal intubation (the process of placing a breathing tube to protect my airway and control breathing during the administration of general anesthetic), became very difficult because of various anatomical issues unique to me. A fiberoptic bronchoscope had to be used after several unsuccessful attempts at direct larngoscopy and glidescope.

Surgery went well initially, using an internal mammary artery and another artery from my left leg, but then there was increasing difficulty controlling bleeding. I had a number of transfusions. In fact, after my sternum was wired and the chest stapled, there were further signs of internal bleeding so for the first time in recent memory, Dr. Katz had to reassemble his OR team and go back into the wound. This carries a risk of course and it is why surgery is as much an art as it is a science.

Thankfully, he was able to control the bleeding at this point, but I had been through the wringer and back again, and had to have half of my body's blood replaced. As I had so much anesthesia, my recovery was to be equally slow and for four days I had that breathing tube down my throat as I went in and out of consciousness. My throat had been lacerated and was now excessively swollen. Waiting for my throat to return to normal, mittens had to be put on my hands so I wouldn't grab the tube when I had brief borderline awareness. Ann said during those moments I was waving my arms, gesturing with my boxing glove hands and giving everyone the fish eye. No wonder.

When I finally came to, I was in intensive cardiac care, pretty much unable to move, and having been unconscious for four days, would now probably be awake for at least two days. Those nights were the most difficult, not being able to move much, trying to get into a comfortable position, forced to lie on my back. I could hear almost every precious heart beat and sometimes the creaking of my sternum which was wired together. Deep into those nights you are left with your thoughts and fears, regrets and hopes.

I could operate a TV on the wall with a remote. It is not possible to realize how bad late night TV is until I became dependent on watching it all night, unable to sleep. I thought it ironic that juxtaposed to my surgery was all the rhetoric on the news shows about shutting down the government because of the lack of a budget compromise, all the posturing and huffing and puffing by the wolves in Washington, the propaganda about "entitlements" and the inexplicable inability of rolling back some of the Bush tax cuts as one part of dealing with the growing deficit. A subject for another entry, but, this is what I listened to as I was personally benefitting from an excellent healthcare system and no doubt a very expensive one, the very one some of our politicians would like to turn over to the insurance companies.

There is no way to describe everything that had to be done to me and for me to pull through. Medicare, in spite of all of the shortcomings of the program, works. As one of the most civilized countries in the world, such care must be available to all. And of course, throughout all of my 15 days and nights lying in that hospital bed, I was looked after by a revolving crew of highly trained nurses who literally kept me alive changing vital fluids, making me as comfortable as possible with all the tubes and apparatus attached to me and using all their skills and experience to help me survive my arduous surgery. There is no way I could ever thank them properly enough for their dedication and professionalism.

My breathing tube was gone by the time I came to. The third chest drain was yanked out (yanked is the correct word) by Dr. Katz as he diverted my attention to a discussion of where I grew up and my familiarity with Jahn's, a favorite teenage hang-out in Richmond Hill. Strange to be talking about Jahn's "kitchen sink" some fifty years later while a chest drain is being removed. Finally my urinary catheter was removed as well.

Another complication was a sudden spike in fever when I finally got to the regular cardiac unit, so for the next two days I was tied to massive intravenous antibiotics. No one could explain this spike which disappeared as quickly as it appeared other than it being somewhat par for the course.

So now I have been home for a little over a week and thanks again to Medicare, have been closely monitored by an attentive nurse and physical therapist putting me through the paces in the house. I now have follow-up Doctor appointments and have been given the green light to return to cardio rehab next week. While bypass surgery has relatively good prognosis, the fact that I had complications, new blockages, etc., results in some anxiety. I eat a healthy diet, exercise, have always been active, but as I said in my prior entry on the Widow Maker, hereditary factors seem to prevail over everything. Will my therapy and new medications offset this deficit? That is the hope.

To friends and family who might be reading this, thank you for all your heartfelt support, for me, and my wife who has been valiant through all of this. Ann was calling, emailing everyone, coming home from the hospital near exhaustion.

Well, here I am eight years later, so I guess my exercise and med-
ications are working. Of course, during the time immediately
following the foregoing entry I had no idea whether I would
have a sudden relapse. Nonetheless, I forged on recording my
reactions to the changing political and economic landscape,
although more and more entries, not included here, had to do
with the theatre, travel, family, and literature. I think I was
trying to "get everything down" while there was still time. It
is mind boggling to reread some of the following entries, as if
I am in a time warp, some of the same political rhetoric as in
the air today.

Sunday, April 24, 2011
Natty Bumppo Economics
The recently completed $38 billion battle of brinksmanship over
next year's federal budget is going to look like child's play in comparison to the upcoming showdown over the need to increase
the debt ceiling. So, so much more is at stake, including the
dollar's status as a reserve currency. And yet, our congressional
"leaders" have declared a recess until sometime in early May,
only a couple of weeks before the Treasury hits the debt ceiling.
No doubt the recent move in gold and dollar weakness reflects
an increasing anxiety that the United States Government could
actually default. S&P has put the US on credit watch. Without
Congressional action we will simply greatly increase the cost of
inevitably having to borrow anyhow when Armageddon comes
knocking at our fiscal door, and who will want to lend to a dead-
beat government? Why would our politicians even play such a
game? Is it a form of political conspiracy to bring the government to its knees?

　　Agreed, carrying unsustainable debt is a sure death knell
as well. But debt on the balance sheet comes not only from
making poor judgments and being profligate; it also comes from

failing to raise revenue. Both sides of the income statement—expenses AND revenue—need to be examined by our absentee representatives.

It is wishful thinking, particularly as the economy has been on life support through the Federal Reserve since the 2008 financial crisis: that we can grow enough to offset the tax cuts that have been implemented since the Clinton years. US taxpayers with the highest adjusted gross income have watched their federal tax rates fall from about 30 percent in 1995 to 17 percent by 2007. No argument that we need to simplify the tax code, but tax revenues need to be higher, simple as that. We need to revisit those Clinton rates again, a graduated tax rate without the loopholes. Close as many doors as possible to the underground economy. Eviscerate tax avoidance strategies.

We also need to shore up Social Security by increasing the wage limits for SS taxes—or how about a similar "donut hole" we give to seniors for their drug needs, taxing wages for social security to a certain limit, then no tax until another higher limit is reached, and then resume taxing for social security revenue. On the expense side of the income statement, means testing will have to be instituted and the retirement age slowly moved back.

The ideas put forth for privatizing Medicare will slowly kill the program, so desperately needed by the middle class. Cost containment measures have to take first priority. A voucher program is smoke and mirrors. Can you imagine the average senior having to make such decisions with insurance companies pulling the strings?

And Medicare being entirely turned over to the States, many of which can hardly make their own budgets balance? Disaster for the poor.

These are huge issues and I don't mean to simplify any of them, but defaulting on our debt is NOT the first step in resolving any of these problems. It will be our last.

The amazing thing about this "movement"— if it is fair to call it that—is some of the people who would be hurt the most just say "bring it on, let the government fail." Perhaps this notion harkens back to the idealized Natty Bumppo from James Fennimore Cooper's *Leatherstocking Tales*. But this is not a mythical tale of American rugged individualism and "one shot, one kill." It is about cooperation and compromise. We need our representatives to do the hard, serious work they were hired to do without all the political posturing and partisanship, and without the brinksmanship of the twelfth hour.

The first time I mentioned Trump's name in my blog came on the occasion of marking the killing of Osama bin Laden. Little did I know, what I thought was basically a joke, would accost and consume our very consciousness only a few years later, unthinkable by "everyman."

Tuesday, May 3, 2011
Credit Where Credit is Due
The killing of Osama bin Laden brings back the memories of that terrible day of 9/11 and a feeling of closure and admiration for the persistence of our intelligence community and brave men and women in the military. Ironically at the White House Correspondents' Dinner traditional "roasting" over the weekend, President Obama was joking about Trump's decision to fire a "celebrity apprentice" as the kind of thing that would keep him up at night, while this operation was being planned. It was a daring one, and not involving Pakistan was a calculated risk. Can one imagine if it had failed, as Carter's rescue of the Iranian hostages did, and the ensuing invectives that would have been launched at Obama? President Obama inherited a decade of overspending, tax cuts, wars on multiple fronts, an elusive bin Laden, and continuing unrest in the Middle East. What a lousy

hand he was dealt, but, as that Correspondents' Dinner showed, he has managed to retain a sense of humor while his intelligence never fails to shine through.

It remains to be seen whether bin Laden's death will have an effect on future Al-Qaeda efforts or, more importantly, the unrest sweeping the Middle East where Al-Qaeda is conspicuous by its absence. If anything, there are signs that self government, even along democratic lines, is being valued more than Muslim extremism. It's almost as if our electing our first biracial President, one who lived in a Muslim country briefly as a child, was a symbolic call to the world of "tear down these walls"—no less potent than President Reagan's challenge to Gorbachev at the Brandenburg Gate.

Tuesday, June 7, 2011
The Financial Crisis Reaches Out to the Arts
The tentacles of the Great Recession and financial malfeasance run deep, as evidenced by the demise of one of the great theaters in the area, Florida Stage. While their move to the Kravis Center this year was a positive development, everything else seemed to be a negative for this local, but well-established theater company, its revenues shrinking because of declining contributions (partly due to the aftershock of the Madoff scandal which hit this geographic area particularly hard), reduced interest income, and changing demographics as well. When we first began subscribing to Florida Stage, more than ten years ago, I remember remarking about the average age of the audience, wondering whether succeeding generations will appear to take their (now our) place. It seems like great theater has taken a back seat to Twitter and Facebook in that regard, Florida Stage's subscription base declining from a peak of 7,000 to now only 2,000 (including our prepaid subscription for next season which now will not be).

Florida Stage was daring enough to put on many original plays and musicals, not content to take the "easy way" as many theaters do in Florida, serving up the pabulum of Broadway revivals or touring companies as a staple. Of course, it is one thing to be daring during good economic times and strong subscriptions, and another to steer that course when the tide is running against you. I thought this season's offerings could have been stronger, maybe they should have served up a classic play or two to appeal to its audience. *Ghost-Writer*, I thought, was their best play of the season, with their opening play, *Cane*, the weakest.

All in all, there have been stronger seasons at Florida Stage, but it is doubtful whether that would have saved the company in face of all its other macro adversities. A really tragic moment for the arts and for the West Palm Beach area.

And this eliminates, still, another venue for new plays; one that I've learned firsthand from experience is fraught with difficulties to produce. More than a year ago I began an adaption of four Raymond Carver short stories into a theatrical work, *When We Talk About Carver*. Florida Stage was very much on my mind as a possible venue but it took me most of the year to negotiate and secure a formal permission for non-commercial, non-exclusive stage rights (just to show the work) with the Carver estate.

I had thought the success of "Gatz" which is a six hour acted reading of Fitzgerald's *The Great Gatsby* was an encouraging sign that unabridged adaptations of great literature could make great theatre. As Fitzgerald is to the American novel in the 20th century, Carver is to the American short story, and it is time HIS story and magical power of writing should be dramatically told. Also, interestingly, the new film, *Everything Must Go* with Will Ferrell was based on Carver's short story "Why Don't You Dance." The timing might be right for something more significant by and about Carver.

But without a local theatre that would consider a new work, even one which was essentially written by an established writer of Carver's stature, I now begin a search for a company that is willing to take chances as was Florida Stage.

One can only hope that other such companies can survive these hard economic times, one of the many unintended consequences of putting Wall Street ahead of Main Street (jobs) and failing to address a decade of deficit spending. The closing of Florida Stage is not only a loss for our area; it is a tragedy on a larger scale for the Arts in general.

Monday, June 13, 2011
Substance and Talking Points
I try to set aside Sunday mornings for catching up on some newspaper reading and to watch political shows such as *Meet the Press*, keeping my eyes on the page/computer and my ears on the TV, drifting back and forth depending on what I'm reading or hearing. This week's *Barrons'*, which I've read forever it seems (now online, having forsaken the print version), had a remarkably to the point article by Doug Kass, founder and President of Seabreeze Partners, and well-known "short-seller" which echoes some of what I've written about the subject of the growing abyss between the haves and the have not's and its impact on the misery of the middle class. Kass' term for this misery is "Screwflation" (combing inflation with the screwing of the middle class). Here are some of his bullet points:

"* While ... corporate profits will soon attain a new peak, median real wages have made little recent progress....Moreover ... an unprecedented four years of declining home prices have further weakened the confidence and purchasing power of the middle-class screwees.

* Unemployment has exacerbated screwflation's impact on all but the wealthiest Americans.
* Because there are few areas of the domestic economy that can replace the prerecession strength in real estate, a recovery in jobs will be more difficult than in previous cycles. Work related to real estate accounted for nearly 40% of U.S. job growth in 2001-06—almost all of it middle-class.
* Back in 1980, the richest 1% of Americans captured 9% of national income. Today, the richest 1% receive about a quarter of national income.
* [The] rise [of commodity prices] falls more heavily on low- and middle-income families, who spend most of their money on the necessities of life. Add rising health care, education and other costs to commodity prices, and the result is a poor foundation for growth.
* Difficult fiscal decision ... must be made this summer in Washington. The needs to accelerate job growth and to control the federal deficit seem irreconcilable.
* A shallow and fragile domestic economic recovery may be exposed to and be vulnerable to the need to cut spending— but drastic spending cuts will jeopardize the shallow recovery in jobs. Not moving on deficit reduction holds its own risks, of U.S. dollar weakness, soaring interest rates and higher unemployment....Partisanship already makes a real solution less likely."

Kass concludes with some excellent suggestions, but with Washington in gridlock, even on such major issues of raising the debt ceiling, and in the throes of pre-Presidential election rhetoric (see *Meet the Press* discussion below), one can't be terribly optimistic about implementing them:

"Policies that could help quickly include: extending the payroll-tax cut initiated by the Obama administration; reducing income taxes for the middle class; providing federal funds for infrastructure spending; creating incentives for businesses to make new capital investments; allowing tax-free repatriation of U.S. corporate earnings made abroad, if they are earmarked for the creation of American jobs; the launch of an energy plan that taps domestic resources; and the use of federal-housing financing to slow foreclosures and distressed sales."

While reading that article of substance, I was watching *Meet the Press*, particularly David Gregory's interview with Debbie Wasserman Schultz, the Democratic National Committee Chair and Reince Priebus, the Republican National Committee Chair. Talk about talking points galore.

Gregory immediately baits the debate with so called "facts" such as 59 percent of the public disapproving of the president's handling of the economy. He also cited that unemployment's "up 25 percent since Inauguration Day for President Obama ; the debt's up 35 percent, over $14 trillion; a gallon of gas up over 100 percent, with gas $3.75."

The numbers might be correct but one has to wonder about the "cause" of the "effect." Naturally, both Schultz and Priebus jump on their talking points Schultz rightly citing that before "he was inaugurated, the economy was bleeding 750,000 jobs a month...., and the economy has created 2.1 million private sector jobs, a million of those jobs just in the last six months. We've had 15 straight months of job growth."

Priebus has his talking points: "... We have lost two and a half million jobs since Barack Obama's been president. And of that two and half million jobs, almost 45 percent of those people have been out of work for six months. That number, that number rivals the Great Depression."

Back and forth, your talking points vs. mine. It is a sign of the silly season of an impending election, with the danger that the increasing polarity will result in a stalemate that leaves our economy on the edge of a cliff once again.

But, can they both be "right?" The Bureau of Labor Statistics' Employment, Hours, and Earnings from the Current Employment Statistics survey (National) 2001–2011 confirm that, indeed, we've lost about 2.5 million jobs since Obama was inaugurated, and we've gained almost 1 million jobs in the last six months. But the BLS also shows about 4.4 million non-farm jobs lost in the 12 months before Obama took office. How's that for a talking point?

One can play with all these statistics any which way to "prove" a point of view. The fact of the matter is we had tremendous job growth in the three plus years before the collapse of the economy (and almost the collapse of our entire economic system) in 2008, but those jobs "created" were heavily real estate and construction related during a housing run-up which we now know was merely a chimera. These are jobs that would not have come into existence without the frothy, nothing-down, exotic mortgage real estate market and the complicity of the investment banks and Washington to get those deals done. We simply "borrowed" from the future. Now, those jobs are out of the system with no prospects of returning soon. It is going to be very difficult to have robust job creation if, as Doug Kass suggests, real estate represents 40% job growth without solving our foreclosure and distressed sales issues which is now on such an enormous scale.

And how fair is it to "mark" a President's starting point for job creation as the date of his inauguration? The economy is a leviathan which cannot be turned on a dime. And, by the time Obama was making some headway, he lost control of Congress. Now we have such a polarized government, it is a wonder that any jobs are being created.

And, really, what control does the President have on world oil prices? We could have an army of rigs in the Gulf of Mexico and it wouldn't make much difference in prices as it is a world market for oil. The US cannot affect prices much by creating marginally more supply. Now, controlling the speculative aspect of prices may be a different matter, but financial regulation is habitually resisted by Obama's adversaries.

Agreed, we should have a national energy policy, but for it to have any teeth it will mean some hardship. In Europe, gas is twice the price as it is here. People learn to drive smaller cars, take mass transit, etc. No one would agree to that here so a national energy policy is simply kicked down the road, by both parties.

Finally, the deficit. Does anyone really think that if McCain was elected it would be much different today? President George Bush's 2001 and 2003 tax cuts have been big contributors as well as funding for the wars in Afghanistan and Iraq. Granted, President Obama's 2009 stimulus bill is also in the mix. But that was enacted when the Federal Reserve no longer could cut interest rates (they were already effectively at zero) and there was general agreement that the economy was still in crisis and without a stimulus, it would slip off the cliff again. And no one argues the bill failed to create jobs as intended. No Republicans voted for the act and now that they control Congress, one has to wonder what they will vote for or block. We know the talking points, and Kass makes substantive suggestions, but can Congress even function any longer?

Sunday, July 24, 2011
"A Glide Path to Zero Debt Post 2011"
This "glide path" was forecast in George W. Bush's Feb. 28th, 2001 budget, *A Blueprint for New Beginnings; A Responsible Budget for America's Priorities.*

The centerpiece of the legislation was a $1.35 trillion tax cut over 10 years which was signed into law on June 7, 2001. This cut was supposed to spur growth and thus increase federal revenues in spite of the tax cut (sound familiar?)

The exact wording from *Blueprint for New Beginnings*:

"Over the next 10 years, the Federal Government is projected to collect $28 trillion in revenues from American taxpayers.

The President's Budget devotes roughly $22.4 trillion to extend the Government we have today, including the President's new initiatives. This leaves a $5.6 trillion surplus. The President's Budget takes a cautious approach to allocating this staggering sum, starting by saving the entire Social Security surplus—nearly 50 percent of the total surplus—for Social Security and debt retirement. None of the Social Security surplus will be used to fund other spending initiatives or tax relief.

By devoting these revenues to debt retirement, the Nation will be able to pay off all the debt that can be redeemed—an historic $2 trillion reduction in debt over the next 10 years. The only remaining debt will be those securities with maturity dates beyond 2011. In all likelihood, American taxpayers would have to spend an additional $50 to $150 billion in bonus payments to bondholders to accelerate the repayment of those notes, a wasteful and senseless transaction. It makes more sense to allow the securities to mature naturally, leaving the Nation on a glide path to zero debt post 2011.

By 2011, Federal debt will have fallen to only seven percent of GDP—its lowest level in more than 80 years. Net interest payments on this debt will be less than 0.5 percent of GDP, less than one quarter of today's share and only three percent of the budget. This represents a great national achievement."

Meanwhile, the threat of recession intervened, and the Federal Reserve ratcheted down interest rates. America went on a borrowing and speculation binge, focused on real estate and the building industry. Government, Wall Street and Main Street were all complicit, greedy investors buying up "investment property," Wall Street packaging them as "risk-free" CMO's, and homeowners indulging in the practice of using their homes as a piggy bank, with exotic no money down, no initial interest payment loans, the repayment of which was dependent on future appreciated real estate values. At the same time we continued to outsource our manufacturing capabilities to China and other emerging economies. Why work when Utopia could be achieved by merely borrowing?

So returning to the halcyon *Blueprint for New Beginnings*, another lesson to be learned from China: "Forecasting is difficult, especially about the future." This is why the brinksmanship of raising the debt limit is such political grandstanding. Where was the outcry about the buildup of the national debt during the Bush years or holding Congress accountable for the failure of *Blueprint for New Beginnings*? While the stock market was climbing to new highs by 2007 and real estate prices were soaring, making homeowners and investors feel (not be) wealthy, not one peep about the national debt. We were borrowing against the future.

Depending on how one defines accountability to an administration (which takes control in late January every four years, but really does not have much impact until at least the end of the following Sept. 30 fiscal year), one could argue that Bush administrations were responsible for about a $6 trillion increase in National Debt (9/30/2001 - 9/30/2009) and the Obama administration for about $2.5 trillion thus far.

Of course, debt growth has been more dramatic over the last few years (including the final year of the Bush administration) as Keynesian spending of "saving the world" from a depression soared. In spite of that spending, economic growth has been slow, unemployment persistently high, and real estate and associated industries remain in the doldrums.

These are the serious issues, as well as the national debt, which must be addressed. While I am the first to argue for fiscal responsibility, a balanced budget cannot be achieved overnight and cannot be achieved without some revenue increases via taxes. The best argument against pinning hopes that spending cuts, alone, will achieve a balanced budget is simply to reread *Blueprint for New Beginnings*. Allowing the US to default on its debt is a hopelessly reckless option.

Tuesday, August 9, 2011
Fed Speaks
The Federal Reserve's press release covering its recent meeting begins "Information received since the Federal Open Market Committee met in June indicates that economic growth so far this year has been considerably slower than the Committee had expected. Indicators suggest a deterioration in overall labor market conditions in recent months, and the unemployment rate has moved up." Later, it continues, "the Committee now expects a somewhat slower pace of recovery over coming quarters than it did at the time of the previous meeting and anticipates that the unemployment rate will decline only gradually toward levels that the Committee judges to be consistent with its dual mandate. Moreover, downside risks to the economic outlook have increased."

Its main action point is that the nation's economy is "likely to warrant exceptionally low levels for the federal funds rate at least through mid-2013." Talk about telegraphing what it probably already knows: the economy seems to be slipping into recession once again and the Fed is helpless, meaning continued high unemployment, no remedies for the real estate market and homeowners with mortgages under water, and continued low returns on any savings. And these conditions are not temporary: they are expected to last two years (and unless Congress ever learns to function again, they will last much longer). Imagine, three year Treasury notes (no longer AAA which is another farce from S&P, the folks who brought us triple A-rated collateralized debt obligations) now yield less than a half a percent!

Where this is all likely to end is anyone's guess, including the learned economists at the Fed. The volatile markets are reflecting that uncertainty. Buying dividend paying stocks may be the best option for income, but any severe recession could leave those stocks vulnerable, jeopardizing the return of capital. That seems where the Fed is leading the individual investor.

Thursday, October 6, 2011
Do You Hear the People Sing?
About a year ago I likened the US income distribution to a "parade," the wealthiest appearing only at the very end, demonstrating the parabolic nature of great wealth at the very extreme of the income curve. I was wondering when, finally, the middle class would wake up to this growing disparity and do something about it. Finally, the "Occupation of Wall Street" movement takes up the cause, hopefully all by non violent means.

It is sad that Steve Jobs should pass away at this time. I think of him not only as a visionary technology and marketing genius, but as the greatest entrepreneur the world has ever known. The grass root movements of today, such as Occupation of Wall Street, would not be possible without the mobile devices he had a key part in developing and popularizing. I feel a personal loss of his passing at such an early age, and of the same terrible disease that took my father. And I wonder, if we did have a fairer graduated tax structure, one that would have rolled back the Bush tax cuts, would he have worked any less hard? The "don't-tax-the-job-creator" crowd might so argue.

Steve Jobs worked as he did because it was his passion. Entrepreneurs work with a creative obsession that is not going to be railroaded by a higher incremental tax rate. They are the job creators, not the legions of corporate and banking types, raking it in, paying a lesser portion of their income in taxes than a dozen years ago when the US actually had a balanced budget, CEOs now being paid unspeakable multiples of the average income of workers in the same company. Are higher incremental tax rates and the closing of loopholes the only solutions to the deficit? No, but it's a beginning. And that, as well holding these people accountable for any fiscal malfeasance, is what the growing Occupation movement is all about, the middle class finally awakening to the issue of their being used as puppets by political ideologists.

"Do you hear the people sing?
Singing a song of angry men?
It is the music of a people
Who will not be slaves again!"
Les Misérables, the musical

With the Tea Party squaring off against "Occupy Wall Street" the silly season got underway, the primaries, Republicans grasping for the golden ring. So many entries begin to deal with the absurdity of the process and the deterioration of political discourse and civility. And yet, it was only a harbinger of greater divisiveness in the future.

Sunday, October 16, 2011
Let Them Eat Leftovers
Actually, this is closer to what he meant: "Let the idle poor buy the hand-me-downs of the job creators if they can't afford to pay a 9% national sales tax."

And the non-taxation of used goods is but one feature of Herman Cain's 9-9-9 catchy sounding "plan." Help, I find myself agreeing with Michele Bachmann: "the devil is in the details."

While his 9-9-9 plan is "transparent," it is also transparent that he fails to see it as a regressive tax. It sounds oh-so-fair on the surface, all individuals pay a 9 percent tax on earnings and a 9 percent national sales tax and voila, everything becomes an even playing field. One only has to run an equally simple spreadsheet to see how overwhelmingly regressive such a tax plan would be as at lower income levels, fixed expenses, such as food, shelter, transportation, insurance, health, and, of course, taxes, become 100% of one's earnings. Conversely, even with a national sales tax, very high income tax payers would have even a smaller share of their income taxed unless they spent every discretionary dollar at Tiffany's.

Even if all deductions are removed from the tax code, ones the affluent can more easily access, it is a long way from 9% to the current top 35% marginal rate. And eliminating the 15% capital gains tax is a net gain for those taxpayers. Doing away with the estate tax is another bonanza for the fabulously wealthy (no dispute on my part, though, the estate tax needs reform).

Also if Mr. Cain is going to rely on reducing the payroll tax as a bone toss to the middle class, he is ignoring an increasingly large segment of the population—retired folk who are living on non deferred savings accounts accumulated during their working careers (already subjected to payroll and income tax, and probably at a higher level). They don't get the offset of a reduced payroll tax and in effect this is a means of double taxing and further penalizing savers. And Mr. Cain likes to argue that the removal of the payroll tax is an offset for the average worker that would now have to pay "only" a 9% sales tax, failing to note that half of the 15.3% current payroll tax is presently paid by business.

Overzealous tax reformers advocating a flat tax, or a reduction in income tax, triumphantly use the "growth" card to fill in any revenue shortfall. "Trust me," they are saying, "reduce taxes and the economy will grow to such an extent that everyone will prosper." The "job creators" will work harder.

If, as Cain's supporters contend, the 9-9-9 plan raises as much revenue as the current flawed tax structure, then mostly it is on the backs of working stiffs. And while there are merits in simplifying the tax code, 9-9-9 is not one of them.

Wednesday, October 19, 2011
Chauncey Gardiner Lives!
The Republican debate last night was laughable, sometimes downright embarrassing. Sound bites galore: "Everything is Obama's fault," "I'm a Christian" (choose your deity carefully), "I love

family," "prosecute illegal immigrants and their employers"—
in fact electrocute them! (Who will pick Cain's apples and
oranges?) "Less or even no taxes will create jobs." "9-9-9," "drill,
drill, drill," "blah, blah, blah." If you can't say it, scream it over
the other candidates.

Each has his/her shtick in these "debates" proclaiming a
"plan" (as they like to call it), in 30 seconds or less. One cannot
help but think of Jerzy Kosinski's prophetic novel, *Being There*,
written more than 40 years ago about a simple minded gardener, Chance, who is catapulted to political fame, becoming
"Chauncey Gardiner" when the media mistakes his comment, "I
like to watch my garden grow" as a metaphor for the economy.
That was Chauncey's "plan."

And did the CNN format remind you a little of "American
Idol" or "Dancing with the Stars?" I honestly thought I'd
see three judges emerge with scorecards. Text your winner
America!

Tuesday, October 25, 2011
Show Us The Figures, Rick
By now Rick Perry's opinion piece in today's *Wall Street Journal*
is making some waves. In many ways I agree with you, Rick,
particularly about simplifying the tax code. But that does not
mean a simple graduated tax structure has to be thrown out (in
favor of the regressive flat tax) and it does not mean one has to
entirely do away with capital gains taxation (usually the realm
of the wealthy, so that, too, is another regressive move) or does
it mean that a carefully thought out, and fair, inheritance tax
shouldn't be retained (concentration of wealth doesn't enhance
the American dream, it erodes it). And I'm all for responsibly
addressing the twin Swords of Damocles that loom in our future,
Medicare and Social Security. I'm even for a balanced budget,
but not via Constitutional Amendment (imagine having to raise

$$ in a crisis with congressional bickering stalling the process, not to mention transitional issues).

So while I agree with many of the feel-good measures, Rick, how does your op-ed piece constitute a "plan?" Show us the figures, Rick—how many jobs evolve from massive tax cuts and would those jobs materialize anyhow with the next business cycle? Where is the evidence? Or, is this merely an ideological belief?

And that is my problem in accepting your "plan" as a serious one. Furthermore, Rick, you were not the first Republican candidate with a flat tax agenda. Cain beat you to the Texas punch and Gingrich now says he's for an optional flat tax rate of 15%, which beats yours by five percent. By your own logic, that ought to create even more jobs! And Romney now says he's always been for a flat tax. Sounds like a game of Texas Hold 'em. Are all you Republican candidates in?—place your bets.

There is a pioneering book of social psychology you should read, Rick: Gustave Le Bon's *The Crowd; A Study of the Popular Mind*. Hard to believe it was written in 1895 as your true-believer words "tax cut" could have been used by Le Bon as an example. Think of them in the context of a passage I underlined as a student: "The power of words is bound up with the images they evoke, and is quite independent of their real significance. Words whose sense is the most ill-defined are sometimes those that possess the most influence ... Yet it is certain that a truly magical power is attached to those short syllables" [e.g. tax cut] "as they contained the solution to all problems. They synthesize the most diverse unconscious aspirations and the hope of their realization. Reason and arguments are incapable of combating certain words and formulas. They are uttered with solemnity ... and as soon as they have been pronounced an expression of respect is visible on every countenance, and all heads bowed. By many they are considered as natural forces, as supernatural powers. They evoke grandiose and vague images in men's minds, but this very vagueness that wraps them in obscurity augments their mysterious power."

"Tax cut" is the holy grail for supply-siders—a "mysterious power" indeed when it comes to resulting in more jobs. As Le Bon further says, those unexamined words "become vain sounds, whose principal utility is to relieve the person who employs them of the obligation of thinking." And, that seems to be the new "democracy" of the so-called "debates." As the late preeminent science fiction writer Isaac Asimov said in *Newsweek* (21 January 1980): "There is a cult of ignorance in the United States, and there always has been. The strain of anti-intellectualism has been a constant thread winding its way through our political and cultural life, nurtured by the false notion that democracy means that 'my ignorance is just as good as your knowledge.'"

Tuesday, November 1, 2011
Corporate Governance Gone Wild
Here is something for the Occupy Wall Street crowd to get specific about: CEO salaries have become obscene. Even new shareholder "say on pay" rules have not reversed the tide, shareholders being led by management's "recommendations" like lambs to the slaughter.

By 2009 the average CEO pay at S&P 500 companies was $9,246,697, including salary, stock and option awards, bonuses, pension and deferred compensation and other compensation (like the use of the corporate jet, when reported).

Compensation for these so called "job creators" has risen to 262 times that of an average worker by 2005, up from 24 times in 1965, about the time I entered the work force with my first job in publishing at $100 a week. If I had learned my ultimate boss earned 24 more times than myself, I think I would have understood, but 262 times? Today it takes the average S&P 500 CEO one working day to earn what his/her average employee earns in an entire year.

There are two issues that get wrapped around these facts for the Occupy Wall Street crowd. First how did salaries get so far out of balance? Then, why would a flat tax or any kind of reduced income tax at these lofty levels help the economy and create jobs?

Here is but one anecdotal example which helps address this issue, Eugene M. Isenberg's (the CEO and Chairman of Nabors Industries Ltd., a Bermuda registered drilling rig contractor) severance package of $100 million.

This nifty package comes after compensation of "almost $750 million since 1992, including the value of his exercised stock options" according to Standard & Poor's *ExecuComp*. So that's about $850 million paid to one person over about twenty years, or about $43 million year after year after year. Meanwhile, "the Nabors stock has underperformed the S&P 500-stock index for the prior one-year, five-year and 10-year periods".

It is unclear whether the corporate jet is included in the compensation figures. "Records of Nabors-operated jets have shown frequent stops in Palm Beach, Martha's Vineyard, Mass., and New York, places where Mr. Isenberg has homes. A Nabors spokesman said previously that the company had offices in Palm Beach and Martha's Vineyard and that Mr. Isenberg is frequently in New York on business." Guess there is a need for off shore drilling offices at some of the most upscale neighborhoods in America.

This is but one example of corporate governance gone crazy, Boards rubber stamping their approval of insanely generous compensation packages for CEOs, justifying their actions based on the (wink, wink) peer review system. Hey, look at these other overpaid executives at competitors, we have to keep up with them! Meanwhile (wink, wink), Board of Director positions are in theory subject to shareholder approval, but in practice management has played a major role in selecting and retaining board members. Board compensation of S&P 500 companies is now $234k per year for a few hours work each month and frequently they serve on the Board of more than one company. This compensation package is up 10% from the prior year (how many average employees received 10% increases last year?). So reciprocal scratches of the proverbial back have to be commonplace. Shareholders and Occupy Wall Streeters, unite!

Then, is it reasonable to tax someone who "makes" $43 million a year at a higher rate than his/her average employee making (in this case) probably less than 1/500th of that salary? You bet it is. And is this executive, competent though he may be, creating more jobs because he is taxed less than he ought to be? No way. Innovators and entrepreneurs create jobs, foremost example of course being Steve Jobs, and they are not primarily motivated by compensation and are they are not deterred from their calling by taxes.

Monday, November 21, 2011
Taking One for the Team
Ever since I heard that Hillary Clinton was planning to "retire" I've been thinking, what a waste of skill and experience. My thought was that Obama needs a new running mate, one that can handle the stalemated war of Republican and Democrat ideologues, and what better person than a former, and very effective, Secretary of State. Of course it means true sharing of power at the top, but Obama does not seem to be threatened by that, and as evidence he himself appointed his former rival to the position of Secretary of State.

Today the *Wall Street Journal* Op-Ed piece by Patrick H. Caddell and Douglas E. Schoen, both former Democratic pollsters, ups the ante with their article "The Hillary Moment," which suggests Obama should actually step aside for the good of the Democratic party so Hillary Clinton can run for President, their argument being that Obama will not be able to run a positive campaign based on his [economic] record and even if he wins we will still be left with a highly charged partisan political landscape, something he will not be able to change. In effect, President Obama should take one for the team.

While I might agree with his difficulty in achieving bipartisan consensus (and that is why I thought Hillary would be the ideal running mate in 2012), I have a problem with ascribing every economic ill to Obama. It is impossible to prove an alternative reality, but if Hillary had run in 2008 and won, we would not be in a much different economic place. And if McCain won, we would have been as equally bad off, or worse ("you betcha" if you know what I mean). After all, the economic problems leading to today were long in the making: regulatory failures, ill conceived Federal Reserve actions, the housing bubble with the attendant rapacity of investment banking firms, Bush tax cuts, 9/11, and ill-chosen wars in Iraq and Afghanistan. When you live beyond your means for such a long time, it takes years to repair the balance sheet, especially when dealing with one the size of the United States'. It can't be done overnight and it can't even be done in one four-year Presidential term.

Making such repairs without doing further damage to the economy means compromise, spending cuts and tax increases, ones that do not further exacerbate the steadily growing division between the haves and the have nots, the one percenters and the ninety-nine percenters.

Expecting Obama to step aside is to concede an imaginary failure, undeserved and such a concession would only feed opposition blathering. And that is where you come in Hillary; perhaps you will consider taking one for the team by agreeing to become Obama's running mate in 2012.

I continue to have high hopes for the Obama presidency in a second term. Hillary, I still hear America singing.

Monday, November 28, 2011
Altar of Consumerism
It's become a religion; thou shall pay homage to the God of
Black Friday. With unemployment and economic uncertainty
persisting one would think that consumers would be hunkering
down in their bunkers, but, no, they are out spending in droves,
standing in the dark with their faces aglow staring into iPhones,
awaiting midnight store openings after Thanksgiving, stam-
peding into the stores as the clock strikes twelve. Perhaps it is
counter-intuitive, $52 billion in sales on Black Friday weekend
during hard economic times, but consumers have been conditioned to "feel good" spending, the same kind of feeling that
arises from cathartic prayer.

Our Father™ in consumer heaven,
hallowed be your trademarked name.
Your Black Friday come,
your buying will be done,
at the mall and online.
Give us this day almighty bargains,
and forgive us our debts,
and give bailouts to our debtors.
Leading us away from credit card temptation,
and delivering us from debit card fees.

AMEN

Wednesday, November 30, 2011
Market Melt-Up
Buy, buy, buy,—be it at Target, Wal-Mart or the NYSE. Everything
is coming up roses. Does this mean one can "blame" Obama?
Surely, FOX will have an interesting take on this. "GOP comes
to the rescue of the payroll tax extension!" Or, "GOP forces

China to cut bank reserve requirements to spur world growth!" Or, "GOP threat of not raising taxes on the wealthy leads to the better than expected ADP employment report as job creators plan trickle-down hiring." Or, "GOP considering not abolishing the Federal Reserve as the Fed says it is ready to act if USA hurt by any European banking crisis."

Whatever the reason, stock markets are surging, for this moment at least (DJIA up over 400 points as I write this). But in this see-saw, roulette investment world, one cannot imagine what the future will bring, not to mention even the 4:00 pm closing.

Friday, December 2, 2011
Unemployment Good News
It's finally happened, a significant downtick in unemployment. Does this make a trend? That remains to be seen. But the headline news—The unemployment rate fell to a 2-1/2 year low of 8.6 percent in November and companies stepped up hiring, further evidence the economic recovery was gaining momentum.—is sure to provoke animated "debate" as the presidential election year gathers steam.

But there is some really good news here: "While part of the decline in the unemployment rate from 9.0 percent in October was due to people leaving the labor force, the household survey from which the jobless rate is derived also showed solid gains in employment." And those gains have been underway for four months. Maybe, indeed, the beginning of a welcome trend. And who will take the credit, or, better, who will give it? Perhaps it is merely embedded in the economic cycle, but everyone is quick to blame someone on the other side of the cycle.

This is the lowest unemployment level since 2009, when I was writing "A true recovery requires jobs, jobs, jobs."

A real recovery still seems to be a long way down the road as it took years and years to get to where we are and mountains of debt need to be addressed.

Meanwhile, the reasons for this drop in the unemployment rate will be parsed by the political pundits during the weekend talk shows. Brace yourself.

Tuesday, December 27, 2011
Another Mission Accomplished Moment
It is more than embarrassing. It could be politically devastating, the Obama administration caught in the cross hairs of political posturing as reported by the *Washington Post*, "Solyndra docs: Politics infused energy programs". These documents show "Obama's May 2010 stop at Solyndra's headquarters was closely managed political theater....Meant to create jobs and cut reliance on foreign oil, Obama's green-technology program was infused with politics at every level."

Am I disappointed that Solyndra was allowed to get so out of hand?—yes, but not surprised. There are parallels to the "Bush moment" in 2003 after Iraq had been invaded, when he arrived on the decks of an aircraft carrier in a fighter plane, dressed as a fighter pilot, to declare "Mission Accomplished!"—the navy personnel cheering him on. It doesn't get any more of a political show than that. But, they call it "politics" for a reason.

The worst aspect of these parallel moments is no mission was accomplished. The Iraq war, slogged on while hundreds more Americans were killed, thousands injured, not to mention a multiple number of Iraqis maimed or killed. And, when it is said and done, more than a trillion dollars will have been spent on the Iraq war. No mission accomplished there.

While Solyndra did not cost lives, and will not cost the American taxpayer anything remotely resembling the Iraq war, it also epitomizes a failed mission—a serious detour in the attempt to achieve a modicum of energy independence, and to create jobs. Simply put, the Obama administration misspent valuable political capital on its "mission accomplished" moment.

So, while I understand the political posturing, and do not think Solyndra is out of character with what we have long become inured to, I am dismayed that Obama's first term is being squandered without serious progress in energy independence.

Obama made an interesting remark during his 60 minutes interview: "Don't judge me against the Almighty; judge me against the alternative." Obama chose hope and change as his mantra, a nice thought but unrealistic in Washington. So he is saddled with the sweeping generalization of his "promise" and it is probably why he is so despised by his adversaries. But when I think of the alternatives it makes me hope that he will change.

In the meantime we enter that dreaded season leading up to the presidential election. This year dinosaur Super PACs will be allowed to roam free in the Jurassic political park, organizations that can raise unlimited sums from anyone, including corporations and unions. Be prepared for an unprecedented level of vitriol in this election, with a constant barrage of negative political ads. Even if nothing else comes from the Solyndra debacle, it will feed the PAC beast

And so again the calendar year flips and we're onto the political rhetoric of the presidential primaries in full bloom. There was finger pointing and blame gaming galore, as we've become accustomed to, an assault of propaganda machines on both sides of the isle, an insult to thinking people everywhere.

Wednesday, January 11, 2012
Blather into Matter
Or, as a friend of mine from my academic publishing days called it, feces into thesis.

The political circus is almost on full parade now but when it comes to the economy I can neither give Obama credit nor condemnation. The news media, the Republican candidates, and the administration are obsessed by citing statistics to justify their positions, and if you think you've heard it all, it is just the beginning of stream of consciousness blather. But the fact of the matter is the economy was in a swoon, a serious one, before Obama took office and continued on that route for a while before stabilizing and, even, growing.

Capitalism is a story of inherent cycles. The Federal Reserve was devised in part to mitigate the extremes of the cycles. Unfortunately, the Federal Reserve failed in that mission with the beginning of the 21st century, thanks to the hubris of Greenspan. At the bottom of the crisis in 2008 he confessed to Congress: "I made a mistake in presuming that the self-interests of organizations, specifically banks, were such as that they were best capable of protecting their own shareholders and their equity in the firms. Free markets did break down, and I think that, as I said, that shocked me. I still don't fully understand how it happened or why it happened."

It is amusing to hear all the political rhetoric now that, for the time being, we seem to have been able to drag ourselves off the cliff of a depression. Harking back to those dark days of 2008/9 the CNBC cheerleaders looked stunned most of the time as the Dow was flushing like a broken toilet. Now the market is up about ninety percent from its low and jobs are slowly coming back (agreed, way too slowly, but this is a different kind of recession and a different kind of recovery) and everything is cheery at CNBC except for their opinion of Obama.

The Federal Reserve policy is just one component of the crisis and one can add to the mix the expense of overseas wars, the housing crisis, deregulation (yes, see what Greenspan admitted to above), private profit at public risk, governmental gridlock, all of this exacerbated by normal economic cycles. Oh, also add the multi-generational lack of an energy policy to this colossal conundrum.

The Republicans say that by now Obama "owns" the economy, as if a switch was thrown when he was inaugurated and a dial was set for about three years, the onset of the next Presidential election cycle. Unfortunately for him, he too misunderstood the magnitude of this unprecedented economic cycle, saying the following in an interview only days after he took office: "A year from now, I think people are going to see that we're starting to make some progress, but there's still going to be some pain out there.... If I don't have this done in three years, then there's going to be a one-term proposition." Romney et al have eagerly seized on this gaffe. Expect to hear it over and over again in the next ten months. Likewise, expect to hear Romney's (the presumptive Republican nominee) recent comment that he "likes being able to fire people" over and over again. Sound bite vs. sound bite reverberating on the airwaves thanks to the endless resources of Super PACs.

When it comes to job creation (or erosion) there are limits as to what a mere president can do in a relatively short period of time given economic cycles and the severity of the present crisis. That Romney created or uncreated jobs in the private equity arena are of no particular advantage unless he has the cooperation of Congress with smart policies. Likewise, Obama has little control over jobs without cooperation and policy agreement. It is preposterous to assume that Romney is any more qualified than Obama simply because he worked in private equity. I ran a publishing company for thirty years; that ought to make me more qualified to deal with the economy!

And those policies have to consider the vice grip closing in on this unique moment in US economic history: baby boomers are reaching retirement age at the rate of about seven each minute of each day for the next two decades, expecting the promises of Social Security and Medicare. We all know both sides of the equation have to change, how entitlements are doled out, and how revenue must be raised. This is not something that can be achieved by a Presidential Executive Order (although at times I think our dysfunctional Congress needs to be replaced by a benign dictatorship).

The Republicans do not talk about areas where Obama successfully functioned without having to negotiate with Congress, such as his role in planning Osama bin Laden's death. Remember when John McCain promised voters (in 2008) that he "knows how to capture and bring to justice Osama bin Laden"(although at the time that was a secret he was not going to share with anyone unless elected)? They didn't have the economy to blame on Obama then, so it was his foreign policy "inexperience." Bin Laden sharing the bottom of the North Arabian Sea with the fishes came with no help from Congress, thank you. In spite of his inexperience Obama had the wisdom to send in Navy Seals rather than taking out bin Laden with a drone strike to have proof it was indeed him.

So let the games begin. Blather into matter. Feces into thesis.

Sunday, January 22, 2012
The Politics of Entitlement
Mitt Romney calls it the "politics of envy." "The rich are different than you and me" to quote F. Scott Fitzgerald, but, let me assure you, contrary to Hemingway's rejoinder, it isn't just because they have more money. There is a sense of entitlement, something one (they) can "talk about in quiet rooms" but never in public because the rabble might grumble. The full quote from Fitzgerald's, *The Rich Boy*, beautifully tells about this kind of wealth: "Let me tell you about the very rich. They are different from you and me. They possess and enjoy early, and it does something to them, makes them soft, where we are hard, cynical

where we are trustful, in a way that, unless you were born rich, it is very difficult to understand."

Oh, to be a fly on the wall of Romney's campaign headquarters, advisors pouring over his tax returns trying to determine if they should be released, and, if so, when, how many, in what detail, and what explanations (spin) should accompany them. Bring on the Madison Avenue types to brand and package his wealth as a sort of "Romney Success Cereal." I am "successful" (i.e. "rich"). Vote for me, and you can be like me with a nice looking Father-Knows-Best family thrown in for good measure!

His tax returns are probably hundreds of pages and there may be multiple returns depending on how he has set up Family Limited Partnerships, etc. They probably reflect some form of tithing as by "Commandment of God" Mormons are expected to pay 10% of their gross income to the church—including income from trust funds and food stamps (no chance of the latter) to be a member of the church "in good standing" and therefore receive its "blessings."

While religion should not be an issue in this or any election, and I will vote for any candidate I think best suited for the job, no matter what the religion, even (gasp!) an atheist, undoubtedly this is an issue for the American electorate (which would never elect an atheist), and therefore what is revealed in Romney's tax return may have a bearing.

But, mostly, it will be about how his tax handlers may have manipulated the issue of earned vs. unearned income. And this cannot be determined by one year's return. When asked about his intentions to release multiple years' tax returns at a recent Republican "debate" he chortled with his patented disingenuous laugh, "maybe." In fact, every time his wealth comes up as an issue he looks like a deer in the headlights, trying to portray himself as having lived "real streets of America" and having come from modest means (father, president of American Motors, and later Governor of Michigan).

The greater the wealth the greater the opportunity to shift income between "earned" (taxed up to the maximum 35%) to "unearned" (income from investments and in private equity, "the carry" which is taxed at 15%) It was not long ago when those figures were approximately in equilibrium, but the Bush era changed all of that and Wall Street would like to keep it that way. Masters of the Universe, unite! A reasonable measure of economic equality has become a corpse of the American Dream.

This election year is conjuring up the most virulent politics in history, Super PACs having contributed to this, something that should be abolished. Here, in Florida, we are now being besieged by them on the airways, Romney having a presence in political advertising even weeks before. The Republicans would like us to believe that calling to roll back the Bush "temporary" tax cuts is the "politics of envy" and that "class warfare" is actually a tactic in an overarching strategy by Obama to make a "welfare class" dependent on the Federal government and therefore more likely to vote Democrat. Talk about conspiracy theories. Might as bring up the issue of his birth certificate again.

Ironically, if I had to hold my nose and vote for just one of the remaining Republicans, my default candidate would be Romney. But as much as I find wanting in President Obama, he has the right idea when he said "don't compare me to the Almighty; compare me to the alternative."

Jan. 24 Follow-Up:

"The" Return was released—as expected, hundreds of pages but everything legal and above board, an effective tax rate of 13.9 percent. Romney also contributed what would be expected to the Mormon Church, so, on both counts he is absolved of any wrong doing. But if there was ever a clarion call for a more sensible tax code, this is it.

However, I will say the following fearing this point gets lost in all the rhetoric about what motivates people to work: the Republicans argue that lowering the tax rate for everyone (Gingrich proposes a zero tax rate for capital gains) will magically create jobs, economic growth, and therefore the necessary revenue for the Federal Government to do its job, albeit at a reduced level (with cuts in just about every area of social welfare as everyone would "then" be working). But if their theory is wrong, we will be right back onto the same economic precipice at the end of the Bush Presidency.

Romney says his success was due to "working hard." Did he do so because of an effective tax rate of 13.9 percent? At the end of the Reagan Presidency my effective rate was 33 percent. Did I work "less hard" as president of a publishing company than Romney did in private equity? My mistake was to work for a W-2 rather than for carried interest. This kind of tax code games the system so, indeed, the rich can only get richer while everyone else is mired in economic limbo at best.

Jobs do not "happen" because of the tax code alone. They come from education, a passion for working, jobs being valued by society no matter what they are, entrepreneurial vision, and a host of other, more relevant, factors.

Thursday, March 8, 2012
PAC Politics
"Stay tuned, but now a word from the sponsor"—the despicable political advertising condoned by the Supreme Court. The Founding Fathers obviously anticipated ungodly sums of money being raised by corporations and unions for political PACs so elections can be bought and sold by these "people" whose first amendment rights would otherwise be violated. Or at least I guess that is the Court's interpretation.

And to think we are just seeing the tip of the Super PAC iceberg in this Presidential election cycle. The Republican primaries are appalling enough (both in terms of content and political advertising). Just wait until the REAL election gets underway.

The American electorate is electronic media addicted; broadcast emails, streaming video, Tweets, YouTube, network and cable TV. Outside sleep and work, "video consumption" is the #1 activity, or, if written, preferably 140 characters or less please. Robocalls are part of the political media bombardment. Sound bites over substance.

When motivational research was being pioneered by the likes of Ernest Dichter and James Vicary in the 1950s and popularized by Vance Packard in his *Hidden Persuaders*, little did they know that some of those principles would become part of a giant advertising machine aimed at buying elections. Advertising 101: sell the emotion, not the pragmatic benefit of the product.

And, so in this political season, we're selling religion and all the emotions that are attached to the same (and in a negative way, not the way it was used in WW II advertising to spur solidarity and sacrifice):

But the real selling job is just getting underway. Sell fear. Just wait until the Super P's roll out their shadowy images of their opponent bathed in a light to look like Jack the Ripper.

The firestorm unleashed by the misogynist "entertainer" Rush Limbaugh regarding Sandra Fluke's testimony to Congress fits the bill as well. Talk show radio is just another media circus of highly charged emotional invectives. This elaborate infomercial is then recycled on the Internet, passing for fact. No sense commenting on vile Limbaugh as the definitive word was posted by Jim Wright over at *Stonekettle Station* in his recent "The Absurdity of Rush Limbaugh." But while Limbaugh's blather has led to some lost advertisers (probably temporarily), the Gingrich "Winning our Future" Super PAC signed on for more advertising! Way to go to win our future!

It is no wonder that a society that consumes movies that are more computer animated than acted, and cannot live without 24/7 video is a perfect target for Super PAC persuasion. Just fork over the bucks and try to buy an election! Sanctioned by the Supreme Court, the same folks who "sponsored" the results of the 2000 presidential election.

Monday, March 12, 2012
Game Change a Game Changer
Last night we went to a "Game Change" dinner with friends to view the much talked about film that is based on the best-selling book by journalists John Heilemann and Mark Halperin. The film focuses on just one part of the story, the selection of Sarah Palin as John McCain's running mate and the subsequent campaign which revealed how woefully under-vetted Palin was.

As a movie, it is terrific, with great acting, starring Julianne Moore, who plays Sarah Palin so accurately (not as a Tina Fey caricature—but rather so realistically that one would be hard pressed to tell the difference between Moore's portrayal and Sarah Palin herself), Ed Harris as John McCain and Woody Harrelson as his campaign strategist, Steve Schmidt, The supporting acting was also first-rate, particularly Sarah Paulson as Nicolle Wallace the senior advisor for the McCain campaign who had to suffer as Palin's "handler." Jay Roach, the director, kept things moving at a lively pace so there was never a dull moment, an interesting film to add to his prior credits such as the Austin Powers films! The characters are so believable, Moore, Harris, and Harrelson being almost exact facsimiles of the people they portray.

So, how much is the film (and therefore the book) a facsimile of the truth? Much of the "truth" relies on the recollections of

Steve Schmidt the chief strategist of the McCain/Palin 2008 presidential campaign, but Danny Strong, the screenwriter, also independently interviewed scores of people to corroborate the facts. One has to admire Schmidt for fessing up; the truth being Palin was selected for her gender and pizzazz. If she thinks North and South Korea is the same country or Britain's head of state is the Queen instead of the Prime Minister so be it. To Schmidt's credit, his regret at having gotten the Palin ball rolling led to his disclosures, particularly after Palin's *Going Rogue* was published, basically freeing him to talk.

An excellent follow up to seeing the film is the C-Span panel discussion on the film adaptation, consisting of the book's authors, Heilemann and Halperin, Roach, the director and executive producer, Steve Schmidt, and Danny Strong, screenwriter and co-executive producer. Particularly interesting is Roach's comments on the selection of Moore, Harris, and Harrelson, the perfect serendipity of it all. One of Roach's favorite scenes in the film is Moore as Palin watching a YouTube clip of SNL's Tina Fey portraying Sarah Palin, commenting that he's hoping Palin will see Game Change, watching Moore portraying her watching Fey's portrayal. An infinity of mirrors, befitting her media star status.

For me, the film just underscores the ludicrousness of Presidential/VP candidate selection and election campaigning that seem to rely upon the gullibility of the American electorate and their susceptibility to mass persuasion. And this is not just to finger point at the GOP as the same kind of machinations undoubtedly go on in the Democratic camp. But the GOP primaries have been especially transparent in this regard, a stain on the democratic process.

The film concludes with the not so prophetic remark of Rick Davis, McCain's campaign manager, "she'll be forgotten in a couple of days." But we all know the rest of the story. And the film, *Game Change* is a game changer in that it's probably all true, quite unlike much of politics itself.

Looking back, I'm amazed that my aversion to the prolifera-tion of military style weapons did not surface until this point in time in my blog. The mass shootings, the Florida Stand Your Ground laws, weapons in the classroom subjects became an obsession. I failed to cover one of the most horrid tragedies, the shooting at Sandy Hook in December, 2012 on a concurrent basis, although mentioned later in my entries. I remember the shock of it, right in my old back yard in Connecticut. We know people who live there. I was speechless, but my anger towards the NRA (not the 2nd amendment) festered, and I began covering this insanity, considering it one of the most serious failures of the federal government, to have sensible gun control laws.

Wednesday, March 28, 2012
Running Through the Jungle
That jungle is here. The U S of A. The conservative mind would like us to believe that we'd all be safer carrying a weapon (or at least, "feel" safer). When John Fogerty wrote (and the Creedence Clearwater Revival recorded) his prophetic 1970's, Run Through the Jungle, it was thought that, along with many of his other songs, the jungle he was referring to was Vietnam. Wrong. It was his plea, still unanswered, that some gun control sanity transpires—here. The lyrics refer to 200 million guns—then the population of the United States....

"Run Through The Jungle

Whoa, thought it was a nightmare,
Lo, it's all so true,

They told me, "Don't go walking slow
'Cause Devil's on the loose."

Better run through the jungle,
Better run through the jungle,
Better run through the jungle,
Woa, Don't look back to see.

Thought I heard a rumbling
Calling to my name,
Two hundred million guns are loaded
Satan cries, "Take aim!"

Better run through the jungle,
Better run through the jungle,
Better run through the jungle,
Woa, Don't look back to see...."

Now, only forty years later, there are 300 million people who could be armed, locked and loaded. Wouldn't you feel safer?

And toward that end, in Florida we have "Stand Your Ground," Yeehaw!!!

With the tragic killing of unarmed Trayvon Martin, by a "crime watch volunteer," George Zimmerman, Florida's "Stand Your Ground" provision has proven to be the gun-slinging cowboy's best friend. This NRA supported measure says "a person who is not engaged in an unlawful activity and who is attacked in any other place where he or she has a right to be has no duty to retreat and has the right to stand his or her ground and meet force with force, including deadly force if he or she reasonably believes it is necessary to do so to prevent death or great bodily harm to himself or herself or another or to prevent the commission of a forcible felony." "Reasonably believes?" Does a hooded black youth give cause to "reason?"

Life imitating art? It conjures up the Bertolt Brecht play, *The Exception and the Rule,* a parable for these times, in which a merchant hires a coolie to help him cross a desert to close an oil deal, but near the end of the journey, when the exploited and abused coolie offers his boss some water, the merchant mistakes the gesture for an attack and shoots him dead. He is put on trial but acquitted as the court concludes the merchant did not know the coolie meant no harm and therefore the killing was pardonable. If the one with power kills, he may do so merely out of fear. One has to be armed to have that power and Brecht saw that as an issue in class warfare.

Let's escalate this insanity further. Guns in classrooms. The Colorado Supreme Court recently upheld a state law that allows residents to carry concealed weapons, finding that the University of Colorado's campus gun ban violates the "law." Colorado is not the only state with such a law and guns are not the only "approved" concealed weapons. In some states such weapons "may" include one or more of the following: Brass knuckles, Slingshots, Martial arts weapons, Knives, Swords, Spears, Daggers, Clubs, Electronic dart guns, Blackjacks, Sand bags, Razors. Sounds like a scene from West Side Story or Blackboard Jungle. Or something out of Medieval "Fechtbuchs." Including "sand bags?" Ouch!

My old college buddy, Bruce, who was the chairman of a high school English Dept. in Massachusetts, and also a Vietnam vet who knows first-hand the consequences of brutal gun force, was stunned to read Jeff Jacoby's March 21 piece in the *Boston Globe*, "A Safer Society with Guns"

With forced logic and anecdotal statistical evidence, Jacoby happily concludes that it is OK for students to carry guns, as "having a gun makes many people—for good reason—feel safer." Yeehaw!!!

In disgust, Bruce dashed off a letter to the *Globe*, but as his comments are steeped in sarcasm, perhaps the *Globe* thought it disrespectful and elected not to publish it. Legacy media ought to rethink its policies if it is to survive. Here is Bruce's response....

"Thank you, thank you, Jeff Jacoby, for standing up for a student's right to carry a concealed weapon. We've known all along that such sound arms policy would only make our schools and our nation safer, kinder and gentler. As a teacher, I have always advocated that my students be able to carry concealed weapons.

Though I live in Massachusetts where the benighted populace still prevents students from carrying concealed weapons or even visible ones (typical liberal policy that ignores the need we all have to defend ourselves in the classroom—Obama's fault for sure), I can finally hope that one day I will be able to teach in Colorado. In the meantime, I can only hope that perhaps among my students are an enlightened few, who are courageous civil libertarians, carrying concealed weapons in defiance of Massachusetts law.

I myself would like to be able to carry an M16 in the classroom or perhaps an M60 machine gun, and I dream of the day when this will be possible. To be sure, I would not be concealing those weapons but would be using my desk in the front of the room to mount the M60. (I note here that large arms carrying laws across the nation need to be changed. We vitally need to be able to carry automatic rifles and other large arms, locked and loaded. But that's an issue for discussion at a later date.) As for myself, I could work out some camouflaging technique if we can get some reasonable laws passed for concealment. With columnists like you Mr. Jacoby leading us out of the unarmed wilderness and with, I'm sure, the backing of the NRA, perhaps all students and teachers will one day be armed.

Thank goodness for the sound reasoning of the conservative voice backed by the statistics you gave us showing reduced crime and kill numbers in jurisdictions where people can carry. Thanks for not showing statistics from other pusillanimous

societies that haven't the courage or the manhood to carry. Who would want to know that those sissy societies don't kill nearly as many men, women or children with firearms as we do? Thanks for knowing what in addition to weapons needs to be concealed. Thanks, and thanks again."
— Bruce Rettman

The presidential primary rhetoric was now coming into full bloom with the usual posturing and preening and PAC induced advertising invectives. Meanwhile the zero interest rates combined with government support, really began to take hold in the economy.

Sunday, June 3, 2012
Anecdotal Headlines Redux
One of the advantages of writing a blog is to be able to understand what I was thinking (or not thinking) at a certain point in time. It can be satisfying, or amusing, or downright embarrassing looking back. We are all adrift in an ocean of information, the seas fomenting more than ever, that affecting our perception of the horizon, when we can see it at all. Sometimes, the headlines of the *Wall Street Journal* seem to cry out a general national Zeitgeist and this weekend's edition was such a moment. I've noted this phenomenon before, first on Wednesday, December 10, 2008, "Anecdotal Headline Annotations," which I prefaced with a sentence that could exactly apply to the most recent edition, three and a half years later: "If I was handed a copy of today's *Wall Street Journal* only a couple of years ago, I would have thought the headlines were a forecast of an ethical and economic Armageddon. How otherwise does one interpret the following captions, from just one day's newspaper?"
    Then, a little more than two years ago, Friday, April 9, 2010, I posted another such moment, "Anecdotal Headlines," writing at

the time: "...while the Dow basks in the glow of massive liquidity injections in a low interest rate environment, approaching 11,000 as I write this, and investment bankers are rewarding themselves with record bonuses, the economy swims on against the tide of high unemployment (much higher than reported), kicking the state/municipal finance crisis down the road, and rising foreclosures."

Usually, extreme headlines happen at inflection points. Certainly the Dec. 2008 posting was one as far as the stock market is concerned (the Dow bottoming three months later), but the April 2010 posting was during the market's ascent. However, the so called "market" seems to be disconnected from the economy and jobs and whatever recovery there has been of Main Street mostly has been induced by the Federal Reserve and other government stimuli. Some like to finger point, believing that recent deficit spending is the cause of our economic malaise. I don't like deficit spending any more than they, but it is overly simplistic to think that if we ran our government like a responsible family, sitting around the ole' kitchen table, budgeting our expenses, tightening our belts, all will be OK. Running a country is not like running a household, and without the stimulus, who knows where we would be today.

We are going to hear a lot about the economy, everything being Obama's fault (note now that gas prices have fallen in the last few weeks we no longer hear about his being responsible for those) but another benefit (there are not many) of writing this blog is some of the documentation it provides. The Monday, September 22, 2008 entry, "This Fundamental is Whining" is worth revisiting in this regard. Senator Phil Gramm, who had then become a lead economic adviser for McCain's presidential run, called us (the American public) "a bunch of whiners," saying the only economic problem we have is a "mental recession." Well we now know that this little "mental recession" was real, could have been a depression (who knows, it still might become one), and it was set in motion long before Obama took office.

Nonetheless, at the time McCain was already blaming Obama for the economy, saying "We've heard a lot of words from Senator Obama over the course of this campaign ... But maybe just this once he could spare us the lectures, and admit to his own poor judgment in contributing to these problems. The crisis on Wall Street started in the Washington culture of lobbying and influence peddling, and he was right square in the middle of it." Obama was to blame even before he became president! And today, we not only have the residual effects of our own economic problems baked into the cake, there is also the exogenous factor of Europe's slow-motion economic collapse—something we have no direct ability to control, even if we could agree on anything. Then, there is the sun-setting of the Bush tax cuts, a fiscal cliff that desperately needs our malfunctioning government to agree on something. What are the chances?

Unfortunately, presidential elections do focus on how people feel at the time, and while we were feeling lousy in 2008 and "hope" was a mantra we eagerly seized, now we will be asked to "hope" some more, or rely on the magic wand of a private equity bailout specialist, Mitt Romney. It is a nice fantasy (the magic wand), and as the Federal Reserve may be running out of its own magic bullets, the economy and the leading economic indicators will dictate the election, no matter how much tinder the Super Pacs throw on the campaign fires.

The headlines of today are not much different in tone than those that preceded them, two years ago, and almost four years ago. Two of my favorites from 2010 are: "Greek Bond Crisis Spreads and Fed Chiefs Hint at Low Rates Possibly Into 2011." Where is Yogi Berra when you need him? "It's déjà vu all over again." But he might have got it wrong with, "The future ain't what it used to be."

So, how are we to divine our economic and moral future from today's headlines, a few of which are cited here just from the first section of the *Wall Street Journal* June 2/3 2012?

"*Grim Job Report Sinks Markets
*As Costs Soar, Taxpayers Target Pensions of Cops and Firefighters
*State Takes Fresh Crack at Mortgages
*Campaign's Focus Turns to Grim Data
*Fed is Sure to Step Up Debate on More Stimulus
*Euro-Zone Reports Deepen Gloom
*Asia Weakness Heightens Fears of Contagion
*Brazil Loses Steam As World Slows
*Cyprus Is Close to a Request for Bailout
*Japan Gives Warning on Yen"

Friday, June 8, 2012
Some Good News?
To offset the abundant "bad news" of the last entry, here is an interesting article from *Marketwatch* on the deleveraging progress: "U.S. debt load falling at fastest pace since 1950s; Despite surge in federal deficit, America is deleveraging"

Some salient points:

"* Little by little, our economy is reducing its debt burden, slowly repairing the damage caused by 10, 20 or 30 years of excess.
* Total domestic—public and private—debt as a share of the economy has declined for 12 quarters in a row after surging over the previous decade.
* The level of public debt is indeed worrisome, but it's not as big a worry as the economy's total level of debt—public and private.

* As much as we hear politicians, pundits, tea-party patriots and the Congressional Budget Office obsessing about government debt, it was excessive private debt—not public debt—that caused the 2008 financial meltdown. And it was private debt—some of it since transferred to the public—that lies behind the current European debt crisis.

*According to a study by McKinsey published earlier this year, U.S. households may have two more years of deleveraging left before their debts are sustainable again. If McKinsey is right, the U.S. economy may have to endure a couple more years of slow growth."

Another little mentioned factor is that while the public debt has surged during the past few years, maturing debt is being replaced by new debt with coupons (interest rate) of one half or even one fifth the maturing ones. For instance, the US Treasury 30 year bond issued in 1982 had coupons of some 15% while the most recently issued US Treasury 30 Year bond was issued at 3.06%. Ten year yields are now less than two percent, replacing US Treasury Notes in the 4 - 5% range. Servicing the debt is actually getting cheaper, although these savings are probably offset due to the expansion of borrowing that has been needed to fend off a depression. The low rates also leave investors with a continuing dilemma.

Saturday, June 30, 2012
Supreme Decisions
PAC ads are now running ceaselessly. How many times have we heard that hushed voice, solemn in its accusatory tone, "In 2008, Barack Obama said, 'We can't mortgage our children's future on a mountain of debt.' Now he's adding $4 billion in debt every day, borrowing from China for his spending. Every

second, growing our debt faster than our economy, Tell Obama, stop the spending."

Last week the Supreme Court made two major decisions, the really BIG one—perhaps in part to ensure the Court's integrity as a non-partisan institution—was to uphold the Affordable Care Act, but in a less publicized one it also declined to reconsider the Citizens United decision that has led to viral PAC advertising by corporations and wealthy individuals. Montana had challenged the decision by contending its century-old Corrupt Practices Act might be applied to PAC advertising in state and local elections. Not so, said the Supreme Court: let the PAC advertising flow, with all its inherent sound bites and vapid fury!

And concerning the Supreme Court's courageous decision to uphold the Affordable Care Act, our local *Palm Beach Post* columnist/humorist, Frank Cerabino, wrote a wonderful satire In this age of posturing over substance, he shows how it could be used as a political harangue from any viewpoint, merely by twisting a few words in each sentence. I quote the beginning paragraphs....

"My Dear Fellow American:

The U.S. Supreme Court's (historic / activist) decision to uphold (the Affordable Care Act / Obamacare) is but a temporary (victory / setback) in our long fight (for access to health care / against government intrusion) in (America / the marketplace.)

The law that the Supreme Court upheld on Thursday will mean that scores of (uninsured / reluctant) Americans will be (covered / forced) in a system that provides the kind of (care / costs) that the rest of the (civilized / Socialistic) countries of the world already (enjoy / are saddled with).

(Unfortunately / Fortunately), the Supreme Court's decision won't be the last word on this (triumph / travesty) of justice. There are already (sinister forces / courageous voices) who are prepared to take this battle to Congress, which can (subvert /

stop) the health care law through (vindictive / corrective) legislative action."

Tuesday, July 24, 2012
Milestone and Miscellany
After my last post, Google informed me that was Lacunae Musing's 300th entry, a milestone of sorts. When I began this blog almost five years ago, I had no idea where it might lead or, even, whether it would merely be a passing dalliance. I had discounted writing about investments, something I know enough about to be dangerous, or about publishing, which, when I retired, I knew a lot about, but by the time I began to write in this space, the publishing world had changed dramatically. Nor did I want to espouse only political views, although I've posted my share on the topic. No, I wanted to write something that simply expresses my interests (as well as my views) and experiences (including some family history) and, perhaps, along the way make a small contribution on the WWW. The one thing I wanted to avoid is turning it into a job; I have no hidden agenda, no source of income from this effort. There is only the satisfaction from writing, and having a "written trail"—a form of accountability, an intellectual balance sheet that is auditable.

As far as blogs go, mine is but a minor star in a minor universe. Comparing this blog's statistics to those of my blogging "hero"—to me the "father" of the investment blog—Barry Ritholtz's *The Big Picture*—shows the stark differences between a blog written by an erudite professional such as Ritholtz, and an unfocused personal blog. It is like comparing the *New York Times* to a mimeographed newsletter (does the mimeograph still exist?).

Late in the game I began to add labels to the entries as the eclectic nature of the blog needed some sort of thread to tie everything together. Unfortunately, as much of this work was done retrospectively, it isn't a true index because of inconsistencies. But it does give a handle on the contents with more than 350 labels.

The political season is heating up and I'm so disgusted with Super Pac advertising, and the unbearable rhetoric from both sides of the aisle that I doubt whether I will be as engaged in these blog pages as I was during the last presidential (and historical) election cycle. To make my personal views clear, I think President Obama, given he is a mere mortal, has done about the best he could given the economic mess he was handed and the political roadblocks thrown at him. But his campaign rhetoric has also worked against him, promising too much. Also, I've criticized some of his priorities in these pages, so it is not as if I am a raving liberal. I like to think of myself as a fiscal conservative and a social liberal and one might say that the two are not compatible; I think intelligent compromise can transcend many of the disagreements that are aired like dirty laundry in the media. Of course, there are also the lunatic fringes and there is no compromise possible with them.

In fact, I recently learned, there is actually a word to describe this endless obfuscation of the truth—Agnotology: Culturally constructed ignorance, purposefully created by special interest groups working hard to create confusion and suppress the truth.

And to whom do I give a hat tip for this morsel of incredible insight?—Barry Ritholtz! (Who, in turn gives full attribution to the word's creator, Stanford historian of science Robert Proctor.) Ritholtz uses the term as but one element in his recent entry "Defective Government By Design" asking the rhetorical question, "Is it democracy or plutocracy when less than 200 people drive election spending in a nation of 300 million?"

This entry is about the rise of corporate power and the Super Pac—implications that are onerous for democracy. I've written about it before.

Agnotology. You hear and see its practice every day......say the lie often enough, and in as many forms as possible and voila, it suddenly becomes "the truth". In fact, innuendo works as well or even better than saying the lie straight out.

Here's an example, the *Daily News'* agnotological headline, "How many more must die, Mr. President?"—as if the horrific tragedy in Colorado is somehow the President's fault. If Obama had a magic wand, he would probably outlaw assault weapons, but he has a Congress to deal with, the NRA, and, of course, State's rights. It was the Supreme Court of Colorado which upheld a state law that allows residents to carry concealed weapons, even in schools! But a glance at the *NY Daily News* headline plants an agnotological subliminal message.

That is the brave new political campaign world for 2012, different than it was in 2008, although that one too was quite ugly. I will be relying on Fact Check.org to winnow truth from agnotological fiction.

Tuesday, August 14, 2012
Romney and Ryan and a Hope and a Prayer
Although I had promised myself that I would not write much about the upcoming presidential election (or at least as much as I did some four years ago), I have to say something about Mitt Romney's VP choice of Paul Ryan. When Sarah Palin was picked by McCain to be his running mate, I thought it was one of the most unconscionable, politically motivated choices he could have made. Palin simply did not have the knowledge or experience to be a heart beat from the presidency.

Now, another GOP choice four years later seems to be as politically motivated to appeal to the conservative base. While Ryan is no Palin, his economic "plan" is the typical hope and a prayer of supply-siders: lower taxes for the "job creators" and that will inexorably lead to spectacular economic growth. Didn't we try that last when Bush's tax cuts went into effect after budget surpluses under Clinton? What was the outcome of that along with the deregulation of the banking system? I guess Romney thought his own lack of specifics would be easily clarified by adopting Ryan's plan, at least in spirit.

Ironic, isn't it, the GOP accuses Obama of engaging in social engineering, but the essence of Ryan's plan is social engineering in reverse? The Obama camp has called it a form of social Darwinism. Indeed, the survival of the fittest, all others be damned! ("At this festive season of the year, Mr. Scrooge, ... it is more than usually desirable that we should make some slight provision for the Poor and destitute, who suffer greatly at the present time." / "Are there no prisons?" / "Plenty of prisons ..." / "And the Union workhouses.....Are they still in operation?" / "Both very busy, sir ..." / "Those who are badly off must go there." / "Many can't go there; and many would rather die." / "If they would rather die, they had better do it, and decrease the surplus population.")

The personal irony is I would be better off with Romney and Ryan's economic plan. Imagine, not having to pay any taxes on dividends, interest income, and capital gains! Bring it on, but how many jobs is this retired ex-publisher going to create? And, then, the double irony of the hard-working middle class getting conned by all the staged patriotic hoopla the handsome R&R team projects, and then voting against their own best interests!

I'm as much against a big government welfare state as I am a government based on *Atlas Shrugged*, but I'm afraid that is how this presidential campaign is going to be framed. The PACs will have a field day with hyperbole.

Saturday, October 20, 2012
The Alternative Reality
It's easy to be cynical in this presidential election year, the rhetoric and posturing of the scripted, agnotological "debates," the

Super PAC ads, the robo-calls, the deluge of direct mail, sending out those sound bites to "the undecided." But what would this election cycle be like if McCain had won in 2008? Ironically, it would have been the Democrats finger pointing about the economy because we'd probably be in a similar situation, or worse, who knows—it's impossible to prove an alternative reality, but we can speculate.

The debt Romney carps about was first ramped up by the Treasury Department of the previous administration, not by Obama, with the enactment of the Troubled Asset Relief Program (TARP) in 2008 to stabilize the financial system and it was quite necessary at the time. Jobs were falling off the cliff before Obama took office. Our financial system was in melt down. And what would have been a McCain administration response as that crisis just continued to deepen? Go into an austerity spending mode? Cut taxes? No, that would have been impossible. The time for government to reign in its spending is when the economy is NOT falling off the cliff and even a Republican administration would have had to take similar action (and the Federal Reserve's Ben Bernanke was an appointee of the Republican administration as well).

Reviewing some of the more distant past, Clinton enacted tax increases in 1994, mostly on high income earners. Eventually, those, as well as a booming economy (note, no loss of jobs due to raising taxes on the upper 1%), turned around President George Bush Sr.'s deficits into surpluses. After three consecutive years of national debt reduction under Clinton, the surplus in 2000 amounted to $230 billion.

The first fiscal year impacted by George W. Bush's tax cuts was 2002 when the surplus swung to a $159 billion deficit, a $286 billion negative change from the previous year. True, we were now embroiled in the war on terror, but the administration persisted on raising the stakes with tax cuts. Bush said while campaigning for a local Alabama congressman. "In order to make sure that our economy grows, in order to make sure the job base is strong, you need to have a congressman who will join me in making sure that tax relief plan we passed is permanent and doesn't go away." Where were the jobs after nine years of this "temporary" but massive tax cut, mostly benefiting the upper 1%?

When Paul O'Neill, Bush's Treasury Secretary, argued against a second round of tax cuts, VP Cheney purportedly said "You know, Paul, Reagan proved that deficits don't matter. We won the mid-term elections, this is our due." This was Cheney speaking, not some liberal Democrat. O'Neill said in an interview "It was not just about not wanting the tax cut. It was about how to use the nation's resources to improve the condition of our society. And I thought the weight of working on Social Security and fundamental tax reform was a lot more important than a tax reduction." For that view, O'Neill was eventually fired.

Obama clearly underestimated how long it would take to reverse years of deficit spending, not only his administration's (necessary as the private sector was not spending), but his predecessor's as well. (He also didn't anticipate being stonewalled by Congress.) But if McCain had defeated Obama in 2008, he would have inherited the same mess and today we might have Hillary Clinton running against McCain (or Palin or Romney) making some of the same arguments about fiscal responsibility being spun by Romney.

As I said, it is hard not to be cynical about this particular election, but I respect Paul O'Neill's admonishment: "It was not just about not wanting the tax cut. It was about how to use the nation's resources to improve the condition of our society." That is why I support President Obama and hopefully in a second term he would have Congress' cooperation to achieve some fundamental tax reform and make inroads in controlling the growth of entitlements.

And last night, as I was preparing to post this, a bit of serendipity led me to watch the 1957 classic A *Face in the Crowd* on Turner Classic Movies. Directed by Elia Kazan and written by Budd Schulberg, it depicts Larry Rhodes (Andy Griffith), a drifter who is found in a jail by Marcia Jeffries (Patricia Neal), who she enlists to sing and talk on a local Arkansas radio station, he ultimately rising to the pinnacle of media demagoguery. He is nicknamed "Lonesome" Rhodes by Marcia, and she goes on the journey with him from obscurity to fame to fall.

The relevancy of this film, made more than fifty years ago, to today is striking. Lonesome is drawn into the political arena, and is brought in to help transform the film's Senator Worthington Fuller into a Presidential candidate. Lonesome instinctively and sardonically understands the manipulative power of language and media.

When he first meets the Senator, he advises him to abandon his stiff personality and give himself over to Lonesome's control: "... Your problem is getting the voters to listen to you. Getting them to like you enough to listen to you. We've got to face it, politics have entered a new stage, television. Instead of long-winded debates, the people want slogans. 'Time for a change' 'The mess in Washington' 'More bang for a buck'. Punch-lines and glamour....We've got to find a million buyers for the product 'Worthington Fuller'....Respect? Did you ever hear of anyone buying any product beer, hair rinse, tissue, because they respect it? You've got to be loved, man. Loved....Senator, I'm a professional. I look at the image on that screen same as at a performer on my show. And I have to say ... you'll never get over to my audience not to the millions of people who welcome me into their living rooms each week. And if I wouldn't buy him, do you realize what that means? If I wouldn't buy him, the people of this country aren't ready to buy him for that big job on Pennsylvania Avenue....I'm an influence, a wielder of opinion ... a force. A force."

To Marcia he says :"This whole country's just like my flock of sheep!....Rednecks, crackers, hillbillies, hausfraus, shut-ins, pea-pickers - everybody that's got to jump when somebody else blows the whistle. They don't know it yet, but they're all gonna be 'Fighters for Fuller'. They're mine! I own 'em! They think like I do. Only they're even more stupid than I am, so I gotta think for 'em. Marcia, you just wait and see. I'm gonna be the power behind the president - and you'll be the power behind me."

An actor on Rhodes' show asks him about Senator Fuller: "You really sell that stiff as a man among men?" Lonesome Rhodes replies: "Those morons out there? Shucks, I could take chicken fertilizer and sell it to them as caviar. I could make them eat dog food and think it was steak. Sure, I got 'em like this ... You know what the public's like? A cage of Guinea Pigs. Good Night you stupid idiots. Good Night, you miserable slobs. They're a lot of trained seals. I toss them a dead fish and they'll flap their flippers."

'Nuff said before next Monday's "debate" after which the "undecided" can flap their flippers.

Friday, October 26, 2012
Gorilla in the Room
Finally it comes out, point blank. No mistake about it, racism in the so called post-racist USA and its possible impact on the election.

One of Mitt Romney's presidential campaign advisors, John Sununu, in an interview on CNN when asked about Colin Powell's endorsement of President Obama for a second term, said, "Frankly, when you take a look at Colin Powell, you have to wonder whether that's an endorsement based on issues or whether he's got a slightly different reason for preferring President Obama." When asked to clarify what that issue might be he said "well, I think when you have somebody of your own race that you're proud of being president of the United States, I applaud Colin for standing with him."

Does that mean Sununu supports Romney, not based on the issues, but because of race? It is not too farfetched to wonder why. According to Reuters/Ipsos polling conducted October 1 to October 7, likely white male voters favored Romney 55.5 percent to 31.9 percent."

An earlier entry mentioned that I was reading the last of the "Schmidt trilogy" by Louis Begley, the current one being *Schmidt Steps Back*, published this year but probably written over the two prior years. I think of Begley as being the intellectual equivalent of John Updike, who coincidently was Begley's classmate at Harvard, both graduating summa cum laude in 1954. From there, their careers diverged, Updike becoming a writer and Begley an international lawyer. But Begley is now a full time writer, and to me, writes with the intellectual ease of his classmate and, like Updike, follows a character in multiple novels over years (Rabbit and Schmidt).

There is something from *Schmidt Steps Back* which has a direct bearing, on "the gorilla in the room." One of the characters in the book, Mike Mansour, an ultra wealthy and powerful international financier, gives voice to the issue: "... he revealed to Schmidt more than once, to the effect that Obama's presidency, however much he personally wished it to succeed, was doomed. The question is, he insisted, the question is can he make American politicians do his will. The last Democrat able to accomplish that was LBJ. He'd grab them by the balls....and they said, Yes Mr. President, before he'd even begun to squeeze ... But Obama is black! Black in the most racist country in the world."

Another character reminds Mansour that Obama was just elected by a landslide. Mansour opines "... Obama has to be such a good guy that his hands and feet are tied. You watched him debate McCain?....You saw him smirk whenever Obama talked? Not once, not twice, but every time. LBJ would have said, Wipe that smirk off your face or I'll tear your head off. Barack can't do that. You can't have a black man telling off the Man. Please, there is no place here for angry black men! Obama has to be polite and make nice, and you know what they say about nice guys—they finish last."

It will be a close election as the one in 2000 decided by the Supreme Court....

Finally the election, and back to politics as usual. This section begins with the result and then a rare "guest editorial" by my former teacher in high school, Roger Brickner. Imagine, still being in touch with one's high school teacher after all these years. And a new year starts.

Wednesday, November 7, 2012
The People Have Spoken: Compromise!
It is amazing how close the anecdotal survey mentioned at the end of my last post came to predicting the 2.2% popular vote plurality for Obama (only a tenth of a percent off). I wonder how many professional polling pontificators were as accurate! Assume Florida is finally called for Obama, and that seems most likely at this point, the final Electoral College tabulation will be 332 for Obama vs. Romney's 206. Here the survey of 289 vs. 249 was too pessimistic, although calling the winner.

This was no mandate for Obama, nor should it be. His political campaign of 2008 underestimated the depths of the economic crisis and the ability of a mere President to affect meaningful economic change. Too many promises were made, indeed. Perhaps he has a more sober view of reality with the onset of his second term.

Looking at the results vs. 2008 clearly shows that the American public is dissatisfied with the status quo. Obama's popular plurality in 2008 was 52.93% or 2.63% more than 2012. That doesn't sound like much except when you look at the absolute vote itself, with Obama getting 9.6 million less votes than in 2008. Less people voted, showing the disenfranchisement of the country as a whole. We are all sick of the shenanigans of both parties.

But if Obama is listening, hopefully they are across the aisle as well. Senate's Minority Leader Mitch McConnell's gave an ominous post election speech saying, "They [the American public] gave President Obama a second chance to fix the problems that even he admits he failed to solve during his first four years in office, and they preserved Republican control of the House of Representatives … Now it's time for the president to propose solutions that actually have a chance of passing the Republican-controlled House of Representatives and a closely divided Senate, step up to the plate on the challenges of the moment, and deliver in a way that he did not in his first four years in office … To the extent he wants to move to the political center, which is where the work gets done in a divided government, we'll be there to meet him half way."

It sounds like more of the same. Will Senator McConnell and Representative Boehner get the message as well? Boehner said "The American people also made clear there's no mandate for raising tax rates." Doesn't sound encouraging that Boehner is still drawing a line in the sand that there can be no tax increases in any compromise. Another game of chicken with the fiscal cliff and the debt ceiling? Any sane person knows this cannot be merely addressed with spending cuts. There will have to be some tax increases, a more progressive tax scale such as in the Clinton era. Our economy did fine then, why not now? Ok, guys, time to compromise. The election results seem to be shouting that message

Friday, November 16, 2012
Whither Go Republicans ... or Will They Just Wither?
A Guest Editorial by Roger Brickner

My high school teacher from years and years ago, a Republican all his life, expressed his dismay at what has happened to his party in an email to friends, and I have his permission to share it. Roger has studied the American political scene for more than sixty years now, more than 25% of the lifetime of the Union itself. His observations are truly first hand and astute....

"The party wasn't always like that. From 1861-1913 they lost to only one Democrat. Their major successful policies during that period included, the winning of the Civil War, the ending of slavery, the supremacy of the union, meaning the central federal government, the opening up of western lands to pioneers, both domestic and immigrant (Homestead Act), the opening up of the west by encouraging entrepreneurs to build the infrastructure of the transcontinental railway, the land grants to states to establish free state colleges (Morrill Act), the control of greedy capitalists who sought to take at others expense (Trust Busting), they laid the ground and finally passed the Suffrage Act of 1919 giving women the right to vote, they encouraged Prohibition as a way to lessen the effects of wife beating (not all their efforts succeeded). Almost all of these measures, including the last two, were opposed by the Democrats. This was a formula of beliefs which worked for Republicans. Why has the party of today strayed from these successful principles which spawned their own party?

These are questions about their own party which they must answer. It was a party which combined what was good for America with care and compassion with the people they ruled. Why is it so different today? Part of it is that their vision is blurred as they do not fully understand the origins of their own party. Part of it is because policies initiated in the late 1960's moved them away from their roots. Pres. Nixon's "Southern strategy" worked all too well. For 108 years the SOLID SOUTH held for the Democratic Party. Since then the South has voted overwhelmingly Republican. What an incredible reversal! It has transformed the Republican Party on racial and states' rights policies. Its earlier openness to the needs of a diverse nation has become crabbed and resentful.

Given the ever evolving aspect of America it will become more and more diverse ethnically. We are a nation based on the concept that we are united as a democratic society, not as a nation based on one ethnicity. We are therefore not a carbon copy of how Europe views itself. Europe sees itself as countries of a single cultural identity, in spite of their rather unsuccessful attempts to integrate other cultures into their societies. To illustrate, I ask: when will England have a Pakistani ethnic become PM, when will the French have an Algerian ethnic become their leader, and when will Germany have a Turkish ethnic become their Chancellor? Don't hold your breath.

Unless and until the Republican party ... the party of my own proud heritage ... realize who they are and embraces in its heart ALL Americans, I foresee them becoming like the old Whig party which shunned the issues of the day and allowed the great Republican party to succeed it.

When Abraham Lincoln and Theodore Roosevelt can be found again in Republican circles, they may once again become relevant today. Until that happens those great Republican presidents are better reflected in the Democratic party."

Friday, January 4, 2013
Getting Back to Reality
The extraordinary increase (as a percentage move) in the 10 Year T Note yield shows the artificiality and the fragility of market values, everything being propped up by the Federal Reserve in the absence of any sound fiscal policy. The recent Fed minutes

merely hinted at the possibility of reducing asset purchases before the end of this year, and bond investors were left without their bungee cord:

Bill Gross, the "bond king," persuasively writes about the problem in his January letter, a long discourse on why "helicopter money" rained down by the Fed to save the financial system has to end badly in some way.

The artificiality of it all hasn't escaped the notice of corporations, many of which have loaded up their balance sheets with cheap debt, while holding mounds of cash, even to the point of paying massive dividends to their shareholders with borrowed funds. The poster child for this is Costco which paid its shareholders $3 billion and borrowing the funds to do it. Of course that was before the laughable fiscal cliff deal, which raised taxes on dividends to 20% from its present 15% but only for high income taxpayers. They were talking about taxing dividends as regular income which must have freaked out the five largest shareholders who are corporate officers or directors, their take on the special dividend with borrowed funds being almost $12 million. What a country! Borrow the money to pay your top people a huge bonus that is taxed at only 15%. It truly is the microcosm for the contrived and completely unpredictable financial landscape of today.

A few days ago Barry Ritholz suggested a positive way of using today's manipulated market—that is to upgrade and repair our aging infrastructure. Many of our roads are atrociously maintained and bridges are crumbling, not to mention aging water systems, power plants, and a railroad transportation system which is truly 3rd world quality. As Ritholz says: "At some point in the future, your kids are going to ask—'Wait, you could have upgraded _____ and it only would have cost you 2.5% in borrowing costs?!?'"

Isn't that where we should be putting borrowed money to work, creating jobs?

Wednesday, January 23, 2013
Inaugural Day Thoughts
Our friends, John and Lois, hosted a second Inaugural party, some thirty guests to witness the ceremonial swearing in of the President and his speech. What a difference four years make. Last time it was a euphoric party, imagine, a young black president, imbued with liberal ideals, but with an economy that had already shown signs of complete collapse the joy was somewhat restrained by worry.

Four years later, the intransigence of government compromise has given way to more temperate expectations. However, none of this detracted from the day, a remarkable, very moving, and humbling exercise of the democratic process with the pageantry instilling a quiet pride and hopefulness in us and the sea of faces that swept across the National Mall.

Everything about it was just about perfect, even the weather cooperating. President Obama's speech was aspirational and progressive, touching upon many of the themes of his presidency and introducing the sorely needed goal of combating climate change. Perhaps he will make that the hallmark of his second term as universal healthcare was in his first. In spite of the overwhelming need to face this issue realistically, action has been lacking.

This will become yet another clash in Congress. To fully understand the severity of political polarization, one only has to read comments about Obama's reelection such as Texas Representative John Culberson's: "I grieve for the country....We're going to throw the emergency brake on as best we can and fight him every step of the way." Welcome to your second term, Mr. President!

A key phrase from the Inaugural speech, "we, the people, understand that our country cannot succeed when a shrinking few do very well and a growing many barely make it," was also Obama's central point when he was campaigning and will probably be the fulcrum of budgeting and tax reform. But this is going to be a more complex problem as there are systemic reasons behind this widening gap that go far beyond the reach of mere tax reform legislation. The *New York Times* magazine section this Sunday carried a relatively brief but pointed article on "skill-biased technical change:" The rise of networked laptops and smartphones and their countless iterations and spawn have helped highly educated professionals create more and more value just as they have created barriers to entry and rendered irrelevant millions of less-educated workers, in places like factory production lines and typing pools.

Thus, workers having technology skills, mostly those in information industry professions, law, finance, engineering, and medicine, have disproportionately benefited from those skills at the expense of blue collar workers who have been forced into the service economy at lower wages. Having technology skills is tantamount to buying on margin, being able to leverage those skills for much greater compensation.

So when President Obama tries to put through legislation to reverse this course, it has to take into account not only tax reform, but massive educational reform and the effects of that will not be immediate, but rather long term, maybe measured in generations, like the progress made in civil rights. Do we have the fortitude and patience?

And, then there is the deficit and reducing the National Debt. We could embrace the best parts of the Simpson-Bowles plan (so eagerly commissioned by both parties as the National Commission on Fiscal Responsibility and Reform, and then the results so immediately distanced by both). No one wants to face up to their recommendations. Our massive National Debt in part was incurred to save our financial system from ruin, but it did not occur overnight. Quick and easy fixes are impossible. But, if we get the direction right, and gradually phase in some of the Commission's recommendations, perhaps we can then move forward on that front.

But do our politicians have the right stuff? This is where presidential leadership is so sorely needed. President Obama threw down the gauntlet in his speech about the need for action—even "imperfect" action—a veiled suggestion of compromise. There were two beautifully crafted paragraphs about the dangers of taking intransigent positions based on ideology in his speech:

"That is our generation's task—to make these words, these rights, these values of life and liberty and the pursuit of happiness real for every American. Being true to our founding documents does not require us to agree on every contour of life. It does not mean we all define liberty in exactly the same way or follow the same precise path to happiness. Progress does not compel us to settle centuries-long debates about the role of government for all time, but it does require us to act in our time.

For now decisions are upon us and we cannot afford delay. We cannot mistake absolutism for principle, or substitute spectacle for politics, or treat name-calling as reasoned debate. We must act, knowing that our work will be imperfect. We must act, knowing that today's victories will be only partial and that it will be up to those who stand here in four years and 40 years and 400 years hence to advance the timeless spirit once conferred to us in a spare Philadelphia hall."

Finally, a bit of serendipity. Does life imitate art? I had noted that Aaron Sorkin's 1995 classic *The American President*, directed by Rob Reiner, was on TV the same night as the inaugural. We've seen it before but Ann and I, in a "presidential inauguration mood," said, what the heck, we'll watch it again (thanks Encore, no commercial interruptions). Talk about a feel good movie and how incredibly relevant although made almost twenty years ago.

The focus of fictional President Andrew Shepherd's administration is to pass a crime bill (with assault weapon gun control) and an environmental bill that mandates the reduction of hydrocarbon emissions. Meanwhile, a right wing political demagogue, Senator Bob Rumson, is running against Shepherd's reelection, appealing to "family values" of Americans, by attacking Shepherd's relationship with Sydney Ellen Wade (Shepherd is a widower in the film). Have things changed so little in the almost twenty years since the film's making? Unresolved issues of gun control, environmental protection, and campaign character assault go on and on.

The film's President Andrew Shepherd initially takes the high road, concentrating on the issues rather than the personal attacks until he appears at an unscheduled and impromptu news conference and gives an impassioned, unrehearsed speech. Perhaps all our politicians should see this movie once every four years (I realize that Sorkin writes with his own political agenda—even I think that eliminating handguns cannot be lumped in with assault weapons—but taking that into account, still there is much to be gleaned from this wonderful and eerily relevant script). Here is what "President Shepherd" says, but only in part. The entire speech can be found on line:

"....We have serious problems to solve, and we need serious people to solve them. And whatever your particular problem is, I promise you, Bob Rumson is not the least bit interested in solving it. He is interested in two things and two things only: making you afraid of it and telling you who's to blame for it. That, ladies and gentlemen, is how you win elections. You gather a group of middle-aged, middle-class, middle-income voters who remember with longing an easier time, and you talk to them about family and American values and character...."

Listening to the entire speech was the perfect way to cap off Inauguration Day!

Tuesday, April 16, 2013
Riffs
This is a sort of a "catch up" posting, although gun control is deserving of more thorough coverage.

First and foremost, the Boston bombings, deplorable, despicable, cowardly. The stark, almost naked vulnerability of the runners, makes it especially gruesome to me, and on Patriot's Day in Massachusetts, the symbolism of the act is unambiguous. If it was carried out with assault weapons rather than the anonymity of trash can bombs, would it speed national gun control legislation as Connecticut commendably passed? I wonder, but violence in our great land is intolerable and must be dealt with through education and legislation and improved economic opportunity for all.

When President Obama delivered his State of the Union address, he said that the people of Newtown, Connecticut "deserve a vote" on gun control, little did he imagine that a watered down version that focuses mainly on background checks would fail—a shameful example of NRA's control of our politicians. We got our vote. Hopefully, all will remember when those Senators are up for reelection.

And to the city of Boston, great sighs of relief to the refrains of Sweet Caroline.....

"And when I hurt,
Hurtin' runs off my shoulders"

Saturday, May 18, 2013
Infrastructure and Politics Redux
Inevitably, this headline—"Probe begins after Conn. commuter trains crash"—will lead to the conclusion what any rider of the New Haven Railroad could tell you: the tracks are in need of serious upgrade. Yet, investment in the railroad's infrastructure

is one of those things that is constantly postponed—until a tragedy occurs, and this could have been a much more serious accident with loss of life in addition to the injuries. But making this expenditure is a political hot potato; no one wants to take on. Again, until.....

Fact of the matter, not only do the tracks need upgrading, the entire system—which to a degree is still mired in its late 19th century beginnings—needs to be addressed, bringing public transportation for the heavily populated northeast corridor into the 21st century. We are a third world country when it comes to such transportation—ask anyone from China or Japan who visits and rides those rails. And, with easy credit and the need for jobs, it would seem to be a no brainer to make this investment, but do we have the vision and determination?

Meanwhile, on the Florida political front, an apparent self-serving decision by Governor Rick Scott: to deny Amazon. com the ability to build a warehouse in the State as it would appear that he (the Governor) is supporting an Internet sales tax and he wants to be perceived as being against tax increases. Consequently, the Governor has given tacit approval of the commonplace practice of avoiding the payment of "use tax" on such purchases, a law already on the books. In rejecting Amazon's application for a warehouse in the State, he is also foregoing more than a thousand new jobs, an initiative that was the centerpiece of his election campaign. No surprise, he is up for reelection next year, and being perceived as a champion of tax avoidance now seems preferable to job creation.

Friday, June 14, 2013
Flag Day and the Electronic World
Flag Day. A time to reflect on the adoption of the flag we honor, and what it symbolizes. In the world of 1776, it is a nation committed to freedom in its purist form. Oceans separated us from

the rest of the world, difficult for an invading army to breach that defense.

The Second Amendment, giving us the right to bear arms, was passed in 1791, a means of maintaining a civilian militia. ("A well regulated militia being necessary to the security of a free state, the right of the people to keep and bear arms shall not be infringed.") At the time the flintlock musket was the standard weapon. Count on being able to fire it maybe 2-3 times a minute. Arms have evolved to the point where a deranged individual can hoard a surfeit of automatic weapons, making that one person a veritable army.

And communications used to be dependent on the mail, then the telegraph, the telephone, and now electronic everything, marrying all methods of communication from the printed word to video. The Internet has given rise to threats that could not even be imagined by the framers of the Constitution and the Fourth Amendment.

Maybe it is time for a public debate on the issue, but the data mining being done by the National Security Agency cannot be a surprise to anyone. Edward Snowden's so called whistle blowing merely politicizes what most suspected.

If anyone asked us the day after 9/11 whether the government should make use of private electronic communications with the sole objective of preventing any such future event, we would have merely said, where do we sign on? How short everyone's memory is. It is ironic that a liberal constitutional law professor—Barack Obama—now, as President, is carrying forth the NSA program which had been condoned by his predecessor.

The brave new electronic world exponentially enhances the weapons of guerrilla warfare, the preferred tactic of terrorist adversaries. One does not fight this with the tactics of warfare when the Constitution was written, soldiers standing in straight lines right out in the open. Clandestine electronic communications are fodder for equally clandestine data mining. So, let the "debate" begin in Washington, but if it is anything like exchanges over the budget, it is liable to do more harm than good, unless there can be some consensus on an oversight mechanism that still preserves the intent of the program.

In this regard, I can't help but think of Aaron Sorkin's brilliant movie, *A Few Good Men*. When Col. Nathan R. Jessup faces Lt. Daniel Kaffee on the stand, we are all rooting for Kaffee, recognizing the menace that Jessup represents. But that was 1992. With a little editing (my apologies to Mr. Sorkin), I can imagine how this might go today …

NSA to Snowden: "Son, we live in a world of electronic communications, ones terrorists routinely use, and we have to be guarded by high tech surveillance. Who's gonna do it? You, Mr. Snowden? We have a greater responsibility than you can possibly fathom. You weep for your loss of freedoms and you curse the NSA. You have that luxury. You have the luxury of not knowing what we know, that some loss of privacy, while tragic, probably saved lives. And our existence, while grotesque and incomprehensible to you, saves lives! You don't want the truth, because deep down in places you don't talk about at parties, you want us data mining. You need us on that job. We have neither the time nor the inclination to explain ourselves to a man who rises and sleeps under the blanket of the security that we provide, and then questions the manner in which we provide it! I would rather you just said "thank you", and went on your way."

Tuesday, October 8, 2013
Catch 22 in Washington
What is one supposed to expect from Washington nowadays other than a Kafkaesque response to communication? Of the several emails I recently sent concerning the government shutdown and the debt crisis, my favorite exchange was with U.S.

Senator Marco Rubio's office. Here is mine which I tried to keep brief and to the point:

"To use the shutdown of the government and, far worse, the possible default on our debt as a hostage for repealing a law that has already been passed, adjudicated, is the worst kind of governing I can imagine and I blame this on the Republican Party, particularly the fringe elements, a Party I used to admire. This kind of brinksmanship reminds me of the Cuban Missile crisis, but being played out with the full faith and credit of our country as the A bomb (I lived in NYC then and remember the anxiety clearly). Why not deal with the weaknesses of the Affordable Care Act (which is the proper name, not Obamacare) when they become evident during its implication? It makes me furious at my representatives and apprehensive for this country"

One minute later, I got the following response:

"Thank you for taking the time to contact me, please be advised due to the government shutdown, my office is currently closed. My office will respond to your concerns or resume work on your case as soon as the office reopens. In the interim, if you would like to leave a comment for me, you may still do so at 1-866-630-7106 (within Florida) or 202-224-3041.

Sincerely,
U.S. Senator Marco Rubio"

Thus, I first called the Florida number, and it was busy. So I called the Washington number and got one of those happy, professional recordings, one option was to leave a message concerning any legislative matters. So, that is the option I chose.

Then, even a more friendly voice responded, I'm sorry, that mailbox is full. Goodbye.
The end.

PS When I wrote this entry, I had no idea that practically con-
currently President Obama was calling the failure to raise the
debt ceiling an economic "nuclear bomb." Amen to that.

Thursday, October 31, 2013
Boo!
Talk about a scary Halloween. We're fearing little goblins with
Ted Cruz masks, demanding all the Candy or else, the "trick"
being they will stay at our doorstep forever, blocking our exit
until we relent. Other non-Cruz goblins better watch out too,
once the Cruz clan congregates.

Until now, I've been silent on the subject of Ted Cruz. He
burst on the political scene as did Sarah Palin, but Palin was
clearly a hopeless lightweight who was "hired" to play a role. She
is a reality TV star, and that's about it. But Cruz is very different,
and I've been trying to make some sense of him, his views, and
where he might be going.

He is perhaps the most disturbing politician I've witnessed
firsthand (only vaguely remembering Joseph McCarthy from
my childhood). I thought Barry Goldwater was dangerous, but
unlike Ted Cruz I don't remember him threatening to hold the
US Government hostage. Cruz's intransigent political views,
with no compromise possible, is menacing enough. He is clearly
an exceedingly ambitious politician who has all the requisite
American-as-apple-pie views and the mannerisms of a preacher,
attributes that appeal to his Tea Party / Christian Right followers. (His recent hunting outing was amusing, perhaps not as
well staged as Sarah-got-her-gun trained from a helicopter for
moose in Alaska; he was in Iowa, the first stop for the Primary.
And he looks oh so manly with a gun. Furthermore, Cruz is well
educated and one can only assume that his behavior is being
carefully choreographed to achieve the objective of running for
the Presidency of the United States.

His call to shut down the government and have the US default on its debts is a form of economic terrorism, i.e. the "threatened use of force [in this case, legislative force] ... by a person or an organized group against people or property with the intention of intimidating or coercing societies or governments, often for ideological or political reasons." (The Free Dictionary) Or at least the rubric of demagogue might apply—"a political leader in a democracy who appeals to the emotions, fears, prejudices, and ignorance of the less-educated citizens in order to gain power and promote political motives. Demagogues usually oppose deliberation and advocate immediate, violent action to address a national crisis; they accuse moderate and thoughtful opponents of weakness." (Wikipedia)

I can't help but think of Sinclair Lewis' *It Can't Happen Here*, depicting the rise of a Senator "Buzz Windrip" to the Presidency, a campaign built on the back of patriotism and traditional "American values" promising economic reform, and after election appoints his own personal army ("The Minutemen"—perhaps the NRA would apply for the job?), curtails minority rights, institutes kangaroo courts to do his dictatorial biding, while also limiting the power of the United States Congress.

No, I don't believe that is what would happen if the unthinkable occurs, Ted Cruz being elected President, but he has mainly used his Senatorial seat as a bully pulpit for his Tea Party views, so his political ambition seems to know no bounds. And I also can't help but think of this very loose paraphrase of a quote (sometimes attributed to Sinclair Lewis, but no one is sure)—if some form of dictatorship ever comes to America, it will be with a cross wrapped in an American flag. (Whatever happened to the concept of the separation of Church and State?)

One would hope that moderates in the Republican Party can put down this radical, take-all-or-else faction. John G. Taft, who rightly calls himself "a genetic Republican" made the brilliant case for reigning in the likes of Ted Cruz in his Op-Ed column in the October 22 *NYT*. He expresses my concerns exactly.

"... Speaking through the night, Senator Ted Cruz, with heavy-lidded, sleep-deprived eyes, conveyed not the libertarian element in Republican philosophy that advocates for smaller government and less intrusion into the personal lives of citizens, but a new, virulent strain of empty nihilism: blow it up if we can't get what we want.....This recent display of bomb-throwing obstructionism by Republicans in Congress evokes another painful, historically embarrassing chapter in the Republican Party—that of Senator Joseph McCarthy.....There is more than a passing similarity between Joseph McCarthy and Ted Cruz, between McCarthyism and the Tea Party movement...."

So, we now wait until February 7, the next "deadline" for the debt ceiling (it's becoming a Yo-Yo economy with all these kaleidoscopic, Armageddon-like cut-off dates). It will be fascinating (or perhaps even more frightening) to watch Senator Cruz's machinations as that fateful day approaches.

Friday, November 22, 2013
November 22, 1963
Fifty years ago. Can it be? There are few moments of our lives that are indelibly etched in our memories. 9/11 was such a day. But only those of a certain age who can remember that horrid day of Nov. 22, 1963. Such high hopes for our young President, John Fitzgerald Kennedy. These hopes were dashed by what would become the first of other assassinations in the turbulent 1960s, Malcolm X, Martin Luther King, and Bobby Kennedy.

To have borne witness to them all is almost dreamlike, but Friday, November 22, 1963 is emblazoned in my mind's eye.

One would have had to live through the Kennedy era to fully appreciate the anguish of that day, and the subsequent weekend, and ultimately what that day symbolized. My first real awareness of Jack Kennedy (other than his being a Senator and a war hero), was when he ran for President in 1960. I was not eligible to vote as an 18 year old (21 was the age then and it was not lowered to 18 until eleven years later), but as a freshman in a predominately Democratic-leaning college, I was caught up in the Kennedy message. He talked about the future and just did not seem to be content with politics as usual.

My parents were staunch Republicans. Nixon all the way. My father was horrified by my views. And, as I was in the process of breaking from my parent's home, his reaction only reinforced my support of Kennedy. The other tripping mechanism was the Congregational church I used to attend (my parents sent me there for religious training and expected me to go to Sunday service, which they rarely attended). The minister at the time warned his parishioners of the dangers of electing a Catholic, inviting the Pope into American politics. That was the last time I was in a church other than for a wedding or a funeral or to visit one that had historic significance. Anti-Catholicism was as big an issue in that election as racial / birthplace issues were in Obama's.

I think if the Kennedy - Nixon election had taken place before television finally established a major role in elections, Kennedy would not have had a chance. But TV made the difference as Nixon came off looking like a perspiring used car salesman with a cool Kennedy sitting beside him, at home in front of the camera.

And so a new era of politics ensued, but that quickly went downhill as Kennedy had one test after another, first the Bay of Pigs fiasco, which merely foreshadowed the more serious confrontation over Russian missiles placed in Cuba later, and then taking on the steel industry over price increases they had promised not to implement. These were headline topics and both diminished, somewhat, the Kennedy mystique.

But nothing prepared us for what happened in October, 1962, the Cuban Missile crisis. This made the Cold War more than a theoretical event, as Kennedy took the calculated risk that a blockade (actually a "quarantine") of Cuba would give Russia an opportunity to back down, probably the most important decision of his Presidency. We were on the brink of nuclear war and living in a college dormitory in NYC the anxiety ran especially high. Had such a war broken out, Washington and New York would have been first targets. Alternatively, there was talk about an invasion of Cuba and we wondered whether we would soon be enlisting in the Army.

Through skillful behind-the-scenes diplomatic negotiating, the crisis was ended and the following year was relatively placid (except for the occasional mention of Vietnam), with improving diplomatic relations with Russia, a veritable Camelot era the Kennedy mystique had so often suggested. At the end of my Junior year, I was married (June 1963—to my first wife, also a Junior at college) and we moved into faculty / married student apartment facilities in the dormitory, working part time and summer jobs to pay for rent, utilities, and food. So, we were married only four months when the momentous day of Kennedy's assassination took place.

We did not own a TV, but we were friends with a Drama professor, Barbara Pasternak, who also lived in the faculty apartments with her husband, Mel. Barbara treated us almost as colleagues as my wife was acting in the university's theatre department and I was a student in Barbara's Drama-as-literature course.

They had a TV so we spent most of that gloomy aftermath of Kennedy's assassination in her apartment, frequently with other faculty members, watching, stunned, at the turn of events, from Jack Ruby's assassination of Lee Harvey Oswald to sadly watching Kennedy's flag-draped coffin as it moved through Washington on an open carriage. Little did we know what this horrible event would presage, such as the assassinations of Kennedy's brother Bobby, Martin Luther King, and Malcolm X. Or, now from the prospective of 50 years later, add the commonplace local shootings, slaughtering in malls, movie theatres, schools, not to mention wars and terrorism.

Many years later, sometime in the late 1980's my current wife, Ann, and I were sitting on our boat in Block Island and a large yacht was approaching Payne's Dock. The word quickly spread, that it was owned by a friend of Jacqueline Kennedy, and she was aboard (this long after her second husband, Aristotle Onassis, had died). Naturally, everyone was hoping that she would step off the yacht and perhaps walk on the dock, but she did not. Instead, I thought I caught a glimpse of her in the salon through thin curtains, almost like a cameo profile. I'm sure she had wondered, as I have all these years, what could have been. What kind of alternative history would have been written had Nov 22, 1963 been just another, forgettable, day?

Wednesday, November 27, 2013
Reflections of a Relic Investor
I used to think I was a fairly knowledgeable individual investor, watching measures such as the money supply (no one even refers to that anymore), interest rates, and comparing those to the earnings yield on stocks (the reciprocal of the Price/Earnings ratio) to partially determine asset allocation. Alternatively there was also the tried-and-true asset allocation approach, maintaining a fixed relationship between a percentage of bonds vs. stocks in a portfolio. March 2009 presented an incredible buying opportunity with the S&P reaching its nadir of some 676 (vs. 1,800 plus today). If you rebalanced every year thereafter, you would have missed out on some equity appreciation, but, nonetheless, participated in the rise of the S&P with less risk. Buying long term bonds today for balancing now implies taking

on more risk because of the artificially low interest rates. The asset classes would be highly correlated in a period of rising interest rates and declining equity values.

During that same period, the earnings yield on stocks vs. bonds became more and more divergent as the Fed moved from one stage of "quantitative easing" to the next. The impact on both markets can be seen with clarity if five years ago you decided to commit half of your investments to the iShares 7-10 Year Treasury Bond (IEF) and the other half to the SPDR S&P 500 (SPY) and, then, took a five year trip to Mars, leaving the market behind. Returning today, you'd find your 50/50 bond/ equity allocation now at 35/65, simply because of equity appreciation. So, what to do if you don't want so much at risk?

Jason Zweig addresses that question in this past weekend's *Wall Street Journal*. Bottom line, "know thyself." He quotes investment adviser David Salem who said that investors holding large stock portfolios or are considering buying more equities, should be "both willing and able to bear the loss," clarifying that "willingness is behavioral and ability is financial, and you can't know for sure in advance which one is going to trump the other." As the last bear market quickly eroded 50% plus of equity values, a 65% equity weighting puts one's portfolio at higher risk. What one did as that last bear market gathered momentum is a good indication of what one might end up doing if this market, too, ends badly. Of course, it can go higher—in that regard I'm always reminded of John Maynard Keynes' famous comment "the market can stay irrational longer than you can stay solvent."

Today's investment environment is now as foreign to me as the Mars landscape would be. Hostile too. While GDP is hardly growing, and unemployment stubbornly stays above 7%, peak profits are being racked up by major corporations. How can this be? Zero interest rates translate into profits, borrowing at nearly nothing to reduce corporate higher-rate debt or financing stock buy-backs. Corporations have squeezed their workers too, many laid off, a reward to shareholders in the form of increasing dividends. Labor unions are no longer empowered, a major consequence of labor competition from overseas. We no longer "make things" here and even intellectual labor can be harvested overseas, at lower cost, thanks to the impact of the Internet. So, by some measures, the "market" is "cheap." It certainly is cheap if you look at earnings yields vs. bond yields, a spread that has widened with every nail in the QE coffin.

At one time I thought the Fed's actions saved the world from a financial meltdown. Perhaps it did. But sustaining its monthly $85 billion bond buying program ad infinitum, not to mention maintaining zero interest rates, is creating an asymmetrical investment environment with every passing day (I'm avoiding the word "bubble" as the latter I sort of understand). It gets worse: recent Fed minutes implied lowering the interest it pays on bank reserves, which has led banks to warn that such an action might force them to charge depositors for holding money in savings and checking accounts (a negative interest rate!).

Perhaps all of this is being engineered to create a feeling of prosperity from the inflated asset prices of 401Ks, real estate, and equities, hoping that some will trickle down to the middle class via increased spending by the main beneficiaries, the wealthy. (Not surprising, Tiffany & Co. "reported a 50% increase in net earnings in its third quarter ..., largely resulting from 7% growth in worldwide net sales and a higher operating margin.") Or, perhaps, there is something more ominous behind the Fed's actions, a fear of deflation outweighing its concern for (or even desire for) inflation. Deflation would be an investor's clarion call to buy longer term "secure" bonds, even at these low rates, but, then, we will soon see the next round of the shoot out at the O.K. Corral (a.k.a. Congress), when the debt limit debate comes up again in March. So, even US Government Bonds may not be rated AAA given the crazy political environment.

No, all the old rules of investment are out the window in this investment environment, as understandable to me as Bitcoins, the price of which surpassed $1,000 today vs. $30 earlier this year, resembling the parabolic price rise of Dutch tulip bulbs in the 17th century.

Wednesday, December 18, 2013
Passing the Baton
Only a few years older than I was at the time, my son Jonathan is making his first business trip to Japan and China (having traveled extensively on his own in those regions, and having lived there as well). The confluence of his education, business experience, and language abilities has led to this moment. I had no such language skills and whenever I traveled in Japan I needed a translator. This left me at a disadvantage when it came to negotiations which usually entailed a team of Japanese executives on the one side and me on the other, they free to converse among themselves in my presence without my being able to understand a word. It was the collective "them" against lonely "me."

While my son is there on a business mission that doesn't directly involve negotiating, his language abilities are key to his success there. He reports on the number of Japanese women that are now in the executive ranks, a far cry from when I first went there in the 1970s. A 1977 photograph of me at a business meeting shows me with all male executives, a translator to my left. When tea was served, it was brought by women but they were not allowed to cross into the conference room—a sacred domain of the men—instead handing us the cups at the door. Oh, how things have changed there. The Japanese are finally becoming a more heterogeneous society.

From the depth of my files, I unexpectedly came across the speech I made in Japan at the turn of the New Year, 1990 (I had presumed the speech lost to time).

I've reread that speech and am amused by many of its observations. Japan was the economic juggernaut at the time, reveling in a sense of exuberant nationalism that comes with that territory. To an extent I bought into that then, but Japan since—when the Nikkei 225 reached its peak of 40,000, certainly a genuine case of irrational exuberance—has paid an economic price for that incredible bubble, and, making matters worse, their government "zigged" (raising interest rates) when it should have "zagged" (monetary accommodation). It only made their recession and deflation a multi decade affair.

They too have been impacted by the economic rise of China and the creative destruction of the Internet. When I review this speech which I delivered to Tokyo's Rotary Club, consisting of executives of leading Japanese companies at the time, I'm now fully conscious of those two giant forces no one at the time could have fully anticipated. I'm also acutely aware of how China is now in the position of Japan—an economic juggernaut that is also flexing its nationalistic muscles. Just witness its recent landing on the moon, a highly symbolic statement of where it stands today and the rise of its navy.

And the Internet has forged forces of incredible change, breaking down trade barriers that had stood for scores of years, "flattening" the world's labor forces, allowing manufacturing to follow where it might be done best and cheapest. When one looks at the components of a car or a cell phone, one needs a world map to track the many places they come from. And the impact of the Internet on the publishing industry in which I worked for decades are self evident, rendering some of the observations I made in the speech about the future of huge multinational publishing conglomerates more a figment of past imagination. Google and Amazon rule!

Still many of these issues exist, although, now, the trade battle, and our trade deficit, relate to China. The more things change, the more things do indeed seem to stay the same. Over to you, the next generation!

We were away during the beginning of the New Year, January 2014, and the very first political / economics entry at the end of that month was a summary of how we got "here" and "where" we might be going. Towards the end of that entry I mention the gun control issue and our lack of progress which, again, in retrospect now, might be the most serious deficiency of the Obama administration and "signature accomplishment" of the Republican controlled congress. Some subsequent entries during the year show the increasing divide in the nation, the perfect fodder for Trumpism. This culminates in the midterm elections handing over both the House and the Senate to Republican control, an ominous sign.

Monday, January 20, 2014
"Existential Illegitimacy"
We recently returned from a week cruise in the Caribbean. On our way home from the cruise terminal parking lot, between Ft. Lauderdale and our home, a message was flashing on I95 about a traffic alert. I checked Google Maps, and there didn't seem to be any delays but a few minutes later, on an overpass, there was a terribly disorganized "protest" with few protesters in attendance (I guess the authorities thought this would tie up traffic), holding signs for the motorists passing underneath, reading "Obama is a Muslim"). How sad, I thought, wasn't this yesterday's "news" or are these zombies conditioned by the Tea Party media, condemned to be the walking dead for their propaganda?

But it is something deeper, sadder than that, and especially on this Martin Luther King Day it is propitious to be reminded of the racially charged roots of such "protests" (and the "existential illegitimacy" of Obama's presidency). In this regard,

Sunday's *New York Times* carried an especially insightful article by Greg Grandin, a professor of history at New York University, "Obama, Melville and the Tea Party." Melville, you ask? Ironically, one of the books on my "reread" pile is *Benito Cereno*, a short novella that I had mostly forgotten (as I had read it in college ages ago) and Grandin makes the association between Melville's classic and Obama's ongoing problem as a black in a Christian white man's world: "*'Benito Cereno* is based on a true historical incident, which I started researching around the time Mr. Obama announced his first bid for the presidency. Since then, I've been struck by the persistence of fears, which began even before his election, that Mr. Obama isn't what he seems: that instead of being a faithful public servant he is carrying out a leftist plot hatched decades ago to destroy America; or if not that, then he is a secret Muslim intent on supplanting the Constitution with Islamic law; or a Kenyan-born anti-colonialist out to avenge his native Africa.

No other American president has had to face, before even taking office, an opposition convinced of not just his political but his existential illegitimacy. In order to succeed as a politician, Mr. Obama had to cultivate what many have described as an almost preternatural dominion over his inner self. He had to become a 'blank screen,' as Mr. Obama himself has put it, on which others could project their ideals..... Yet this intense self-control seems to be what drives the president's more feverish detractors into a frenzy; they fill that screen with hatreds drawn deep from America's historical subconscious."

Indeed. One of my blog articles, written in May 2008 as the presidential elections were gearing up, was an "Open Letter" to the then Senator Obama, in which I expressed my hope that he would address the mounting national debt, a decaying infrastructure, and the lack of better healthcare and being hostage to oil producing nations. I concluded "racial and religious divisiveness still erodes the fabric of our society and the view of

America abroad has undermined our ability to effectively deal with terrorism and to address global environmental issues."

Since then, I've had my problems with Obama's presidential style, his academic standoffishness (perhaps Governor Christie could have given him a few pointers in good old fashioned strong-arm politics). But, looking back, even with the brinksmanship of Tea Party politics he's had to contend with, there has been progress. The economy is one, unemployment still too high, but slowly declining. And soon after Obama was elected, the Dow dropped a few hundred points and the conservative press was immediately crying, SEE! For months, it was all Obama's fault (although he had nothing to do with it) and now, years later, with everyone's 401Ks flush with gains from a rising market, and real estate making a recovery, not a peep about his being responsible (which I would only attribute indirectly anyhow). And even now that Osama bin Laden has been killed and al Qaeda in disarray (although, admittedly, not entirely eliminated—almost an impossibility due to its decentralized organizational structure), little credit is given to Obama, but only just imagine that if bin Laden was still at large, you'd never hear the end of it from the Tea Party. And Obama supporting the efforts of NSA surveillance to minimize terrorist threats—how many conservatives would have jumped on board that train until they discovered Obama was at the wheel? Meanwhile, hydraulic fracturing has made us more energy independent, something Obama has supported in spite of certain aspects being under assault from environmental organizations.

Obama's signature piece of legislation has been the Affordable Care Act, and the conservative press was delighted at the very poorly planned launch via the government web site. But as a cynic about many aspects of government, I can only attribute that to the "a camel is a horse designed by a committee" syndrome, not to mention the inherent complexity of the entire program. But it is a start.

Are things perfect, or as far along as we would like? No. In the absence of sound fiscal policy from a dysfunctional Congress, the Federal Reserve has had to use monetary policy to stabilize the economy—even to bring us from the brink of a depression (although deflationary clouds still gather). We've substituted soaring public debt for private debt and a banking system gone wild (remember the days of unregulated CMOs?). And another Sword of Damocles hanging over the nation is its inability to balance the legitimate spirit of the Second Amendment—the right to bear arms—and the demands of the NRA. (I say "legitimate spirit" as the weaponry when the Second Amendment was drafted was nothing like today's.)

There have been twenty mass shootings since Obama became president and he is helpless to do anything about it without the complete cooperation of Congress. After the shooting in Newton, Connecticut, only a few miles from where we lived for twenty plus years, there was a ground swell (verbal only) in Congress to do something to control the sale of certain automatic weapons, but by the time the NRA got finished with their lobbying campaign, that effort was AK47ed to death. Explain that failure to the parents of the children slaughtered.

So if Obama's presidency is finally judged as mediocre at best, read *Benito Cereno* to understand the historic etiology of his predicament. As Grandin says, "it represents a new kind of racism, based not on theological or philosophical doctrine but rather on the emotional need to measure one's absolute freedom in inverse relation to another's absolute slavishness. This was a racism that was born in chattel slavery but didn't die with chattel slavery, instead evolving into today's cult of individual supremacy, which, try as it might, can't seem to shake off its white supremacist roots."

The following entry is classified as literature in my blog as it is an interview with, now, the late Philip Roth. It is severely

truncated to focus on the very essence of everything I write
about in this book, how did we get here and where are we
going? I shared Roth's despondency over the facts:

Saturday, March 22, 2014
"Character is destiny, and yet everything is chance"— Philip Roth

An absolutely fascinating, revealing, brilliant interview was
given by Philip Roth to a Swedish journalist, Svenska Dagbladet,
for publication there on the occasion of his novel, *Sabbath's
Theater* being translated into Swedish. The interview appeared
in the March 18 *New York Times Book Review* as well.

Asked about his generation of writers and the state of contemporary American fiction, he morphs from fiction to his
feelings about the world we now inhabit. His observations on
today's world are particularly profound: "Very little truthful-
ness anywhere, antagonism everywhere, so much calculated to
disgust, the gigantic hypocrisies, no holding fierce passions at
bay, the ordinary viciousness you can see just by pressing the
remote, explosive weapons in the hands of creeps, the gloomy
tabulation of unspeakable violent events, the unceasing despo-
liation of the biosphere for profit, surveillance overkill that will
come back to haunt us, great concentrations of wealth financing
the most undemocratic malevolents around, science illiterates
still fighting the Scopes trial 89 years on, economic inequities
the size of the Ritz, indebtedness on everyone's tail, families not
knowing how bad things can get, money being squeezed out of
every last thing....."

His comments on American popular culture are priceless:
"The power in any society is with those who get to impose the
fantasy....Now the fantasy that prevails is the all-consuming,
voraciously consumed popular culture, seemingly spawned
by, of all things, freedom. The young especially live according

to beliefs that are thought up for them by the society's most unthinking people and by the businesses least impeded by innocent ends. Ingeniously as their parents and teachers may attempt to protect the young from being drawn, to their detriment, into the moronic amusement park that is now universal, the preponderance of the power is not with them."

May we hear again and again from Philip Roth, perhaps not in imaginary literature, but in interviews such as this and essays. To me he is still the reigning dean of American literature and intellectual thought.

Saturday, April 26, 2014
Weekend Thoughts
Can you imagine the effrontery of what Georgia's legislature euphemistically calls the "Safe Carry Protection Act"? Just ask any parent of a child who was at the Sandy Hook Elementary School slaughter.

Georgia "Cracker" takes on a new meaning. Crack! Pow! Rat-tat-tat! To what extreme and at what cost of lives do we take the interpretation of the Second Amendment? When the Second Amendment became part of the Bill of Rights the reigning weapon was the Musket, accurate perhaps up to the length of a football field, and if you were experienced, perhaps you could get two shots off per minute. Compare that to today's weapons. Is that what our Founding Fathers meant, the right of every citizen to carry AK-47s which can fire 600 rounds per minute with a maximum range of 30 football fields?

Georgia takes this to another level. Bring your gun to your favorite bar, have a few drinks, and shoot 'em up! Then, go to church with your fellow gun-toting religious zealots and pray! And, bonus time, give a gun to your kid to take to college!

Georgia now joins twenty two other infamous states with some form of "stand your ground" laws as opposed to eighteen states that have laws imposing "a duty to retreat," seemingly a more civilized law that puts the burden on the threatened individual to avoid deadly force where reasonable (like getting the f**k outta there!), only resorting to deadly force where unavoidable, such as being in one's home during an armed home invasion.

It just seems that in the wake (sadly and certainly no pun intended) of the Newtown, CT tragedy, the NRA has simply put state governments in its powerful lobby cross hairs (pun intended). Frankly, although I support the second amendment for hunting and target practice, it's dispiriting that we can't have stronger laws to outlaw automatic weapons and institute laws that mandate registering weapons as we must register automobiles (which can be equally lethal). It's a stain on our legislative resolve (or lack of it to be precise).

Thursday, July 3, 2014
Independence Day Reverie
I've increasingly avoided political topics recently. To what end I've argued with myself. Here we're about to celebrate our independence while, as citizens and voters, we are held hostage by an intransigent Congress that can't even address some of the basic needs of our society. High on my priority list is our decaying infrastructure, inability to control the widespread distribution of assault weapons, addressing immigration reform with some realism, and an economy that is being held together by artificial means. And those are just the domestic issues.

But I'm not alone in ranting with disappointment. Barry Ritholtz wrote an insightful article on this subject for *Bloomberg View*, "Is This the Worst Congress Ever?" I can't wait until he expands on his thoughts as he promises in a future article, particularly on the Federal Reserve's role in this.

Meanwhile, we "celebrate" the 4th with the long drive from Florida to Connecticut. I now dread the drive up I95. In years gone by we actually enjoyed the trip but now it is mostly drudgery having to share crowded roads and hotels with people who rarely smile at you or might even just shoot you, depending on how the dice rolls nowadays. Fewer seem to exhibit some simple common courtesy. It's become worse over the years, or perhaps I've become embittered with age, I can't tell.

It's an in-your-face-I've-got-mine-so-to-hell-with-you attitude, so incongruous with the spirit of the 4th. I was reminded of this on a recent drive to the airport to pick up my son. I saw a bumper sticker on a pickup truck—probably from the time of Obama's 2008 presidential race when he had emphasized it is a time for change. Easy to remember, clever I thought, but a disconcerting way thinking of about half the State it seems: " I'll keep my God, I'll keep my guns, I'll keep my money, YOU can keep the change!"

I'm all for freedom of speech. But this "in-your-face" slogan anecdotally underscores everything that is dysfunctional with our present political system. Compromise and consideration of the other person's point of view be damned! The story of our forefathers' struggle to conceive a new nation out of many points of view is what July 4th must be remembered for the next time we, the citizens, go to the polls to vote. E Pluribus Unum! Unless we can find common ground so our legislature works, and we can stop the march towards divisiveness and corporatocracy, July 4th will be nothing more than a fireworks show for the general amusement of a non-enlightened population.

Friday, September 5, 2014
Big Money Behind Little Dollars
Anyone following the financial headlines has to marvel at the game of steal the bacon being played out by three very

similar companies, Dollar Tree, DollarGeneral, and Family Dollar Stores Their merchandise is consumable products— paper products, cleaners, clothing, gadgets and chachkas and the like—primarily aimed at low- and middle-income consumers. Most of the goods are imported from cut-rate factories in China or 3rd world countries. Basically, Family Dollar Stores has been the object of takeover bids by their rivals, Dollar Tree and Dollar General.

Although we're talking about a generally low margin business, there are a lot of consumers in this category, and the owners of these businesses know it. So what is Family Dollar's 5.36% operating margin and almost $10 billion in sales (that's a lot of purchases at $1.00 each:-) worth to the highest bidder, Dollar General: $9.1 billion. It's amazing that low margin businesses can carry this kind of price, but we're talking about next to nothing interest rates, so just borrow it! And of course there is the magic of synergy.

But if you look at the principals and the major individual stockholders of these three businesses, making millions of dollars personally in compensation and stock options every year, it brings up the issue of the 1% and the huge disparity of income between them, their employees and their customers. That's the sad reality of the issue, the magnitude of that income discrepancy unprecedented until Wall Street overshadowed Main Street.

Maybe all three can get together as General Family Tree Dollar Stores? Cheap goods for the poor and riches for the job creators! Money rules!

Tuesday, September 9, 2014
Obama and ISIS
Apparently, unlike some Americans I support President Obama's careful and deliberate assessment of what to do with the

extremist terrorist group, ISIS. We've heard the knee-jerk criticism of Obama, an understandable emotional reaction to the sickening images of beheadings of journalists on the internet. Why is he on the golf course instead of in Washington devising a devastating and decisive response?!!!! (As if planning and policy comes to a standstill as Obama slices a tee shot. And as if we have an immediate strategy for dealing with all permutations of such groups. And as if we can do anything to make this group simply disappear.)

When President Obama takes to the TV tomorrow we'll hear more specifics about dealing with ISIS. It's pretty clear that this is not a "boots on the ground" war, but one similar to what we've waged against Al Qaeda. ISIS is even better organized and funded. It is unlikely we can "defeat them" in the military sense of the word. They are like a form of the black plague which at best can be forced into remission but is easily activated. It is an especially dangerous group as they know how to court social media and they are positioning themselves as the long sought after Islamic caliphate. We're talking about trying to contend with about 1,000 years of history and religious fervor in that case.

No you don't march on them; you surgically and systematically degrade their capabilities (as has already been said by Obama). And of course we must develop collaboration with European and Arab states for containing ISIS, and especially how it is being financed. Judging by their sophisticated weaponry, more like an army than a fragmented terrorist group, some factions of the oil rich Middle East states would seem to be involved. Is this a middle-eastern incarnation of the protection racket? Intelligence is needed to identify and choke off those funds.

Indeed, those who fail to learn history are doomed to repeat it. As Adam Gopnik recently wrote in his article in *The New Yorker*, "Does It Help to Know History?" "ISIS is a horrible group doing horrible things, and there are many factors behind its rise. But they came to be a threat and a power less because of all we didn't do than because of certain things we did do—foremost among them that massive, forward intervention, the Iraq War. (The historical question to which ISIS is the answer is: What could possibly be worse than Saddam Hussein?)."

Thursday, November 6, 2014
Specialization is for Insects
It's an anniversary of sorts as it's been seven years since I've been writing this blog, this memoir, this record of just one person's views during that period. I've been all over the place with content, mostly starting with some personal history, some postings about my former profession, publishing, on to politics, the economy, the market, lots of postings on our travels and boating, with photographs, my affair with the piano, including some videos, and, more lately, focusing on literature and theatre. I've always considered myself a generalist, jack of all trades and master of, maybe, a few. As such, blog traffic is less than specialist blogs written by "experts", but that's OK. I write for my own pleasure. Recently I updated my profile to include a Robert Heinlein quote which I think best explains my eclecticism: "A human being should be able to change a diaper, plan an invasion, butcher a hog, conn a ship, design a building, write a sonnet, balance accounts, build a wall, set a bone, comfort the dying, take orders, give orders, cooperate, act alone, solve equations, analyze a new problem, pitch manure, program a computer, cook a tasty meal, fight efficiently, die gallantly. Specialization is for insects."

While I can and have done most of these things and could probably learn the rest (would like to pass on butchering a hog—I don't eat hogs anyhow), I mean eclecticism on a more metaphoric basis. My interests take me many places and these are reflected here. I just don't write about one subject. I'm not an insect!

I see that I've mostly avoided politics lately. It's not that I lost interest, but the tide of campaign money had risen to such an extent that we, the voters, have been drowning in distorted advertising, appealing to emotion, twisting the facts, and little about the issues themselves. I have long contended that political advertising should be banned and candidates should have rounds of public debates, but debates in the purist sense of the word where they cannot go to their well-rehearsed sound bites. We learned more from the "debates" between Crist and Scott in the Florida Governor's race about their families than anything else, not to mention whether a "fan" is an "electronic device." And the media was swamped by the endless political advertising and mailers. The number of times I had to hear or see the words "Charlie Crist, Slick Politician, Lousy Governor" was sickening. All this $$ spent across America to promote attack sound bites. I say give it all to charity and make the politicians stick to the issues.

It reminds me of the Manchurian Candidate. The queen of diamonds is beaten into one's brain, and you pull the right (no pun intended) lever on command (oops, we mostly don't pull levers anymore behind a curtain, but mark electronic ballots). Corporations are people! And that is the message of the mid-terms, money prevails and people vote against their best interests. No doubt the Koch brothers are happy. They paid enough, along with the so-called "dark money."

Assault weapon control, immigration reform, and righting fiscal policy are the really big elephants in the legislative room. No, these we avoid. The only good news in the political arena is those endless robocalls, mailings, radio messages and TV ads, all little subliminal negative messages are over for the time being. Good riddance. They should be banned.

Our political system is broken, at the election level and on the legislative level. The midterm elections now turn over control of both the House and Senate to Republicans. OK, it's your turn

Wednesday, April 29, 2015
It's Come to This
I've passed through Baltimore more times than I care to count but never toured the city. I know the Baltimore portrayed by Anne Tyler, a place of comfy familiarity. She must be appalled about what's happening in Baltimore, although it is not surprising. Racial riots and tensions are not new in America. It is reminiscent of the 1992 Rodney King riots in L.A. which followed the acquittal of police officers after a police brutality incident was caught on video tape. But that was a "one off" capture of an incident.

What is new is the widespread use of cell phone, surveillance, and dash board cameras that reveal the everyday nature of the problem. Twitter and YouTube deliver the message to a nation crazed for user-generated content. The more we see, the more inured we become to the root of the problem, racial and economic division.

Meanwhile media firms are pouring endless money into creating "shows" designed to be watched on ubiquitous mobile devices, the holy grail of streaming Internet firms such as Netflix. We've become a nation of somnambulists, cynical about the political process (ironically revealed by Netflix's *House of Cards*—does life imitate art or vice versa?). According to a study done two years ago, "by 2015 Americans are expected to consume media for more than 1.7 trillion hours, or an average 5.5 hours per person per day, again not counting workplace time."

2015 is now. My wife recently boarded an aircraft from Atlanta and most people were watching videos on their laptops or iPods or even cell phones and although anecdotal evidence at best, many were of interactive games or slam-bang explosive Hollywood films. Imagine, most of your waking hours consuming media of this nature?

What happened to reading? Same answer as to what has happened to education. As long as we put a premium on consuming video content while minimizing education, there really is no answer to the racial and economic tensions that will play out in the future. Along with rebuilding our infrastructure, and our inner cities, education must be this nation's highest priority to provide opportunity where people feel there is none. Better police tactics are needed, and research and education is required there as well. No wonder there is such despondency.

Easier said than done naturally, and having a dysfunctional government is not helping. As presidential electioneering gets underway the failings of the whole process will become even more apparent, thanks to Supreme Court sanctioned unlimited campaign contributions by corporations and individuals: it's a few mega billionaires and corporations vs. the rest of us.

And it's come to this in Baltimore today: the Baltimore Orioles will play the Chicago White Sox in an empty stadium—our National Pastime with no spectators allowed because of safety concerns. Eerie symbolism of things to come? Is that how we want to live our lives?

The following entry might be considered an "odd ball" given the topic of the book, but religion is endemic to the politics and economics of this nation. "God" is claimed to be the ally of most nations, even those at war with each other, claiming God-condoned righteousness. It's your God against mine. Gun violence in this country frequently finds religion or religious and ethnic discrimination at its roots. Likewise, the entry after Labor Day marks the meaning of work in our society, and what it meant to me. Perhaps not a perfect fit, but working and religion are part of our socioeconomic landscape.

Thursday, July 23, 2015
Hitchens' Final Thoughts on Religion
It's a masterpiece of logic and free thought: *God is Not Great; How Religion Poisons Everything.* In the small world department, it's dedicated to his close friend and one of my favorite contemporary English novelists, Ian McEwan, with whom he no doubt extensively discussed the book's contents as it was being written.

I've never forgotten Cal Thomas' reprehensible "Christmas message" extolling the death of the atheist Hitchens who died of esophageal cancer more than three years ago. As a secularist, I'm predisposed to Hitchens' arguments, but as I've only read some of his essays in the past; it was time to read the book which Thomas castigates. While Hitchens carefully builds his arguments free from external dogma, Thomas uses the bible as his reference source. Hitchens would have annihilated him in a public debate.

Hitchens' book begins with two brilliant introductory chapters. The first, "Putting it Mildly," sets out his fundamental arguments: "How much vanity must be concealed—not too effectively at that—in order to pretend that one is the personal object of a divine plan? How much self-respect must be sacrificed in order that one may squirm continually in an awareness of one's own sin? How much needless assumptions must be made, and how much contortion is required, to receive every new insight of science and manipulate it so as to 'fit' with the revealed words of ancient man-made deities?....."

What are the alternatives to organized religion? "Literature, not scripture, sustains the mind and—since there is no other metaphor—also the soul. We do not believe in heaven or hell, yet no statistic will ever find that without these blandishments and threats we commit more crimes of greed or violence than the faithful....We are reconciled to living only once, except through our children, for whom we are perfectly happy to notice that we must make way, and room. We speculate that it is at least possible that, once people accepted the fact of their short and struggling lives, they might behave better toward each other and not worse. <u>We believe with certainty that an ethical life can be lived without religion</u>". [Emphasis is mine— Ann and I were married at NYC's Ethical Cultural Society which practices the "religion" of humanism—valuing the importance of each individual, celebrating diversity, and believing that our collective deeds create our own heaven or hell right here.] "And we know for a fact that the corollary holds true—that religion has caused innumerable people not just to conduct themselves no better than others...."

No wonder Thomas went off the deep end reading this book. The title of the second chapter is "Religion Kills" and is self explanatory. How many people have died because of, or in the name of, religion? How many wars were fought with both sides praying to "their" God to annihilate the other?

Much of the rest of the book examines religion by religion, showing the contradictions and logical fallacies of their scriptures, their inherent harshness, and indoctrination procedures. Get them while they're young. In fact one chapter questions whether religion could be considered child abuse. I felt that way during my "religious training." "How can we ever know how many children had their psychological and physical lives irreparably maimed by the compulsory inculcation of faith....[We] can be sure that religion has always hoped to practice upon the unformed and undefended minds of the young, and has gone to great lengths to make sure of this privilege by making alliances with secular powers in the material world."

As I said, I speak from experience. I was baptized in a Presbyterian Church (as it was nearby the apartment my parents then lived in), and although my grandparents went to a Lutheran Church (I think occasionally, not regularly), for some reason I wound up in the Congregational Church across the street. My parents rarely went, but I was sent there for "religious training," something to make me a better person. This included training during "release time" while I was in grammar school. Kids had Wednesday afternoons off to go to their churches for even more religious instruction. So public schools were in this indoctrination scheme as well. I was "confirmed" into the church as a 13 year old, but continued to go to Sunday school.

I'm not sure whether it was unique with my particular Congregational church or it is a basic tenet of the sect, but Calvinism ran deeply in its teaching. Hard work and good deeds will get you into heaven. That part of the equation was OK by me at the time, but the corollary, the burning in hell part for eternity did not—even for the slightest of "sins." As a young child I had nightmares about the devil and hell.

The last time I went to church was when the minister urged the congregation to vote for Nixon as he warned that voting for Kennedy would mean control by the Vatican, just another missile thrown in the war of Protestants and Catholics. (The Irish short story writer, William Trevor, deals with this issue in many of his writings, in particular "Lost Ground" where a Catholic saint appears to a Protestant boy and the outrage it creates in the town—"Why should a saint of [the Catholic] Church appear to a Protestant boy in a neighborhood that was overwhelmingly Catholic, when there were so many Catholics to choose from?") Other than attending weddings and funerals, organized religion lost its hold on me then and there.

Hitchens is an equal opportunity exposer of religions, analyzing the hocus pocus of each. He is most familiar with Christianity, but is well schooled in other religious texts, particularly the other Abrahamic religions, Judaism (he found out later in life that his mother was Jewish) and Islam. Fascinating—his analysis of the schism within Islam—and I'm wondering what he would say about ISIS, the latest incarnation claiming to be the caliphate.

Unlike other religions, the Islamic tenet is that the Koran can never be translated and therefore be open to free inquiry by "non-believers." "This is why all Muslims, whatever their mother tongue, always recite the Koran in its original Arabic.... Even if god is or was an Arab (an unsafe assumption), how could he expect to 'reveal' himself by way of an illiterate person who in turn could not possibly hope to pass on the unaltered (let alone unalterable) words?"

I understand why a very religious person may dismiss this as a polemic, but anyone with an open mind will perhaps agree that organized religion just seems to complicate everything, and extreme interpretations of the scriptures, whether Christian, Muslim, etc. add violence to the equation. I've always wondered how any religion can claim to be the "true" one when there are so many other ones including splinter sects claiming the same. Surely, at least the majority is wrong if not all. Of course, these are individual decisions and I try to respect all religions provided they are non-violent and do not proselytize. In fact, there is something to envy about someone who is so confident that there will be a happy afterlife instead of the nothingness from which we came.

Thursday, September 10, 2015
Post Labor Day Thoughts
My good friend and ex colleague, Ron, emailed to wish me "Happy Labor Day" even though we're out in the pasture with the herd of the retired. We proudly earned our branded hides: workers.

As my older son Chris proclaims, "Life is work." We're always trying to find a balance but when your job is enjoyable, and you find it meaningful, life and work negotiate a successful merger. During my career I was tempted to bring it to the next level in a major publishing organization. It would have meant leaving the company I was joyfully building and moving overseas to London, a city we love. But the thought of engaging in corporate politics, vs. the hands-on experience of running a stand-alone publishing company made me hesitate and I'm glad I did.

My favorite section of the Sunday *New York Times* is their Sunday Review, mostly thoughtful, opinion pieces. This past week's had two relating to the above, "Friends at Work? Not So Much" (by Adam Grant) and "Rising to Your Level of Misery at Work" (by Arthur C. Brooks). The former cites factors such as the disappearance of a job for life, flextime, and the rise of the "virtual office" that has potentially impacted the loss of meaningful relationships for life. I always considered colleagues friends as well as fellow workers. There is much to be said about the virtual office but it is a steep price to pay for true collaboration and trust that develops through personal interaction.

The second article also speaks directly to my working years. As the article asks, "Why don't people just keep the jobs they like?" The answer is we are sort of hard-wired to achieve success by climbing the next wrung in the ladder, and then the next, etc. I climbed to the extent that I found a place in the working world that made me happy. Why go any further, indeed? Simply for more money? Bad reason I thought.

I always felt that I was responsible not only to my employer, but to my employees, our vendors, authors, as well, everyone who makes up a publishing company. As the article concludes: "In our interconnected world and global economy, our work transforms the lives of countless others. Sometimes the impact is obvious: Managers and executives directly inflect their employees' happiness and career success. But everyone, in every industry, affects the lives of co-workers, supervisors, customers, suppliers, donors or investors." If we all realize this in our working lives, perhaps work would not be a dirty four letter word.

Speaking of the latter, the prior week's Sunday Review (August 30) carried still another meaningful article on work, "We Need to Rethink How We Work," accurately reflecting on what motivates people. As Barry Schwartz, the author of the article points out, it was Adam Smith's view that people just dislike work, writing in his enormously influential *The Wealth of Nations*, that "it is the interest of every man to live as much at his ease as he can." Schwartz thinks that his notion has clouded the science of management ever since, viewing workers as beasts of burden which a whipping stick, or at least a carrot and a stick might be the best motivators. Hence, employees are being constantly monitored, as the wickedly funny movie *Office Space* satires as the "TPS Reports."

Employees thrive on a measure of independence and fair compensation should be the natural result of people working at jobs they find meaningful. "When money is made the measure of all things, it becomes the measure of all things....[We] should not lose sight of the aspiration to make work the kind of activity people embrace, rather than the kind they shun.....Work that is adequately compensated is an important social good. But so is work that is worth doing. Half of our waking lives is a terrible thing to waste."

I'm currently reading Jonathan Franzen's new novel, *Purity* (thus far, brilliant!). More on that book in a later entry, but early on in the novel there is a techno-utopian view of work expressed by participants in a Wiki-leaks-like cult movement. At one point there is a discussion as to why a person changing bedpans in a nursing home for a $40,000 salary wouldn't want, instead, to be a paid as a consumer at the same remuneration. One of the participants in the discussion comes to the conclusion: "The way you'd have to do it is make labor compulsory but then keep lowering the retirement age, so you'd always have full employment for everybody under thirty-two, or thirty-five, or whatever, and full unemployment for everybody over that age."

Is that the future of work? Sounds more dystopian to me. Franzen's unique social observations have a clarion ring of future verity. Maybe that's where we're heading: let robots do the work, and we'll lay about consuming streaming video all day. Thankfully, that is not my future, but we ought to be careful about what we wish for.

Nonetheless, getting back to Labor Day, I'm now many years into retirement and my working life seems more like a dream some stranger went through for those four decades. I like the way my friend Ron put it: "I have accepted the fact that we were merely hired ballplayers. While working we were respected, valued, and even ostensibly loved as long as we could pitch, field, run, and hit. Once retired, we were just old ex ballplayers. Now, there is hardly anyone at our companies who remember us or would even recognize our names let alone appreciate what we did. It is the way of the world, and I have accepted it." To that analogy I added, in my response, "I like to think we played it well—and now don't even get invited to an old timer's game. I still think I can reach home plate from the pitcher's mound though :-)."

OK, no more pitching for me, but we know what we did and we know that our careers led to thousands of publications that might not have seen the light of day, and those went out into an Internet-less world at the time, and affected change and hopefully progress. And we were part of working communities, dedicated as much to one another as we were to the work itself. As I said, it was a merger of sorts.

Now momentum was gathering towards the primaries as well as a number of gun violence incidents and thus my entries increasingly focused on those topics. And soon there was to be the incredible (still, to me) rise of Donald Trump to the Presidency. How this all came together is documented entry after entry, some downright condescending, the joke being on those

*not believing it could even be possible, me being one of them—
initially at least.*

Saturday, September 12, 2015
And I'll Raise You a Hail Mary
It's that silly season of the presidential primary beauty pag-
eant and with Donald Trump in the Republican fray; there is
no shortage of material for late night comedy hosts. But where
are Jon Stewart and the "old" Stephen Colbert when you need
them? Their cable comedy shows became the real news while
the national newscasts seemed more like the comedy shows.

I've purposely avoided writing about politics for some time,
mostly because it's just too disheartening and I write merely one
person's opinion, not with the clout of, say, a Cal Thomas who
clutches his bible when expressing his political views. I have no
such source of "truth" to cite.

But speaking of the Good Book, there is the recent amusing
exchange between Ben Carson and The Donald, a school-yard
square-off to demonstrate who might be more Christian. Poor
Mike Huckabee; he's been going down the yellow brick Evan-
gelical road for so long and still no presidential nomination,
boo-hoo. I'm more Christian than you are na-na na- boo-boo.
Apparently, Carson casteth the first stone, citing Proverb 22:4:
"By humility and the fear of the Lord, are riches and honor
and life." He continued to say, referring to The Donald as
"him,"—"And that's a very big part of who I am. Humility and
fear of the Lord. I don't get that impression with him. Maybe
I'm wrong."

It must be tough to have lots of humility as a billionaire, particularly one who has monetized his name, not to mention being
born to money, and bullied his way to billionaire status with
financial tactics that would be the envy of Vito Corleone. See
Andy Kessler's article in the Sept. 10 *Wall Street Journal* for the

detail: "The Art of The Donald in 10 Easy Steps—First, be born rich. Then acquire political influence. After that, pile up debt, write books and.... run for office."

But Trump showed his other cheek to Carson in a relatively benign Christian Tweet: "Wow, I am ahead of the field with Evangelicals (am so proud of this) and virtually every other group and Ben Carson just took a swipe at me." According to Politico: "Weeks earlier, he told a crowd of religious conservatives in Iowa that he couldn't recall ever asking God for forgiveness, though he said he has taken Communion. 'When I drink my little wine—which is about the only wine I drink—and have my little cracker, I guess that is a form of asking for forgiveness, and I do that as often as possible because I feel cleansed,' Trump said."

Now he might have criticized Carson on something more substantive such as Dr. Carson's belief in creationism and his denial of climate change, but, instead, I suppose Trump had a little wine and a little cracker to cleanse the matter.

This is what the candidates talk about when running for The Presidency? "God" forbid the pious rhetoric if an atheist ever runs.

And let's not forget the Democrats in the two ring circus, and the plight of poor Hillary who was considered a shoo-in for the Democratic nomination not long ago. The Clintons always get in trouble with denials rather than stepping up to the plate and admitting to a mistake. I did not have sex with that email server!

Let the games begin again!

Friday, October 2, 2015
Carly Sidesteps
I'm still stunned by the *Meet the Press* interview with Carly Fiorina last week, and how it juxtaposed to an interview on the same program with Hillary Clinton. Chuck Todd kept Hillary

on the defensive over her private server and the missing emails. Nothing much else was discussed. He would not let it drop and she answered him to the best of her ability ("I'm not a techie!"), although, admittedly, chameleon-like in many respects.

The interview with Carly Fiorina was in stark contrast. She was cleverly and clearly on the offensive, being able to make whatever claims she wanted (although Todd picked up on those, she simply ignored his questions and countered with her well-scripted talking points). First there was the claim of the existence of a Planned Parenthood tape where fetus body parts were being auctioned. Todd picked up on that saying, "well, the footage you describe at best is a reenactment. The people even— the people that made the videos admit its stock footage. Yet, you went right along and said, 'It's Planned Parenthood.'"

Fiorina condescendingly ignored Todd's statement with a generalization: "Chuck, Chuck, Chuck, Chuck, Chuck. Do you think this is not happening? Does Hillary Clinton think this is not happening? So sad that you missed the opportunity to ask Mrs. Clinton why she said, 'Late-term abortions were only performed for medical purposes.' That is patently false. This is happening in America today. And taxpayers are paying for it. That is a fact. It is a reality. And no one can run away from it." That's an answer to a specific question regarding Planned Parenthood and that footage?

In response to Todd's comments about her track record at HP, she said: "I think people are looking for a president who will run to the problems that this nation faces. Yes, I led HP through a very difficult time. The NASDAQ dropped 80%. Some of our strongest competitors went out of business all together, taking every job with them. We saved 80,000 jobs. We went on to grow to 150,000 jobs. We quadrupled the growth rate of the company, quadrupled the cash flow of the company, tripled the rate of innovation of the company. And went from lagging behind to leading in every single product and every single market. I will run on that record all day long."

How many "Pinocchios" is that statement good for?

In the last "debate" Fiorina denounced one of her critics on her job record, Jeffrey Sonnenfeld who is the senior associate dean of Leadership Studies and Lester Crown Professor of Practice Management at the Yale School of Management. Of course he was not there to defend his views. She simply proclaimed that he is a "Clintonite" and therefore his views are false. Sonnenfeld answered her in Politico in his article: "Why I Still Think Fiorina Was a Terrible CEO:" "She can diss me all she wants on live TV, but personal attacks won't take her from colossal business failure to leader of the free world."

I had thought that Fiorina was in the race as a logical VP candidate if Hillary does indeed become the Democratic candidate. Although that still might be the case, I'm not so sure anymore that she will be satisfied with "only" the VP nomination.

Switching gears to one of the major issues of our times, gun control. It is sad that we make no progress in this area and now, still, another mass slaughter, this one at the Umpqua Community College in Oregon. CNN now reports that the police have identified thirteen (!) weapons connected with the murderer.

As President Obama wearily declared in his news conference, these incidents have become routine in this country and our response is routine: commiserate with the families and do absolutely nothing to diminish the problem. Thank you NRA and its obedient congressional cronies.

I'm no Pollyanna when it comes to this subject. People should have the right to have registered weapons for target practice and hunting, and for self protection (with licensing akin to getting a driver's license, testing etc.), with stringent background checks before any weapon could be bought. Assault weapons should be banned. Would those steps eliminate the problem? No. But it's a start. On a macro basis, it is a cultural problem (just look at popular culture which glorifies violence and guns), as well as educational and income inequality feeding the problem. These must be addressed as well.

Saturday, October 24, 2015
In Our Back Yard
Back to the Florida "stand your ground" law, and about racially provoked incidents. Generally, these issues have not been in our community, but last Sunday Corey Jones' vehicle broke down at the nearby Interstate 95 exit ramp in Palm Beach Gardens. He was a drummer in a band and therefore routinely traveled late at night. He was shot and killed by a police officer who emerged from an unmarked car and who was not in uniform while Jones was waiting for a tow truck.

This has attracted national attention as potentially another example of a contentious police action. It is certainly at least a police indifference to an alternative protocol which may have obviated any shooting and it is too early to rush to judgment regarding whether it was racially provoked in any way. It seems the incident was fundamentally a deadly cocktail of circumstances.

Corey Jones' vehicle broke down on his way home from a gig in Jupiter, just north of where the incident took place. He called a friend who tried to help him get his car started around 2:00 am, but without success. He called for a tow truck and although his brother called to offer to pick him up, he didn't want to abandon his car because of the valuable drums he was carrying. So around 3:00 am as he was waiting for the tow truck, he was accosted by Nouman Raja, a plain-clothed police officer who was driving an unmarked vehicle with no police lights.

Corey Jones had a hand gun with a concealed weapon permit and probably thought he was about to be robbed and perhaps when the police officer saw the "suspect" with a gun, the ingredients were suddenly there for a deadly confrontation. Apparently, Jones never fired his weapon, but instead was trying to run away, his weapon being dropped half way between his car and where he was shot (three times according to the initial reports).

Jones was known as a law-abiding, church-going young man with a passion for music. Only a week before he purchased the gun legally. He was concerned about his late working hours and that his usual compensation was in cash.

So it all possibly comes down to mistaken identity, his not knowing that Raja was a police officer and the police officer not knowing whether Jones was a burglary suspect (an activity for which he was on stake-out duty nearby).

Perhaps the most significant question that needs to be answered by the Palm Beach Gardens police is why Raja didn't call for a marked police car to check out the vehicle. Given incidents in Florida involving fake police officers, bad guys who mount a red light on their dashboards and can stop a citizen with impunity, to rob the motorist or have an accomplice steal his car, how is one to know the legitimacy of being stopped? If Jones had been approached by a uniformed officer from a marked police car, it is unthinkable he would have gone for his pistol.

Particularly disturbing is the slippery slope of gun ownership. Here is a case of merely possessing a legitimate gun being a possible causative factor in a needless, horrifying death of an innocent young man, a passionate musician. The more people who carry weapons, the more gun violence, and therefore more people feel they need a gun, a vicious cycle, intolerable in a civilized society. And it will become increasingly likely that "mistaken identity" will involve the police use of guns.

We grieve for Corey Jones, for his family, and for our antiquated interpretation of the 2nd amendment. And currently moving through two Florida Senate committees is a proposal to allow Floridians with concealed weapon permits to carry them openly in public, including on college campuses and universities. There are about 1.4 million Floridians with permits. If this insanity becomes law, we'll soon be having fast draw shoot outs like in the old west, each person claiming that he was merely "standing his ground."

There are obviously no simple answers but given the number of concealed weapons, many of which are carried in the glove compartments of a car, one would think that a plain-clothed police officer in an unmarked car should call for back up before approaching an occupied vehicle on the side of the road late at night. It is highly likely that Corey Jones would be alive today if that was the standard protocol. This sad unspeakable tragedy was so unnecessary.

Tuesday, December 8, 2015
It Can't Happen Here?
Sinclair Lewis' novel *It Can't Happen Here* and Philip Roth's *The Plot Against America* tell tales that seem impossible, demagogues being elected President of the United States and the violent consequences, minorities being persecuted, hunted, fanaticism and mass hatreds abounding. It's an old formula—stir fear among the populace and then promise to protect them. Donald Trump showed his cards last night and got his South Carolina audience worked up into almost an evangelistic state. His message is simple: Muslims in America are dangerous and he'll protect us, classic demagoguery—"a person who appeals to the emotions and prejudices of people in order to advance his own political ends."

Trump has stirred a dangerous pot, just what ISIS wants. If one was a conspiracist, perhaps it could be said that he is merely a Trojan horse for Ted Cruz, who independently stated: "We will utterly destroy ISIS. We will carpet bomb them into oblivion. I don't know if sand can glow in the dark, but we're going to find out." If Trump drops out, Cruz will inherit the far right fringe of the Republican Party. Was that the "plan" all along? Does Cruz know that carpet bombing usually implies leveling an area, civilians and all? It sounds more like revenge than a strategy, something to make his followers "feel good."

Unfortunately, the horror of the recent mass shooting in San Bernardino has fed into all of this, "legitimizing" such dangerous rhetoric and escalating it to personal attacks on President Obama (who now has low polling numbers about keeping America "safe," the exact inverse of what those numbers were after bin Laden was nailed)—and subsequent accusations that any call for stronger gun control laws is merely politicizing the San Bernardino tragedy.

But such calls have gone on for years with fierce Republican and NRA opposition. I do not naively believe that better gun control laws and enforcement would magically eliminate such tragedies, especially in the short term. But I do believe that the Second Amendment, which was written in the days of musket rifles and flintlock pistols, needs serious updating.

At that time, we needed an armed militia and also the founding fathers believed that an armed citizenry would be a deterrent to the rise of a despotic government. The world has changed since then, weapons of war unimaginable to our forefathers, and, now, mostly in the hands of the military and law enforcement. To make some of the same weapons legitimately available to the citizenry no longer serves the purpose of protecting us from a despotic government as the military will always have superior weaponry (is an AK-15 adequate protection against a tank?). The proliferation of automatic weapons just further endangers us all, giving us a false sense of security by just having one in our closet.

No, this is a country of laws and checks and balances and we have to depend on our tried-and-true institutions as well as the much maligned (by Trump in particular) fourth estate to keep our government transparent and trustworthy. If some fringe element threatens us in our homes and public places, we need better intelligence to prevent it and rapid response law enforcement to protect us.

Fully automatic weapons (ones that operate as a machine gun) need to be banned, and guns should be registered just like a car, an equally dangerous thing. That means getting a license, passing a rigorous background check and license renewals (a gun owner having to report if it is sold, just like a car). Guns for self defense, hunting and target practicing are understandable but how can one argue that an automatic weapon is needed? Certainly not for hunting (where is the sport in that?). Do we really want our neighbors to be totting an automatic weapon citing Florida's ambiguous "stand your ground" law as a justification?

Will that keep guns out of the hands of the "bad guys" as the Republicans like to call them? No, but it's a start and of course the devil is in the details of how such gun control is administered.

Tuesday, January 26, 2016
Hopalong Cassidy America
It is the best of times; it is the worst of times, to paraphrase Mr. Dickens. Technologically speaking, it is wondrous. As a kid our Philco radio (which was actually a piece of furniture) brought me into the world of the Lone Ranger and Hopalong Cassidy, graduating to a big Dumont TV (well the cabinet was big but the screen minuscule), where I could finally see my cowboy heroes. We had a party line telephone and had to wait for our neighbor to get off their call to make a call. No dialup. You spoke to an operator to make a call, and telephone numbers began with a word, in our case "Virginia." When dialup arrived and party lines disappeared, the first two letters of the word preceded the number. I still remember ours: VI-6-3134. Unthinkable, making

or taking a call from a tiny device on your wrist, or from one hanging on your belt, or in the comfort of your car. This was the stuff of science fiction, although it was commonly thought that by the 21st century everyone would be driving flying cars.

This time of innocence was belied by the increasing tensions of the cold war with regular air raid drills in school, hiding under our desks as the shades were drawn to thwart the effects of a Russian nuclear attack. We thought of it as protection, but it was part of the propaganda, that the threat of a sudden attack was real and we shouldn't worry, the government would somehow look after us (e.g. the drawn shades). The McCarthy hearings and communist witch hunting were just part of the scheme to whip up fear to justify the investment in a giant nuclear arsenal.

Back then, though, there was the rise of a real middle class, the American dream realized which started with the GI Bill after WW II. Hard work really did pay off then, and company loyalty and affordable housing abounded, although other social issues lagged, in particular; racial equality, long held prejudices were still ingrained in our institutions.

Fast forward to the present with the wonders of technology which have changed our lives, and have given promise to a future of driverless cars, robotic assistants, and the colonization of planets (we'll have to eventually get off this one).

Mankind seems hell bent on destroying those future benefits. Imagine, the reality of global warming still being questioned, politicizing the very existence of our species (quick get me to Mars where I can feast on potatoes, but please don't run out of ketchup : -). Even if we agree to solve this primary issue, we still have a dysfunctional government which cannot agree on matters of gun control, a decaying infrastructure, reeducation of the depressed middle class to replace their disappearing factory jobs with those in the technology, health, or service sectors, and how to properly deal with terrorism and immigration policies, income inequalities, and that is but to name a few.

The ingredients seem ripe in the forthcoming Presidential election for the tipping point into downright dystopianism, the stuff of fiction until now, *1984, Brave New World, Fahrenheit 451, Clockwork Orange*, and *The Road*. I think of the latter two in particular in relation to what is already happening in Michigan, the Flint water fiasco, and the condition of the Detroit public schools.

Read David Brooks' insightful piece in a recent *New York Times* editorial in particular his comments on Donald Trump and Ted Cruz: "Worse is the prospect that one of them might somehow win. Very few presidents are so terrible that they genuinely endanger their own nation, but Trump and Cruz would go there and beyond. Trump is a solipsistic branding genius whose 'policies' have no contact with Planet Earth and who would be incapable of organizing a coalition, domestic or foreign. Cruz would be as universally off-putting as he has been in all his workplaces. He's always been good at tearing things down but incompetent when it comes to putting things together."

Imagine if Bernie Sanders does beat Hillary Clinton and Trump or Cruz wins their party's nomination. I don't think this nation is ready to elect a Jewish politician who has socialist leanings. And of course Clinton has her own issues so she isn't a shoo-in. Maybe the Democrats at the last minute can draft Al Gore who won the election in 2000 if it was not for the Supreme Court? (Parenthetically what would our world look like now if Gore was allowed to win? Would 9/11 still have happened? Would we have gone into Iraq? Would there have been better controls over bank risk taking which might have at least mitigated some of the 2007 collapse? More progress on reversing global warming?). Or, as Michael Bloomberg recently hinted, perhaps he'd run as an Independent if Sanders gets the Democratic nomination and either Trump or Cruz runs as the Republican nominee. But that would further split the progressive vote, making the Republican candidate a more likely winner even with a minority of the popular vote. I'd support Bloomberg.

So, if we find ourselves a year from now waking up to a President Trump or Cruz, would we, as Brooks contends, be in a position of having a new President genuinely endangering our own nation? A self-aggrandizing, poll spouting, reality TV star (to watch Trump squirm as Sarah Palin rambled on invectives and gibberish would be as funny as Tina Fey portrayed, if it were not so tragic—that's what our political system has come to: reality TV star endorsing a reality TV star), or a borderline fascist, a real tough guy (his persona reminds me of Senator Joe McCarthy in many ways) who as Supreme Court Clerk, made the death penalty his cause and who would carpet bomb the sand of the Middle East until it glows in the dark.

Either Cruz or Trump might have us strapping on guns as our "Constitutional right." And if everyone was so armed, shouldn't it be a safer America, where we can shoot the "bad guys" and "stand our ground?" Hopalong Cassidy America!

Art and life have a tendency to be intertwined. Some of the best literature arises out of social commentary, and so it was with a book I read which defines the Trump base, long before he was elected. Thus this "review" with liberal quotes describing this phenomenon is included here.

Monday, February 15, 2016
American Rust to American Politics and Art for the One Percent
When I heard the praise heaped upon Philipp Meyer's *The Son* which was a finalist for the Pulitzer Prize for Fiction, I was curious about his first published novel, *American Rust*. It is a work of merit and promise, and a good read, close to a dystopian piece of fiction, the inverse of the American Dream, depicting

the demise of the middle class and the seismic changes to the American landscape. It is also a Bildungsroman, the protagonist, Isaac English, having to embark on an odyssey to escape the "American rust" of the Pittsburgh valley and its failed steel industry and his father as well, having to endure beatings, starvation and exhaustion during his journey, but ultimately returning home to save his friend Poe, and to find salvation.

This is a well-crafted character driven novel with each carrying a piece of the story, frequently that piece unknown to the others, at least in its entirety, and leaving the reader the omniscient observer. Meyer skillfully maintains the suspense, making the book a page turner, to me one of the marks of a good writer.

The other characters are intertwined with the 19 year old Isaac English who was expected to go to any top college of his choice as he excelled in high school, as did his older sister, Lee, who went on to Yale on scholarship, and married wealthy right out of school. Isaac stayed behind in the prison of his environment, to care for his father Henry who is in a wheelchair and also to be with his only friend, Billy Poe, two years older than Isaac, a star football player in high school who was expected to get an athletic scholarship to college, but ended up hanging around the dilapidated mill town mainly out of loyalty to his mother who is divorced, and living in a trailer. There is the chief of police, Bud Harris, who loves Billy's mother and has moved mountains to keep Billy on the straight and narrow. And to further add complexity to the plot, there is the residual love affair between Billy and Isaac's sister, the now married Lee, who returns to check on her father and finds her brother leaving.

I'll not go into more details of the plot which brings all of this together but there are acts of sacrifice and love that ultimately set Isaac and Billy free. Lurking in the background at all times though, are the remnants of the steel towns, the low-paying jobs left behind for those who have stayed and can find them, a future without a real future and violence. The same feelings were invoked when I read about the empty mill towns of Richard Russo and the trailer parks of Russell Banks. But Meyer's writing is his own, and clever as he builds his novel chapter by chapter, from those different viewpoints, converging at the end. There is a little bit of modern day Kerouac here and even Salinger (such as the way Isaac in stream of consciousness refers to himself in the third person as "the kid").

What came to mind over and over again is this election year. Here we have two revolutionary yet entirely polarized players, the "democratic-socialist," Bernie Sanders, and the "alpha male, say-anything-you-want" Donald Trump. Each in their own way has forged a strong connection with the disenfranchised white middle class, or the young. What used to be a mainstream American Dream now exists mostly for the deliriously wealthy. The phenomena of today's Republican and Democratic primaries is the "do-you-hear-the-people-sing" voice of those who have been left holding the bag as we've morphed from a manufacturing economy to a techno-service based one.

In this regard, Philipp Meyer's *American Rust* speaks like John Dos Passos' *USA Trilogy*, or John Steinbeck's *The Grapes of Wrath*. The topography of the problem is laid down in similar social commentary. Lee is driving her father for a medical appointment and Meyer observes: "Farther along she couldn't help noticing the old coal chute stretching the length of the hillside, passing high over the road on its steel supports, the sky visible through its rusted floor; the iron suspension bridge crossing the river. It was sealed at both ends, its entire structure similarly penetrated and pocked by rust. Then it seemed there was a rash of abandoned structures, an enormous steel-sided factory painted powder blue, its smokestacks stained with the ubiquitous red-brown streaks, its gate chained shut for how many years, it had never been open in her lifetime. In the end it was rust. That was what defined this place."

Migration jobs like the ones offered to Billy Poe involve constant traveling to dispose of the flotsam of shutting down our manufacturing facilities and its environmental impact: "There was an opening at a company that did the plastic seals for landfills. Traveling all over the country. At new landfills they would lay down the plastic liners in preparation for garbage to be dumped there, to prevent leakage into nearby streams and such. At the old landfills they would seal them up, it was like a giant ziplock, a heavy layer of plastic overtop the garbage and then they blew them up with air to test them, just before they dumped the soil on top you could run across the acres of plastic, bouncing, it was like running on the moon ..."

Lee's teacher in high school had come to the town decades before when the steel mills were thriving. He "moved to the Valley to bring socialism to the mills, he'd been a steelworker for ten years, lost his job and become a teacher. Graduated from Cornell and became a steelworker. There were lots of us, he'd told her. Reds working right alongside the good old boys. But there had never been any revolution, not anything close, a hundred and fifty thousand people lost their jobs but they had all gone quietly. It was obvious there were people responsible, there were living breathing men who'd made those decisions to put the entire Valley out of work, they had vacation homes in Aspen, they sent their kids to Yale, their portfolios went up when the mills shut down. But, aside from a few ministers who'd famously snuck into a white-glove church and thrown skunk oil on the wealthy pastor, no one lifted a hand in protest. There was something particularly American about it—blaming yourself for bad luck—that resistance to seeing your life as affected by social forces, a tendency to attribute larger problems to individual behavior. The ugly reverse of the American Dream. In France, she thought, they would have shut down the country. They would have stopped the mills from closing. But of course you couldn't say that in public ..."

Which brings us to the present, the "ugly reverse of the American Dream ... you weren't supposed to get laid off if you were good at your job" and the consequences, a barbell society, lots of people at the one extreme, a select few at the other, and the vanishing middle class in between. Indeed, there are "ramifications" reflected in the contentious presidential debates, the right moving further to the right and the left moving further to the left, not exactly what our founding fathers envisioned.

And speaking of how the other half of the upper 1% live, this past week featured the annual Palm Beach Jewelry, Art & Antique Show which we like to visit but with a look-but-do-not-touch mind-set. Actually, it's with an "unable-to-touch" approach as some of the works of art there are priced at $250k plus although there are some nifty pieces for "only" $10k. It is like an eclectic museum and it appeals to my idiosyncratic taste in "art."

We attended it on "President's Day" weekend. Here is yet another change in American Life. We used to celebrate Washington's Birthday on February 22, but that fell on unpredictable days of the week and there was Lincoln's February 12 birthday to consider, so it became a compromised holiday, conveniently on a Monday for the benefit of blockbuster "Presidential" mattress and automobile sales. Sorry, General Washington.

Friday, February 26, 2016
In Your Face
It's against the law to advertise tobacco products as their use might KILL you. But no such ban against advertising guns which might KILL you as well. So there it is, right in your face, some nifty hand pistols as pictured and advertised in our local *Palm Beach Post*. Buy them on credit with six months to pay! Nothing down! Step right up, come and get 'em!

It is an interesting dilemma. To buy a gun or not to buy, that is the question. The gun industry, our society in fact, wants you to feel unsafe UNLESS you have a gun. We know people our age who have hand guns; they keep them in the car when they travel up and down the I95 corridor. Should I feel safer or more unsafe because they and thousands of others like them have guns, ones that can be stolen, or be used ineptly by their owners? What are the chances that some armed thug will be at a disadvantage because they have a .38 caliber pistol hidden somewhere? Balance those probabilities against the chances of a gun being used against you in an instance of road rage or you becoming a collateral victim of a gun fight between a "good guy" and a "bad guy."

Do we want our children to routinely see ads for guns? It implies an acceptance by our society. Yes, I know, the 1st and 2nd amendment, blah, blah, blah. But must they be advertised in local, family newspapers? Cigarette advertising is forbidden, but guns are fair game?

Tuesday, March 1, 2016
The More things Change
The more they stay the same. Well, not exactly.

I've been winnowing my old files. The stuff I come across sometimes amazes me, things I wrote that I don't remember or don't remember saving or why. Two recent discoveries remind me that over the decades I have witnessed an amazing span of history, technological developments, a world that has evolved with increasing complexity and interconnectiveness. Yet, still, some of the old political issues are not old at all. They have merely festered and changed their spots.

I found copies of two letters I wrote in my salad days, the first to the *New York Times* commenting on their editorial on Barry Goldwater's nomination, a man who, in retrospect, seems tame by today's conservative / tea party crowd. However, at the time of his presidential candidacy in 1964, he had not ruled out the use of tactical nuclear weaponry against our Cold War nemesis, the Soviet Union, and anyplace where communism was being supported. Johnson beat him handedly in 1964. Interestingly Goldwater moderated in his later years as a statesman, and in my mind redeemed himself, although always a staunch conservative in the classic intellectual sense, not the bible-thumping variety of today.

In any case, at the height of Goldwater's rise to the nomination in 1964, the twenty one year old sophomoric me wrote the following to the *New York Times*:

"July 19, 1964

The Editor
New York Times
New York, New York

To the Editor:

'Disaster at San Francisco,' indeed, may yet become a disaster for America. Your firm editorial stand against Senator Barry Goldwater must be continued to help defeat this dangerous radical, so that we may prove to ourselves and to the rest of the world that 'it can't happen here.'

As Hitler made use of Germany's post-World War One frustrations, Senator Goldwater is a political demagogue who similarly, but more subtly, intends to capitalize on the frustrations of many Americans, frustrations that have arisen in the ashes of domestic racial problems and the tensions of the Cold War. Goldwater tells us, as Hitler told Germany, that we are the strongest country in the world and we should stand up to the opposition (who he vaguely refers to as "the Commies"). This simple, but realistically absurd suggestion, appeals to those who are unable to bear the responsibility of living in these modern times. Unfortunately, there are still many 'good citizens' of America who believe that if we act as if it is still the 'good old days,' we will recreate those days.

If we are to preserve democracy in our country and continue to encourage democracy abroad, we must condemn political extremists who present oversimplified, irresponsible, and inherently contradictory solutions to complex issues, solutions which would isolate us from our friends abroad and which, conceivably, could destroy the world as we know it."

Its contents mention some of the same issues Americans face today, particularly as espoused by Donald Trump and Ted Cruz. The latter of course bills himself as a true conservative, but he is the very kind of conservative who I think Goldwater himself would have condemned. In fact where is Barry Goldwater when we need him : -)? Here is something Goldwater said to John Dean in 1994: "Mark my word, if and when these preachers get control of the [Republican] party, and they're sure trying to do so, it's going to be a terrible damn problem. Frankly, these people frighten me. Politics and governing demand compromise. But these Christians believe they are acting in the name of God, so they can't and won't compromise. I know, I've tried to deal with them." How profound is that, Mr. Rubio, Mr. Cruz?

And my files coughed up a letter I wrote three years later to Senator J. William Fulbright during the height of the Vietnam War. Again, different times, different war, but still relevant in many ways:

"August 6, 1967

Senator J. William Fulbright
Chairman, Senate Foreign Relations Committee
United States Senate
Washington D.C.

Dear Senator Fulbright:

I am just finishing your book *The Arrogance of Power* and I felt obligated to immediately express my support of your thesis.

The Vietnam situation is truly tragic. The noble ideals of our great country are belied by our actions. How can we expect the world community to look to America for leadership while we drop millions of tons of bombs on a small country of mostly peasants, support dictatorships, even as we seem incapable of resolving many of our own domestic problems?

While I do not feel that we can just abandon our Asian commitments, we need to discard our military's "search and destroy" philosophy in favor of seeking a solution over a conference table—which may demand compromise, but ones also compatible with democracy.

In addition, I believe that the United States has more to lose by endeavoring to become the world's policeman. An Asian conflict should be resolved, in the most part, by the Asians and/or the United Nations, with the encouragement of the world's great powers. Our military involvement in the affairs of other nations only tends to weaken the fabric of the U.N. and secures the animosity of other nations toward us.

I encourage continuing your efforts to reestablish the system of checks and balances provided for in the Constitution so a more realistic foreign policy can be devised and implemented.

With great admiration of the courageous and sensible stand which you have taken, I am, Sincerely yours."

So, there you have it: the "mini- me" of some five decades ago writing about some of the same issues of today.

And now the present brings us into a political environment ripe for extremism, as evidenced by the unexpectedly strong primary showings of Donald Trump and Bernie Sanders, polar opposites but in many ways playing to the same base, the disenfranchised. In early December I wrote a piece "It Can't Happen

Here?" (the very words I wrote to the *NYT* fifty two years earlier) suggesting that Trump was merely a Trojan horse for Ted Cruz. Still might be (or for Rubio), but now two plus months later Trump is not only still in the Republican race, he's in command of it, and in fact could be much closer to becoming the Republican nominee after today's primaries.

And who knows where Hillary might be if her email morass deepens, but assuming she is the nominee, what if some of Sanders' supporters, particularly the disenfranchised young, join up with the Trump crowd (who Trump now likes to celebrate as being the short, the tall, the skinny, the fat, the rich. the poor, the highly educated and the poorly educated—making a particular point that he LOVES the poorly educated). Those two groups could become a potent base.

Trying to connect all the dots in my mind—how can a phenomena such as a Trump come into being? An epiphany: I remembered my long-ago reading of Eric Hoffer's classic *The True Believer: Thoughts On The Nature Of Mass Movements*. For a more detailed recollection, I went to Wikipedia's description. Hoffer is eerily on the mark. It could serve as a textbook explanation of Trump's appeal, other than the merger of "reality TV" and the presidential primaries. From Wikipedia.....

"Hoffer states that mass movements begin with a widespread 'desire for change' from discontented people who place their locus of control outside their power and who also have no confidence in existing culture or traditions. Feeling their lives are 'irredeemably spoiled' and believing there is no hope for advancement or satisfaction as an individual, true believers seek 'self-renunciation.' Thus, such people are ripe to participate in a movement that offers the option of subsuming their individual lives in a larger collective. Leaders are vital in the growth of a mass movement, as outlined below, but for the leader to find any success, the seeds of the mass movement must already exist in people's hearts.

While mass movements are usually some blend of nationalist, political and religious ideas, Hoffer argues there are two important commonalities: All mass movements are competitive and perceive the supply of converts as zero-sum; and all mass movements are interchangeable. As examples of the interchangeable nature of mass movements, Hoffer cites how almost 2000 years ago Saul, a fanatical opponent of Christianity, became Paul, a fanatical apologist and promoter of Christianity. Another example occurred in Germany during the 1920s and the 1930s, when Communists and Fascists were ostensibly bitter enemies but in fact competed for the same type of angry, marginalized people; Nazis Adolf Hitler and Ernst Röhm, and Communist Karl Radek, all boasted of their prowess in converting their rivals."

It is unlike any presidential election cycle I've ever known, even the Goldwater era which from this point in the future looks placid, even sane. The macho trash talking of the Republican "debates" leaves me bewildered, but that testosterone also extends into policy—make America "great again" by building up the military (we should be building our infrastructure instead).

"Your beliefs become your thoughts,
Your thoughts become your words,
Your words become your actions,
Your actions become your habits,
Your habits become your values,
Your values become your destiny."
Mahatma Gandhi

Wednesday, March 16, 2016
Be-twitched Bothered Bewildered
I'm still recoiling from *Meet the Press* last Sunday, in particular Chuck Todd's brief interview with Ted Cruz. If Donald Trump is

a symptom of a malignancy in American politics, Cruz is part of the disease itself.

Todd ran a tape of President Obama saying: "And what's been happening in our politics lately is not an accident. For years, we've been told we should be angry about America and that the economy's a disaster. And that we're weak. And that compromise is weakness. And that you can ignore science and you could ignore facts and say whatever you want about the president. And feed suspicion about immigrants and Muslims and poor people and people who aren't like us."

Cruz reacted : "You know, Chuck, Barack Obama's a world class demagogue. That language there is designed to divide us. No, Mr. President, we're not angry at that. We're angry at politicians in Washington, including you, who ignore the men and women who elected you. Who have been presiding over our jobs going overseas for seven years? Who have been cutting deals that are enriching the rich and powerful, the special interests and the big corporations, while working men and women are seeing their wages stagnating? And he talks about immigrants and Muslims. Mr. President, we're mad at a president who wants to bring in Syrian refugees who may be infiltrated by ISIS. And you're unwilling to be commander in chief and keep us safe. So don't engage in attacking the people, like the president did."

Wow, it takes a demagogue to call someone a demagogue. Psittacisms for the masses, from both Cruz and Trump.

It was the self proclaimed intention of the Republicans to be the Party of No at the onset of Obama's Presidency and then gathering even more momentum with the first mid-term elections.

This brought Mr. Cruz into power as a leading Tea Party advocate. His obstructionist voice has been a leading one during his Senate occupancy, effectively shutting down any hope of compromise. No wonder the President had to resort to his much criticized use of Executive Orders, although his use of such orders has averaged less than George Bush's.

And, yet, there is the whiff of truth in some of what he says, no, not about Obama being the cause, but about a long-building anger, much longer than Mr. Cruz et al would like it to be known. Bernie Sanders taps into similar angst. At the heart of that fury is the American socio-economic landscape which has changed over the years, but you could count them in decades. The last seven years were more of the same for the disenfranchised middle class, watching their earning power and employability decline in relation to better educated, higher income families. Consequently, wage inequality has grown, but this has been going on for thirty five years, well documented by the Economic Policy Institute (EPI).

Unfortunately, there is no easy panacea for this other than for our country to come to grips with the reality of today's world. The industrial revolution has morphed into a cyber revolution, where geographic borders do not exist. Workers are being displaced by technology, robotics. It is not a question of bringing manufacturing jobs home anymore; it's the challenge of educating workers in new skills. Any politician who holds out the trade war card is delusional, playing a simplistic card to get elected. We're a country after a quick fix and it sounds good, make "tough" deals with China, tax their goods sky high. Wait until the quick fixers see the new prices at Wal-Mart. None of them will like that either (unless a President Trump makes Wal-Mart reduce their prices! :-)

Many of the recommendations suggested by the EPI for turning the tide of income inequality were also advocated by the Obama administration but have been cut off at the knees by the Party of No, one for example enacting public investments in infrastructure to create jobs. And there are others.

But nothing rings truer for the disenfranchised than the Trumperian throwaway that in 15 minutes he'd solve the trade deficit. Our trade agreements have evolved over years of negoti-ations and it's not that simple Donald (or Ted). Admittedly the currency manipulations on the part of governments all over the world throw aspects of trade agreements under the bus, each region fighting for a larger piece of a pie that is growing only oh-so-very-slowly. We have the "advantage" of having (at least seemingly) the currency of last resort, and this is yet another factor in the strong dollar, but that further contributes to making foreign goods cheaper and our exports more expensive. It is the inverse of the early 1980's when the dollar was cheap and interest rates were double digits, inflationary fears running amuck. Today there is little inflation with whiffs of deflation.

This is all in the wake of the most dangerous economic crisis we have faced since the Great Depression. In the absence of Congress being able to agree upon fiscal policy the temporary fix was radical monetary policy engineered by the Federal Reserve. Someone had to act. But the Fed now is blamed by the Party of No.

Nonetheless we are left with debt; it could have been less with sounder fiscal policy, but that was not to be. Where would Ted Cruz's flat tax plan and tying the dollar to the Gold Standard leave us? And the Trump solution? "Trust me, I make good deals." Whatever that means.

For anyone who has read thus far, I leave the reader with an "out-of-the-box" review on the subject. It is the most cyn-ical analysis I've ever read, authored by *Cognitive Dissonance*, "Down the Trump Rabbit Hole - Manufacturing Consent. "

It attempts to explain Trump in light of the "system" which *Cognitive Dissonance* equates to "The Empire," its purpose to always move forward, to consume. "Everyone within the empire serves the Empire, including its individual and corporate 'citizens'. This especially holds true for its upper level civil 'servants', political appointees, elected office holders, state and federal judges, the military at all levels including 'civilian police officers, the oligarchs and elites. And most importantly, the President of the United States. All are beholden to the Empire and constitute the court of the Empire. While the president may be considered the Chief Executive Officer, the president works for the Empire and is controlled by the Empire's court. The power of the president flows up from the Empire's court, not down from the president."

So how does this relate to The Donald? "When your credibility is suddenly called into question and people begin to seek alternative 'authorities', give the people what they want ... though not exactly what they want, just what you have conditioned them to believe they want. Or as is the case with our current situation, since anyone who is presently an authority is not to be trusted, give people the antithesis of the existing authority structure." In other words, The Donald.

Cognitive Dissonance goes on to argue that as Clinton is a "child of the court," she cannot deliver what the Empire's subjects perceive to be needed for the Empire's very survival. Only the anti-establishment holds that power but expect Trump to concoct "some mighty reforms which will bleed and permanently weaken the middle class even further. You didn't expect the elite and court to actually pay for the reforms ... did you?"

I would like to believe that this cynicism is merely an exaggeration of the truth, and we're better than that, and reasonable people can come to long term solutions. Yes, more and more time will be needed as the can is kicked further down the road. To deal with the national debt we first have to work towards a balanced budget. A tall order in today's world, one that will exact pain, particularly for the Plutocracy, but in the end for us all. We've lived long enough by borrowing against the future. Do we have the fortitude, the patience, and above all the willingness to make compromises?

If not, *Cognitive Dissonance* might be right on the mark.

On the other hand, *Stonekettle* has hit it out of the ballpark once again. I've mentioned this blog before. Its views are compelling, brutally honest, no holding back for Jim Wright, the blog's author. His take on the topic was published in two parts, the latest being his "The Latter Days of a Better Nation, Part II."

"Far too many Americans still think of Trump's campaign as a joke and they keep waiting for the laugh ... but somehow the punch line never comes.

It never comes because, you see, the joke is on us. All of us, conservatives and liberals, republicans and democrats and the independents.

In effect, to understand Trumpism, look in a mirror. We've given rise to him." As Wright concludes, "if you want a better nation, be better citizens."

I thought I was done with this. In the process of posting this entry President Obama was delivering an eloquent speech, nominating Merrick Garland to the Supreme Court. Mitch McConnell now responding in the background, with "let the people decide." We did in 2012. So, the beat goes on ...

Monday, May 9, 2016
IT has Started
In Florida, the presidential election robo-calls have begun (put this number on your blocked call list if you are so inclined: 646-891-2992). It was Donald Trump calling!—his recording about the "emergency" of defeating Hillary Clinton and then another voice seeking contributions as, he claims, the Trump campaign is no longer self-funding (do they need funding at all as the mass media and the world of "Tweetledum and Tweetledee" seem not to get enough of him?). The follow up voice said that by contributing $25 you get a nice elect Trump sticker (guess the hat, "made in America" but mostly by Latinos, Mexicans, and Salvadoreños, is too expensive) and if you feel generous enough to

contribute $1,000 you get a signed photograph of him "suitable for framing." So it begins. Where do I puke?

Wednesday, May 25, 2016
Being There with the Donald
Donald Trump on climate change: "You have storms and you have rain and you have beautiful days." But his denial of the effects of global warming does not extend to his own properties.

Chance the Gardener: "In the garden, growth has it seasons. First comes spring and summer, but then we have fall and winter. And then we get spring and summer again."

The latter is from Jerzy Kosinski's prophetic novel, *Being There*, written more than 40 years ago about a simple minded gardener, Chance, who is catapulted to political fame, becoming "Chauncey Gardiner" when the media mistakes his comment, "I like to watch my garden grow" as a metaphor for the economy. In response to Chance's statement, the President comments: "I admire your good, solid sense. That's precisely what we lack on Capitol Hill." So, Donald for President and Chance for Vice President?

Duplicitous Donald also has embraced the NRA. Perhaps climate change denial and ownership of assault weapons go hand in hand. Guns for all (except for those on his own properties)! Oh, Donald et al., no one is trying to abolish the 2nd amendment. We're just trying to rid society of military style weaponry.

Finally, Google "Trump University," a Donald-blessed bait and switch counterfeit "university" leading the gullible to believe they could become "rich" if they enrolled and paid up to $35,000 to learn his "secrets." Some 5,000 are now pursuing a lawsuit which Trump and his legion of lawyers have successfully buried until after the November election. These are the same disenfranchised middle class people he promises to help. The only secret is his tax return.

And yet these contradictions and machinations only seem to vitalize his supporters. Chauncey Gardiner is alive and well!

Wednesday, June 8, 2016
An Even More Dangerous Turn in Political Events
In the wake of Trump's demagogic displays, I thought it would be instructive, ironic, and as I discovered, somewhat disheartening, to read Barack Obama's inaugural speech when he first took office. Such idealism, only to be ambushed by a political party which, as evidenced by their new standard bearer, Donald Trump, would prefer that America be frozen in a snow globe or a Norman Rockwell painting.

From the onset of Obama's presidency he was challenged by the Republican base and this morphed into a stone wall of opposition, no matter what the consequences were to this nation. It was an invitation to disrespect the mere office of the Presidency, perhaps even because it was now occupied by a man of color who said in his inaugural speech: "This is the meaning of our liberty and our creed—why men and women and children of every race and every faith can join in celebration across this magnificent mall, and why a man whose father less than sixty years ago might not have been served at a local restaurant can now stand before you to take a most sacred oath."

Is it any wonder that an ego-maniacal mass-media caricature of a presidential candidate should rise like a Phoenix from the ashes his own party created?

"Let's make America Great Again?" By alienating, or, worse, eliminating by deportation or excluding with walls—physical as well as immigration blockades—minorities he declares unsuitable? I thought that was appalling enough until his now well-publicized comments about District Judge Gonzalo Curiel, whose parents are from Mexico, accusing the Judge of having a conflict of interest as he considers lawsuits against Trump

"University." Instead of recognizing that this is a serious transgression of the separation of powers, and an act of racism, Trump turned the table on the press, suggesting that reporters who ask about the matter are the racists by merely asking the question—yet another attack on the fourth estate.

Trump's world view is there are only winners (him) and losers (anyone he chooses to call as such). He doesn't want to appear to be weak, and therefore be "kicked off the island." No, to show his "strength" he even suggested that if he becomes President he'll pursue a civil case against the judge, the argument being that his Mexican heritage is an "inherent conflict of interest." Ironic, how many presidents have been schooled in law and now we have a candidate who uses his wealth to routinely litigate or threaten to litigate to bully things his way. We all know how preposterous his litigation threat is and he may think as President he might be able to manipulate the separation of constitutional powers. He's already said "I consult myself on foreign policy, because I have a very good brain." So who needs advisers, and for that matter Congress, the Judiciary, and the Press?

It is a severely flawed personality trait, one that does not belong in the Office of the President. It is a form of blame shifting, even paranoia. Weakness is a trait of a "loser;" thus he must appear powerful by blaming others or circumstance. "All I'm trying to do is figure out why I'm being treated so unfairly by a judge," he said on Fox News. About his refusal to release his tax returns: "I have friends that are very rich....They've never been audited." He's a victim!

This is seriously scary stuff. During my publishing career I reprinted Gustav *Gilbert's Psychology of Dictatorship* in which he said "throughout history social movements of far-reaching consequences have been decisively influenced by leaders, and that the behavior of such leaders is necessarily motivated to some extent by psychological tensions rooted in their individual character development. We must further recognize the fact that the personalities of political leaders, like all human beings, are largely the products of their cultural mores and social tensions, and that they become leaders only if they effectively express the aspirations (or frustrations) of significant segments of their contemporary society." Although these words apply to all kinds of societies, they were particularly aimed at those that gave rise to dictators, narcissists who tap into a discordant societal vein.

Contrast Trump's call for denying any Muslim immigration to what Obama said when inaugurated: "To the Muslim world, we seek a new way forward, based on mutual interest and mutual respect. To those leaders around the globe who seek to sow conflict, or blame their society's ills on the West—know that your people will judge you on what you can build, not what you destroy. To those who cling to power through corruption and deceit and the silencing of dissent, know that you are on the wrong side of history; but that we will extend a hand if you are willing to unclench your fist." Perhaps overly idealized, but some of these words could be directed to Trump himself: "know that your people will judge you on what you can build, not what you destroy. To those who cling to power through corruption and deceit and the silencing of dissent, know that you are on the wrong side of history."

Monday, June 13, 2016
Flag Day and Post Orlando Massacre
I've been too stunned by the attack in Orlando to fully gather my thoughts, but I ought to publish this before the subject becomes entirely politicized. I've learned that after years of writing this blog and having expressed over and over again my belief that automatic weapons, the kind that was used in the Orlando massacre, need to be outlawed, that mine is but just one lonely voice. Nonetheless I must write what I think. The NRA would

have you believe that this puts our nation on the slippery slope to repealing the 2nd amendment. That slope is as preposterous as outlawing automobiles, which are simply regulated. I don't know any responsible members of either political party who believe that the 2nd amendment needs to be repealed. It needs updating to take modern day weaponry into account, killing machines our forefathers never imagined at the time of the 2nd amendment.

The math is pretty clear; this no one can dispute. Pack a lot of people into a relatively small space, as in the Paris or Orlando attacks, and anyone with military designed weaponry can kill a lot of people.

Banning the sale of such weapons, making them illegal to own (paying current owners to turn them in), is not going to eliminate them. I'm not stupid. But they will be harder to obtain. Go to the next level by requiring licenses and registrations for guns as we do for cars, would be another step in the right direction. Will that suddenly make everyone safe? Again, I'm not that stupid.

This attack in Orlando is not only about guns, it's about the LGBT community, our way of life, and the potential it has for still hardening the line about a particular ethnic minority group. The Islamic religion is essentially a peaceful one, and to ostracize practicing Muslims will only lead to more radicalization, the very objective of ISIS. So this is the time to indeed rally around our flag, the very symbol of E Pluribus Unum—that we are a nation of diversity and should celebrate that diversity and mourn for the LGBT community and for us all.

Here there is a long break in political entries, not even covering the Presidential debates as they literally sickened me, Trump stalking around Clinton as a hunter toying with his prey. Poor Hillary, she never knew what hit her from all quarters, the leaked emails, her unpopularity even among democrats (including the FBI stating that they were reopening that investigation only eight days before the election), the impact of social media, if not the Russians, on swinging key states. But my main reason for being quiet was we were "on the road" and I was preparing for a major operation two days before election (we had voted by mail). I managed to get off a very brief note the day after the election: "Home the day after in some pain and residual stupor from four hours under anesthesia. But nothing can compare to waking up this first morning home to the election results, with ominous implications for the world order and the environment. We should be careful what we wish for but as difficult as it is, time for coming together as a nation and giving the new administration the chance to work for all people. More when I feel up to sitting at my computer." That day arrived the following week.

Nonetheless I timidly expressed the willingness to wait and see but how quickly that mindset was changed within a month of his being elected. From there, it was and continues to be all downhill, my very fears being validated by his actions and tweets.

Monday, November 14, 2016
Blackened, Blue, Bewildered
Finally, I can sit at my keyboard with minimal pain from surgery. Also, my head is clearer than when I wrote my last entry.

This is a two subject piece but they are related as I've come out of surgery pretty beaten up, dark, angry purple bruises on both legs and staples holding the "wound" together on my chest, with limited range of my right arm, essentially a metaphor for how I feel about the election.

We all now know that if it were not for the arcane Electoral College method of electing the president, Clinton was the clear winner. So Trump was right in saying beforehand (haven't heard it after the election from him, wonder why?) that the system is rigged. Can you imagine if the results were exactly opposite, Trump winning the popular but losing the EC? Instead of the relatively peaceful protests we've seen spontaneously erupting around the country; we'd have Trump's heavily armed militia in the streets. Revolution and bloodshed. So, in a way, for the safety of our citizens at least short term, this outcome has that one benefit.

Long term, it's a different deal. There are so many issues where an unrestrained Trump presidency can wreck the future of this country and the world, that it would be senseless to detail them all here.

First, though, as much as I thought Trump's candidacy was a joke during the initial months of the primaries, I took it quite seriously later, my fear growing in direct relation to his Teflon ability to say anything and, what used to matter, our 4th estate—the Press—having little effect to act as a foil. If I was in a prolonged coma and came out of it to hear a presidential candidate talk about shooting someone on 5th Ave. with no consequences, grabbing women by their pussies, etc., I would have thought the Press would have been able to eviscerate that candidate long ago.

But cyber bullying was the factor in this campaign which made it unique. Facebook and Twitter had more to do with the outcome of this election than all the newspapers and TV news media combined. Trump's attention span is ideally suited to 140 character tweets and his reality TV personality gave him entrée to TV coverage whenever he wanted it, gratis. And in spite of his racist overtone, he did carry a persuasive populist message, the forgotten plight of the white middle class male. Whether he can make good on promises to that minority group is highly unlikely, especially with his tax cut proposals which will benefit his own economic class most. (I don't believe in trickle down prosperity. The "wealth effect" is to make the wealthy wealthier.)

So based mostly on anecdotal evidence, I thought Trump had a better chance than the polls reflected.

I grew up only a couple of miles from his neighborhood in Queens, NY and we're almost the same age. Although more than 50 years have passed since I've lived there, if I close my eyes when Trump speaks I hear street talk I'm familiar with. Between his celebrity status and his strong appeal to the middle class, people were willing to overlook the big picture and especially loved the way he took down the ruling oligarchy (including the now vestigial Press and traditional mass media). And given the unpredictability of what people do in the privacy of the voting booth (perhaps ashamed to be backing Trump publicly, but will pull the lever for him privately), I went into surgery thinking that this election was a tossup, especially with the FBI making unprecedented statements to Congress and Wiki Leak's one sided email revelations, so ripe for Trump's conspiracy campaign (imagine if the RNC's emails were similarly exposed).

Thus, nothing about election night truly surprised me. In fact I called the outcome at 9.20 PM, turned off the TV and went to bed with the residual effects of anesthesia still in my system. I woke up in pain throughout the night but refused to look at the TV or phone to confirm "my call." The next morning my heart sank, in spite of being prepared for the outcome.

So here's the existential dilemma: how does one, as a citizen of a country he/she loves, support its new leader, while having complete disdain for that leader, his policies, his narcissistic disorders, and fearing the damage he and his administration might do?

While I could go into a long litany of all the specific issues, I'm trying to look at this from 50,000 feet so they don't overwhelm. To me, I see a world undergoing turbulent change, hastened by a technology revolution. The industry I came from—publishing—is just one example of the incredible forces of creative destruction that technology has fostered. More books are being published (including e-books) using far less labor than in the past. The majority of book titles are now printed on demand. Warehouses are not needed for those and the process is completely automated. The whole landscape has changed. Robots now make the majority of heavy industry products. This trend is only accelerating. Capital finds the most efficient venues for its deployment.

Anyone who believes that Trump can simply bring back manufacturing jobs like we once had is self-deluded, abetted by the master manipulator himself, Donald Trump, who told the victims of disintermediation what they wanted to hear.......that things would return to the way they were.

I do believe there is a path to expanding jobs and prosperity for the forgotten middle class, but it means abandoning the past and embracing the future. America's export is intellectual capital and technology. Our educational system needs to reflect those realities and build our industries with those as a foundation. Let the manufacturing of goods that require handwork reside in low cost labor countries, such as those which made Trump's hats.

Going further up from a 50,000 foot overview you see a planet whose delicate atmosphere which protects us from the sun's ultraviolet light and governs the balance of glaciers, oceans, and climate—all under siege. Can we afford to aid climate denial forces in our society, simply because it is the easy, short term answer to some of our economic ills? Here again is both a threat and an opportunity, an opportunity to develop the alternative energy and mass transportation industries, a win-win situation, jobs and a healthier environment for future generations. America has to lead other countries in this effort.

We seem to be at a Malthusian tipping point in the history of the world. Population is growing exponentially but while Malthus was concerned about the food supply keeping pace, little could he foresee the other factor, now a bigger part of the equation of whether humanity can survive changes to the environment itself because of our addiction to fossil fuels.

So these are just some of the big picture things I'm concerned about. I want to support my President but I fear that progressives will have to fight tooth and nail, hoping the country can hang on for four years.

If I'm around then, it will be because of incredible medical technology, the kind that allowed me to survive my fourth pacemaker implantation with the removal of existing leads being the most dangerous part of the operation. New leads then had to be implanted, these being MRI compliant which my old leads were not. As I age, an MRI is inevitable. First they had to connect me to a temporary pacemaker as I am 100% dependent on the ventricle pacing by threading leads through each of my legs and then to a temporary pacemaker during the operation. Then they opened my chest to remove the existing pacemaker and begin the long arduous task of removing the existing leads, an operation of great delicacy to not injure the heart. Unfortunately, a small part of the lead in the atrium broke off and the surgeon felt it was just too dangerous to go after that last piece and thus I lost the MRI compliant feature. Overall the operation went well and now I'm trying to rest and rehabilitate,

I'm grateful to family and friends who expressed so much care and particularly to my wife, Ann, who stayed with me in the hospital room, sleeping on an uncomfortable cot, and watched over things for me, shaving my chest, stomach and legs and helping me take the first of two antiseptic showers before the operation. I can't say enough positive things about the nurses at the University of Miami Hospital. To me they are as important as the surgeon, maybe more so.

Thus, I am slowly getting back to form, but to a political landscape that has been shaped by fear and intolerance. I have low expectations that Mr. Trump can suddenly function as the leader we all need to help us coalesce as a nation. His narcissistic personality must be fed and that is going to be a constant obstruction to doing the right thing, such as selecting Cabinet members who are NOT just yes people or those connected to his business interests or family. Can one imagine Sarah Palin, a climate change denier as Secretary of the Interior as rumored? He's already appointed a denier, Myron Ebell, as the head of the EPA transition team.

As H.L. Mencken prophetically said nearly 100 years ago: "As democracy is perfected, the office of president represents, more and more closely, the inner soul of the people. On some great and glorious day, the plain folks of the land will reach their heart's desire at last, and the White House will be occupied by a downright fool and a complete moron." Perhaps that time has come.

Nonetheless I'm desperately trying to end this with something positive: Trump is now going to become OUR President and I for one will try to give his administration a chance to do some of the right things for the nation as a whole.

That metaphoric peace pipe didn't even last to his inauguration as everything from his mouth and Twitter feed was so non-presidential following the election. I had already given up hope before his administration began. Maybe I still had some thoughts that his behavior would change once sworn in, but the proverbial handwriting was on the wall.

Monday, December 12, 2016
He Was Right!
Before the election we heard Donald Trump say it over and over again, "Folks, the election is rigged." His victory tour has been silent on the subject until recently when the CIA "in a secret assessment" (I wonder how long they had been hanging on to that) said that Russia was involved in the WikiLeaks email

releases of the Democratic National Committee (DNC), possibly to swing the election results in his favor. While the Trump campaign embraced the FBI's resumption of reviewing Clinton's emails only eight days before the election (clearing her once again only two days before), his Tweet response to the CIA's assertion was to discredit the Agency saying "these are the same people that said Saddam Hussein had weapons of mass destruction."

Trump's pre-election rally in Green Bay, Wisconsin on Oct. 17 pretty much summarizes his stump speech about "a rigged election," repeated like an Anvil Chorus in other speeches: "Remember, we're competing in a rigged election. This is a rigged election folks, OK? The media is an extension of the Clinton campaign as WikiLeaks has proven. And they don't talk about WikiLeaks, they just keep talking about Trump, Trump, Trump. They want to put nice, sexy headlines up even though nothing has happened, nothing took place, even though it's a total fabrication. They even want to try rigging the election at the voting booths, and believe me there's a lot going on. Do you ever hear these people? They say 'there's nothing going on.' People who have died 10 years ago are still voting. Illegal immigrants are voting. I mean, where are the street smarts of some of these politicians?" Talk about "fabrications."

In spite of Trump's claim that he won in a "landslide" just that little bit of tailwind of the FBI's bringing up the Clinton email affair again right before the election, and WikiLeaks providing the DNC email may have provided enough of a boost for Trump to marginally win these three swing states: WI, MI, and PA. I've done some of my own number crunching on this. Clinton's national victory margin of 2.6 million votes or nearly 2% more than Trump became a hundred thousand total vote deficits in those three states, less than a percent difference. Had those states gone to Clinton, she would have won the electoral vote and she would be President. So much for Trump's "landslide" victory but the one truth he told was the election was rigged, although not the way he asserted, thanks to Russia, WikiLeaks, and the FBI.

Steel, coal, and low-skilled manufacturing are not coming back in those rust belt states like the 1950's. He knows it. He now reneges on his words unabashedly, even admitting they were only said to get himself elected, such as during his "victory tour" in Grand Rapids when the crowd was jeering "lock her up" "he said: No, it's ok. Forget it. That plays great before the election. Now, we don't care, right?"

Or "Buy America, Hire America" just another get-elected slogan, his businesses routinely buying overseas and hiring less expensive foreign labor. As our local December 8 *Palm Beach Post* headline spelled out "Trump again hires non-U.S. club staff." His Mar-a-Lago Club in Palm Beach routinely uses the federal government's H-2B visa program to hire foreign workers for the season instead of domestic ones. Nothing makes a difference in his celebrity revered, post-truth world.

One would think our democracy is immune to demagoguery because our forefathers created a governmental structure of checks and balances. Alexander Hamilton even adopted the safeguard of the Electoral College, a buffer of sorts, to ensure our Presidents are "pre-eminent for ability and virtue." One could argue that if there was ever a time when the Electors should reconsider an election, this is the one. But that isn't going to happen with Trump and his 17,000,000 Twitter followers, possibly locked and loaded. Electors who vote their conscience do so at their own personal peril.

That is my fear over the next four years, the potential to circumvent those checks and balances, including the traditional press, via social networks and fake news. As he said on 60 Minutes, "I have such power in terms of numbers with Facebook, Twitter, Instagram etc, ... [They] are great form[s] of communication." He knows it and we better watch out.

PS The evening after posting this article I read the *New York Times* and discovered that Paul Krugman wrote a very similar assessment, making some of the same points ("The Tainted Election"). Lest I be accused of plagiarism, I wrote my first draft two days before, letting it sit as I am prone to do with any political entry, and then editing and posting it. I have long admired Paul Krugman and feel in good company that the facts drew us to similar conclusions!

Ironically, the New Year opens with the complaint that the, now, President-elect's constant bizarre behavior was making us inured to his very behavior and to a world that was becoming accustomed to gun violence as an everyday occurrence. Little did we know what was in store for us all.

Saturday, January 7, 2017
Another Day, Another Horror
A mass shooting at an airport, the denial by the President Elect that his "victory" had anything to do with Russia's revenge plot against Hillary Clinton (even though he, himself, used the very fake news Russia implanted)—just an ordinary day in the U. S. of A. The normalization of such events inures us to it all. How much can we absorb each day of reports of violence and a President-to-Be who is consumed by his monolithic view of how events affect our perception of HIM rather than how events (such as the Russian involvement in our election) impact the nation Putin prefers HIM to lead? The distrust of Clinton that was baked into the election by Russian hacking and Trump's demagoguery was probably enough to shift those relatively small margins in WI, MI, and PA that gave him the Electoral lead.

Trump's call for "Congressional Hearings" (sorry, wrong venue, Donald, try the FBI) to investigate why NBC allegedly received intelligence information before he did, reveals his world view. He disparages "intelligence" and our intelligence professionals on the one hand ("I'm smarter than all the Generals"), but wants to first receive what he considers misinformation before a network against which he has a vendetta. Look forward to government by retaliation. As he would Tweet, NOT NICE!

As to gun violence, the ubiquity of guns, and our failure to connect that issue with mental health challenges and intelligence needed to keep nut jobs off our planes (even allowing them to check weapons in their luggage), there is just growing legislative intransigence. After Sandy Hook one would think we'd have stricter gun laws. Instead, the nation is gravitating to "open carry" including such a movement in my state, Florida. Its insanity, especially with Florida's "Stand Your Ground" law. I've written about gun control ad nauseam, so no sense repeating everything here. And, no, I'm not for repealing the 2nd amendment and neither was Hillary Clinton as accused by Trump.

Will Trump ever get serious beyond his Tweets? His actions even before taking the Office of the Presidency makes one already think about future impeachment on the grounds of Treason (giving aid and comfort to the enemies of our country).

These were my thoughts as I made coffee this morning only to discover I was so deep in thought (sort of writing this entry in my mind) that I had forgotten to put the coffee pot under the drip so I found myself in damage control, going through half a roll of paper toweling, moping the counter and the floor: a microcosm of the mess we're in.

Friday, January 20, 2017
LA,LA,LA, In La La Land
It might seem disrespectful. In many ways it was, a silent protest, seeing the movie *La La Land* instead of our new President's

inauguration, the first one we've missed in decades. It seems like yesterday when we were filled with hope as evidenced by what I wrote exactly eight years ago.

After watching the never ending ennui of the Republican primaries and the solipsistic behavior of our new President-elect, how could anyone welcome his presence in the oval office? And I'm referring to his behavior, not necessarily his policies, which, to be fair, remain to be seen.

We had hoped Obama would have been more effective, but how could he given the illegitimacy narrative so infused by the right and particularly by the new President himself? All those years contending he was not born here, that he is a secret Muslim, ad infinitum. It was their objective to block any and everything and for the most part they succeeded. Still, the unemployment rate has dropped from 9.3% when he took office to below 5% and the Dow has tripled (although I am not naïve enough to singularly credit President Obama for these changes, but his leadership had an impact). Obama was not a "perfect" President, particularly in foreign affairs, but he was a decent, rational person. Can we say the same, now?

And now there are accusations of Trump being an "illegitimate" President because of Russia's interference (not to mention Comey's). As there is no evidence that ballot boxes were hacked, he is not illegitimate in the legal sense of the word, but one can reasonably conclude the election was tainted. One cannot prove an alternative reality but no doubt these events impacted the election results.

I had to laugh (or cry) at Trump's assertion that "we have by far the highest IQ of any Cabinet ever assembled." You would therefore think that his pick for Treasury Secretary, Steve Mnuchin, would have a better excuse for his failure to reveal $100 million in assets and links to a tax haven company, than saying "as you all can appreciate, filling out these government forms is quite complicated." After all, isn't he a genius like all the rest of the Goldman Sachs ringers appointed to the Cabinet? Not that I have anything against Goldman Masters of the Universe other than when Trump was running he equated them with the "swamp" of the establishment, paying Hillary Clinton for speeches.

But I've now read Trump's Inaugural address which, when read, sounds like many of his impromptu electioneering stump speeches, but pulled together into one dystopian narrative. I'm ready to embrace a stronger economy, jobs for all, but we've been on that trajectory for years now. Rather than rebutting some of the speech, point by point, NPR has done a good job with fact checking. Not that facts matter anymore in this post-factual, reality TV world.

So, to us the perfect antidote to the malaise of fear and despair over the election was seeing La *La Land* while the new President was sworn in and fêted. The movie is a sweeping reaffirmation of the power of music and the arts, and a declarative statement that the American film musical is back. It's wonderful that a new generation is ready to embrace this art. There's a lot to be said about living in fantasy when one goes to a movie theatre, but it's another matter to live one's real life in the real world with leadership in serious doubt. I hope President Trump transcends all these concerns.

Friday, January 27, 2017
Protect Our Free Press
Amendment I. "Congress shall make no law respecting an establishment of religion, or prohibiting the free exercise thereof; or abridging the freedom of speech, or of the press; or the right of the people peaceably to assemble, and to petition the government for a redress of grievances."

"The media has zero integrity, zero intelligence, and no hard work. You're the opposition party. Not the Democratic Party. You're the opposition party. The media's the opposition party."
Stephen Bannon

"You [the press] always want to go by what's come out of his mouth rather than look at what's in his heart."
Kellyanne Conway

"I have a running war with the media. They are among the most dishonest human beings on earth."
Donald J. Trump

"Never forget. The press is the enemy. The establishment is the enemy. The professors are the enemy. Professors are the enemy. Write that on a blackboard 100 times and never forget it."
Richard Nixon to his national security adviser Henry Kissinger in a taped 1972 Oval Office conversation

We all know how it ended in the Nixon administration when he was forced to resign in August, 1974.

But it's different this time as Trump and his ministers of propaganda are "crazy-makers." There is a concerted effort to make the lie indistinct from reality. Responsible journalists must stand united with the facts, clearly pointing out the dangers to the Republic. We, the citizens, must take up each and every infringement of the Constitution and iniquitous Executive Order with our representatives, focusing on the mid-term elections to bring about an effective opposition Congress—and the removal of the "ministers of propaganda."

Fortunately some former congressional staff members have put together "A practical guide for resisting the Trump agenda." It is better to read that, join local groups, than reacting to every Presidential tweet and proclamation, chasing our tails with frustrated tweets and retweets. Even though it's been only a week since the inauguration, it seems like a lifetime in dog years.

Thursday, February 16, 2017
Trump's Truman Show
Once upon a time one's life meant having some time to one-self. Presidents were there but mostly in the background except during critical times. Now we are all exhausted from less than a month into the Trump presidency. Why? He is omnipresent; no matter where you look, to whom you speak, online, news-papers, or TV, big brother is there, "100%" as HE is fond of saying. Now we are subjected to the anxiety and ennui of Trump reporting 24-7.

I can't help but think of the movie *The Truman Show*. Our existential hero of the film, Jim Carrey, is an orphan who has been raised by a corporation to live and be watched, without his knowledge, on a reality TV show 24-7—until he discovers this and tries to escape. In this latter respect we're in Carrey's pos-ition, but this is an environment HE doesn't want US to escape from. As the Narcissist -in-Chief HE enjoys being watched in his own simulated reality TV show, a terrarium of which the contours are "alternative truths." Our role is to be spellbound. Before I merely thought this behavior "crazy making" but it may be more—preparation for almost anything, totalitarian rule by the Plutocracy, religious wars, the demolition of the Republic, a nuclear winter, or all rolled up into the Trumpocalypse ("the catastrophic destruction or damage of civilization following the election of Donald Trump as president of the United States of America."—from *Urban Dictionary*)

Instinctively, even if we survive we all know this will not end well. I hope I am very wrong, and that the next four years will be

bigly amazing, devoid of losers, with tremendous, terrific winners, but I fear it's not gonna happen, zero percent

Saturday, March 4, 2017
Syrian Refugee: 'Who Picks Their Country?'
The headline struck me. Indeed, who gets to pick their country?
For most of us it is an accident of birth. I keep in touch with
my old home town, Westport, Ct. through *WestportNow.com*.
A Syrian refugee, Mohamed al Maassri, spoke to the Westport
Sunrise Rotary Club about his experience of settling his family
in Norwalk, Ct, fleeing the carnage in Syria. Although his tale is
anecdotal, the typical rigorous background checking already in
place is not. Here is a refugee who would be denied the opportunity to pursue life, liberty, and happiness in a nation that has
welcomed so many fleeing their countries for political or economic reasons—all because of the accident of his birth. What
kind of a callous country are we becoming? This is the face of
the "new nationalism"? It is an ugly one. Mohamed al Maassri's
experience of US officials knowing "more about me than I did"
is already the standard. Surely, vigorous vetting is a better solution to protecting our nation than Trump's dictum of excluding
ALL refugees from specific countries

Wednesday, April 5, 2017
Trump Ennui
It is bad enough that he is omnipresent like a Cheshire cat on
the airways, on line, wherever you turn, but to have him as a
"neighbor" as well is pure overload. I suppose he misses the
gold-plated Mar-a-Lago and the opportunity to play on his own
golf courses in the sun. More likely, it is the procession which
draws him here, the parade of pomp and preparation, and his
brand being brandished.

Days in advance our local newspaper breathlessly announces his highness' arrival, expectantly and cautionary as it causes total disruption in the area. This coming visit involves Chinese President Xi and his entourage who will be staying at the Eau Palm Beach which used to have the more hotel-like name of Ritz Carlton. I once stayed there for a big corporate conference myself. It's palatial, but I suppose Trump's Mar-a-Lago gives it a good run for its money. So you can catch Xi at the Eau.

Palm Beach County—and in particular Palm Beach itself—will be a traffic nightmare. Thus far the expense of these numerous Trump visits is borne by the County. Trump makes a big deal of donating his $78k quarterly salary to the US National Parks Dept, while cutting its parent Department of the Interior's budget by $2 billion. According to my math, it'll take him more than 6,000 years of donating his salary to make up the difference. Maybe I have an extra zero someplace, or missed a zero as it seems like a VERY long time but if he lasts 6,000 years in office, all the more power to him. It could happen as everything he does is amazing, big time, etc.

He refuses to pick up Palm Beach County's expense of guarding him so he can play golf in the sunshine. Perhaps the County's officials should read "his" *Art of the Deal* and walk away from the table, go protect yourself, Donald. It might be the only way they/we can get reimbursement for those expenses. But the County officials like to delude themselves that as Trump's visits put Palm Beach County in the limelight that will increase tourism and thus drive tax revenue. Do you want to visit PBC because Trump is frequently here? I guess Washington DC's tourism is on the wane as the star is rarely there on weekends.

I can't imagine why the Chinese delegation agreed to meet at Mar-a-Lago where Trump can flaunt his ego. After all, there are very weighty issues to be discussed. Where does one get the idea that these can be easily discussed while teeing off on a golf course? Why not stay in the White House where there is a bowling alley? They can discuss the issues while joking about Trump's 7-10 split. Trump is a good golfer (my neighbor is one of his pros) and he probably wants to play games he can easily win. Look at me!

This egomaniacal inexperienced President is now toying with one of the most serious international issues of his presidency, the growing threat of North Korea. Making statements like, we'll go it alone if China doesn't act or Tillerson's inexplicable dropping of the mike simply saying "the United States has spoken enough about North Korea. We have no further comment," does not exactly inspire confidence. We're talking nuclear war here, folks, not jobs for coal-miners. Not that the latter is unimportant but that is in an industry that is dying because of alternative energy supplies, including natural gas. It's going the way horse-drawn carriages when the automobile became dominant. Focus on the right stuff!

The first 100 days are not yet over but it already seems like 1,000. There are so many issues that keep me restless at night, day, whenever, the Syrian humanitarian crisis, the impending Korean disaster, decimating environmental budgets and regulations, the gas lighting of fake news, Russia's possible interference with the election and the general vulnerability that the Internet and social media create, the continuing inability of Congress to function, the callous consequences of misguided immigration and refugee proposals, impracticable building of a wall in the middle of the Rio Grande river while our Infrastructure is falling apart, tax reform which will inevitably favor the rich including the removal of the inheritance tax, unrealistic border taxes (and extremely difficult to articulate and manage), and I can go on and on, but what's the sense?

At midterm elections I will cast my one vote, if we last that long—given the consequences of the ischemic seizure of our entire governing process and the self-serving dilettantes now at the tiller. I've written often about DJT even though I mightily try to ignore him, my resolve weak due to ongoing embarrassment for our nation and, now, just plain fear. I write as a form of catharsis.

Monday, April 24, 2017
Barbarians IN the Gate
It didn't take long to deface The Office of the Presidency, celebrity triviality "trumping" expertise and dignity. To the victor belong the spoils and it is no more in evidence than the recent White House fête personally hosted by Donald Trump, his guests being Sarah Palin, Ted Nugent and Kid Rock, whoever the latter two are. Supposedly, Sarah invited Ted and Kid because Jesus was busy. During their four hour run of the White House including a white china dinner they apparently discussed "health, fitness, food, rock 'n' roll, Chuck Berry and Bo Diddley, secure borders, the history of the United States, guns, bullets, bows and arrows, North Korea, [and] Russia." It is reassuring to know our President is getting such good advice.

According to NPR, Mr. Nugent described the visit as follows: "Well well well looky looky here boogie chillin', I got your Shot Heard Round The World right here in big ol greazya— Washington DC where your 1 & only MotorCity Madman Whackmaster StrapAssasin1 dined with President Donald J Trump at the WhiteHouse to Make America Great Again! Got that?"

For a fuller account of the symbolic desecration of the White House with some official White House photographs go to Sarah Palin's website. This includes a photograph of the three mocking the portrait of former first lady Hillary Clinton. According to the *New York Times*, an unnamed person "asked the three to extend their middle fingers beneath the portrait. 'I [Mr. Nugent] politely declined,' he said. 'Let the juxtaposition speak for itself.'"

Meanwhile, apropos to this topic, a recent *Palm Beach Post* cover story revealed the contributions to Donald Trump's inaugural committee and not surprisingly, some of the larger contributors are right here in the Palm Beach area, the home of the so-called Southern White House (might as well be the White House given the extent of his time here). The leading donor in this immediate area was billionaire Chris Cline whose private company has more than three billion tons of coal reserves. No wonder he was happy to throw in $1million to the inaugural festivities. Presumably such contributions assure a place in the new swamp. It is truly a plutocracy of self-serving popular culture or corporate elitists.

Jim Wright, the author of the *Stonekettle Station* blog has written a related essay on this topic, "The Hubris of Ignorance." Wright used to write obsessively in his blog but over time has turned more to Twitter for his incisive jabs. Thankfully, he'll still post a lengthy, thoughtful essay. This is must reading from an ex-military man who sees the world, and the administration, for what it is. A brief quote from his most recent entry summarizes this issue of expertise (or the lack of it) and "the cultivation of intelligence":

"The Founding Fathers weren't amateurs.

The men who freed this country from King George and then went on to forge a new nation were intellectual elite, the educated inheritors of The Renaissance and products of the Early Modern Age. They were able to create a new government because they were experts in government, educated in war and politics and science and religion and economics and social structures and all the hundreds of other things it takes to build a nation instead of tear one down.

Unlike their foolish descendants, the Founders knew that liberty and democracy and good government take far more than shallow patriotism.

Good government takes intellect, education, experience, curiosity, and a willingness to surround leadership with expert advice and support.

More than anything, it takes the cultivation of intelligence instead of pandering to the lowest common denominator."

Thursday, June 1, 2017
Unraveling of Democracy
It's all so overwhelming, so disheartening, everything this country has stood for through so many presidencies, and now being sold to the highest bidder (I'm talking about principles). A transactional President. Let's make a deal, Trump elbowing his way to the center of chaos, his ego knowing no bounds. How could this have happened? But more importantly, what can be done?

Resist.

Let Congress and the appointees of the Justice Department do their job now investigating possible collusion with Russia in the election, presuming they are not thwarted. I've argued in a previous entry that even without collusion, the gas-lighting, the poor timing of Comey coming out about more Clinton emails, and the exposure of the DNC communications by Wikileaks probably was just enough to tip the scales in four swing states. Russia may have merely been the conductor of this dissonance, or, worse, perhaps the financial ties of the Trump empire to Russian oligarchy run deep. Subpoenaing those tax returns that are under perpetual "audit" might do much to make that clearer. Hopefully that lies in the future.

Meanwhile, we are watching the dismantling of decades of foreign policy, trade, and environmental policy agreements, by a know-nothing administration under the cover story of creating jobs at all costs to our allies, and our environment. Why? A show for his base. Corporatocracy. Profit for those in power, sliding towards autocracy.

The withdrawal of the US from the Paris Accord to reduce greenhouse gas emissions puts us in a select group with just two other countries, Syria and Nicaragua. There are some 200 others still in the agreement. Even Rex Tillerson, an ex CEO of Exxon, has advocated staying in the agreement. So why does Trump want to withdraw? Yes, we'll hear about jobs (a canard, pure and simple, more the consequences of automation and that argument ignores the opportunities to create new jobs in technology and alternative energy) but it's probably Trump's ultimate f**k you to the world, something that obviously gives him pleasure. He certainly doesn't care about what people think, but that goes for psychopaths as well.

"It is time to put Youngstown, Ohio, Detroit, Mich., and Pittsburgh, Pa., along with many, many other locations within our great country before Paris, France," he said. "It is time to make America great again." But this is not at the expense of Paris, Mr. President, it's at the expense of the world including our own country. When Mar-a-Lago is knee deep in sea water, perhaps you'll rue removing this country from a position of leadership in climate change issues.

His first foreign trip was revealing. In Saudi Arabia, he obviously felt right at home. In fact, it sort of looked like Mar-a-Lago and his quarters in Trump Tower, the glittering gold, the grandiose chandeliers, the kind of digs and "respect" to which he feels entitled. And he did "deals"—$110 billion in arms. Ka-ching, ka-ching! But outside that comfort zone it was different.

Trump left a "message" in the Book of Remembrance at Yad Vashem, Israel's memorial for the Holocaust." "It is a great honor to be here with all of my friends—so amazing & will never forget!"

"My friends." "Amazing." That's it. Just a few words, so vapid.

Here's what Barack Obama, then in the middle of his first presidential campaign, wrote when he visited in July 2008: "I am grateful to Yad Vashem and all of those responsible for this remarkable institution. At a time of great peril and promise, war and strife, we are blessed to have such a powerful reminder of man's potential for great evil, but also our own capacity to rise up from tragedy and remake our world. Let our children come here, and know their history, so that they can add their voices to proclaim 'never again.' And may we remember those who perished, not only as victims, but also as individuals who hoped and loved and dreamed like us, and who have become symbols of the human spirit."

Is it no wonder he hates Barack Obama? No matter how much wealth he amasses, he will never have an ounce of Obama's humanity or intelligence or capacity for empathy.

His G7 meeting with the Europeans was a disaster, they sizing him up for what he is: the ugly American. Swaggering, braggadocio, nouveau riche, bullying his way past Montenegrin Prime Minister Dusko Markovic for a photo-op, he assumed an alpha male pose and scowl. It inspired the author of the *Harry Potter* series, J.K. Rowling, to tweet "You tiny, tiny, tiny little man." I'm afraid that's what most Europeans now think of us and our leader. Shouldn't that matter to all Americans? These are among (or were) our most steadfast allies.

Frankly, I'm ready to accept a President Pence if impeachment or resignation is the result of the investigation. Never thought I could type those words.

Read Tom Friedman's breathtakingly brilliant op-ed piece in yesterday's *NYT*, "Trump's United American Emirate." It is so succinct, prescient, a sadly true overview of what this country is becoming under Trump.

I've often praised Tom Friedman, even nine years ago writing a tongue in cheek piece advocating him for President. In retrospect, I should have been serious. Here are some of his main points:

"Merkel is just the first major leader to say out loud what every American ally is now realizing: America is under new management. "Who is America today?" is the first question I've been asked on each stop through New Zealand, Australia and South Korea. My answer: We're not the U.S.A. anymore. We're the new U.A.E.: the United American Emirate.....

So any lingering Kennedyesque thoughts about us should be banished, I explained. Let every nation know, whether it wishes us well or ill, that we shall pay no price, bear no burden, meet no hardship, support no friend, and oppose no foe to assure the success of liberty—unless we're paid in advance. And we take cash, checks, gold, Visa, American Express, Bitcoin and memberships in Mar-a-Lago.

The Trump doctrine is very simple: There are just four threats in the world: terrorists who will kill us, immigrants who will rape us or take our jobs, importers and exporters who will take our industries—and North Korea. Threats to democracy, free trade, the environment and human rights are no longer on our menu."

Saturday, June 10, 2017
Let the Games Begin
The "games"—meaning the Congressional Hearings regarding the Russian influence on our election results and the possible "cooperation" of Trump and/or his legion of surrogates.

James Comey laid out his case in great documented detail. Is there enough there to "prove" a case of impeding an investigation by a sitting U.S. President, or even impeachment. No. Not yet at least.

And Trump's reaction was predictable, cherry picking what he liked such as the three times Comey said he was not personally under investigation (he wouldn't be—yet), then claiming other statements were "a lie," such as demanding "loyalty" of Comey.

Trump also said he is "100%" committed to testifying under oath (watch out what you wish for).

It was a one on one conversation, so it boils down to who do you believe, the meticulous note taker Comey, or the off-the cuff reactions of President Trump? Yet, they both may be telling "the truth." How can that be?

At the risk of sounding like an armchair psychologist, simply put perhaps Trump believes his own lies, has created his own reality, and really does not believe he said or meant those aspects of Comey's testimony. Therefore, he can in good conscience testify to that effect. 100%.

As Eric Hoffer, author of *The True Believer* said, "We lie the loudest when we lie to ourselves."

Perhaps future candidates for President should be required to undergo physical AND psychological testing? Aren't we entitled to choose between the healthiest candidates for such an important office?

One possible symptom of sociopathic behavior is the ability to lie but believe the lie is true (from *HubPages*): "In fact, they are so good at lying, many times they become their own lie....If a sociopath can stage himself to believe his own lie and truly live in his own fantasy, how many more people can he convince it is the truth and wreak his havoc and devastation on?"

Pathological lying includes many personality traits that Trump has exhibited time and time again: abusive behavior, impulsivity, narcissism, obsessive-compulsive behavior, etc.

Almost a month ago I wrote to our two Senators (Marco Rubio and Bill Nelson) and our Representative (Brian Mast). This was before Robert Mueller was appointed by the Justice Department as special counsel but right after James Comey was dismissed as FBI Director by Trump. I ultimately received responses from Nelson and Mast, those were after Mueller was appointed and thus their responses were understandably focused on that appointment.

Rubio on the other hand provided an automated response that a reply would be forthcoming and such a reply never did.

I find this interesting as Rubio's questioning of Comey was definitely Trump predisposed. Rubio seems to be committed to appealing to the base that got him elected. This country has devolved into Newton's third law of physics, that for every action there is an equal and opposite reaction. Just flip back and forth between MSNBC and FOX and you can experience the polarity.

Here is our letter first and then the responses.

"May 13, 2017
Dear (insert name of Senator or Representative):

My wife and I, both retired, are distraught and anxiety ridden over the behavior of President Trump. I can think of only two times we've felt so concerned: during the Cuban missile crisis and during the end of the Nixon administration. Luckily, a stable, resolute President Kennedy prevailed during the former crisis and our democracy and separation of powers worked to ensure the preservation of the Republic during the latter.

Where are the courageous Senators to insist on a special prosecutor (now that the FBI has been kneecapped) to investigate the extent of any possible collusion of the Trump election team with Russian operatives? Where are the courageous Senators to insist on a complete examination of Trump's financial dealings in light of the emolument clause of the Constitution or to consider whether his removal is justified by the 25th Amendment to the Constitution based on mental illness?

Perhaps you feel the same existential dilemma we do: how does one, as a citizen of a country he/she loves, support its new leader, given his unstable, even despotic behavior, one who relies on nepotistic advice?

The concept of separation of powers and the role of the 4th estate are being severely tested and we look to the Senate as the last bastion of defense. Will you and your colleagues rise to the occasion or are you going to allow this person to run amuck and jeopardize everything our founding fathers stood for? His behavior is an affront to the dignity of the Office of the Presidency, weakening our country instead of protecting it, something he pledged to do when he was sworn into office.

We will be carefully watching your actions and depending on you to do the morally right thing to protect our country.

Respectfully,"

Replies:

"May 13 at 11:54 AM

Thank you for taking the time to contact me. Your correspondence has been received and I welcome the opportunity to address your concerns. Hearing directly from constituents such as yourself is truly an honor, and your input is much appreciated.

Please look for my response in the near future. In an effort to serve you better, please do not duplicate e-mails into the webform, as it may serve to delay the response to your concerns. If you need immediate assistance with a federal agency, please call (866) 630-7106, toll-free in Florida.

Sincerely,

U.S. Senator Marco Rubio"

"May 22 at 6:40 PM
Dear Mr. Hagelstein,

Thank you for contacting me in support of appointing a special prosecutor to investigate Russian interference in our elections and potential ties to the Trump administration. Your thoughts are important to me as I work to effectively represent you in Congress.

You deserve transparency and accountability in government. We should never run or hide from the truth. If we seek out truth and embrace it then Americans can know we all play by the same set of rules.

As you may know, in addition to ongoing investigations in the U.S. Senate and U.S. House of Representatives, Deputy Attorney General Rod Rosenstein has appointed former F.B.I. Director Robert S. Mueller III as special counsel for the Russia investigation. Like you, I hope that Director Mueller can be looked at as unbiased and that his finding will be respected by all. The American people deserve answers, and I am committed to ensuring a transparent process as these investigations move forward.

Thank you again for taking the time to contact me. If you'd like to receive updates about this issue and other news that's important to our community, please sign up here. To follow along with my work on your behalf, please join me on Facebook, Twitter, Instagram and YouTube. If you have any additional questions, please do not hesitate to contact me again. As always it is an honor to represent you in the United States Congress.

Sincerely,

Brian Mast
Member of Congress"

"May 30, 2017
Dear Mr. and Mrs. Hagelstein:

Thank you for contacting me about ongoing investigations related to the Russian government's efforts to interfere in the 2016 Presidential election.

In March, I called for the appointment of a special prosecutor and/or the establishment of an independent commission to get to the bottom of Russia's interference.

After the President fired FBI Director Comey on May 9, I repeated my calls for a special prosecutor and/or an independent commission. Shortly thereafter, the Department of Justice named former FBI Director Bob Mueller Special Counsel to oversee the Russia investigation. Bob Mueller has the experience to conduct a thorough investigation. Now, he must be provided the resources and independent authority he needs to follow the facts wherever they lead.

The Senate Select Committee on Intelligence has pledged to continue its bipartisan investigation into Russian attempts to influence our election. In addition, I am cosponsoring S. 27, which would create an independent commission to investigate Russia's attempts to interfere with the 2016 Presidential election.

According to the U.S. intelligence community, Russia is responsible for a number of hacks and the subsequent leaking of stolen information related to the 2016 Presidential election, at Putin's direct order. The attempt by an outside power to influence the election and promote a particular candidate is a very serious threat to our constitutional form of government.

On December 29, 2016, President Obama imposed sanctions on Russia in response to these hacks. I am cosponsoring S. 341, the Russia Sanctions Review Act of 2017, a bill that would keep sanctions imposed on Russia for election hacking and other aggression in place until Congress says otherwise.

As a senior member of the Senate Armed Services Committee (SASC) and Ranking Member of the SASC Subcommittee on Cybersecurity, I will continue to support policies that enhance our capability to deter and defend against cyber attacks from all enemies.

Now isn't the time to cozy up to Russia, now is the time to stand up to Russian aggression. I appreciate hearing your thoughts on this issue.

Sincerely, Bill Nelson"

Wednesday, June 14, 2017
Flag Day Despoiled
I was going to write a piece about Flag Day with photos.

Now, the depressing news about the shooting at a baseball practice field of Republican members of the congressional baseball team leads to other thoughts. Thankfully no one was killed other than the gunman. Good riddance to him. And thankfully the brave Capitol Police were there to take him down.

But will this be a time that we pull together long after the incident? Or will it just pull us further apart?

I've heard comments such as Representative Mo Brooks' "It's not easy to take when you see people around you being shot and you don't have a weapon yourself." According to initial reports the deranged gunman had a military assault style weapon. One can understand the helplessness and the impotence felt by Rep. Brooks. It is an outrage that we cannot even enjoy our national pastime without feeling threatened this way. And it is an outrage that political divisiveness should lead to any kind of violence.

But unless we all pull together the subsequent dialogue can go two divergent ways. One could lead us down the path of greater authoritarianism and the call for arming more citizens (although a greater police presence is going to be necessary when many of our Representatives are in public venues). The other path could call for the long-needed ban of military grade weapons. Are we all supposed to be armed with AR-15s on our baseball fields? I'm no Pollyanna and know that such a ban would have little impact on what happens in the near future. I'm thinking long term. This is not about challenging the 2nd Amendment, and it is not about Republican vs. Democrat. It's about common sense banning military weapons, doing comprehensive background checks, expanding our treatment of mental illness, and developing better early warning signs of mentally disturbed people from social networks and prior arrests.

I worry about how this horrible incident will move the country in the future. Will we come together, E pluribus Unum, or be driven apart, politicizing this horror? I look to the flag and wonder and hope.

Again, a long gap in political coverage as we were traveling. I tend to cover those moments on the road with personal entries and try to ignore the litany of transgressions by our very own President. My first entry after returning, though, focuses on those assaults and although since then he's "made nice" with Kim Jong-un, it still remains to be seen whether the "peace" is merely an illusion. Soon thereafter, the Las Vegas mass shooting, gun violence just continuing, ignored by the administration. One could even argue encouraged. Ironic that most shooters are domestic white guys, not people from "the caravans" "invading" our southern border.

Wednesday, September 27, 2017
Who Holds Whom Hostage?
For decades North Korea has crafted a delicate balance, building a nuclear capability while promoting nationalism to perpetuate the Kim Jong-un regime. American Presidents during those years were willing to accept the status quo which was preferable to a military confrontation. Even with conventional weapons, on a first strike North Korea could kill up to a million people in

Seoul, only a few dozen miles from the DMZ. That potential has held the world hostage all these years.

Pressure on North Korea's trading partners, particularly China, to enact stiff sanctions on North Korea has, until recently, been futile. Here China holds the U.S. hostage, owning a portion of our debt and more significantly knowing the American public's insatiable demand for cheap imported goods would prevail over any economic retaliation against China. China was content to have North Korea as a buffer zone until it, too, has been startled by NK's nuclear ambitions.

Indeed, a delicate balance, and then Trump's opening day message at the United Nations, where he threatened to "totally destroy North Korea." We all know what that is code for—the use of nuclear weapons. An American President has said he would use this country's nuclear force as a first strike.

Unthinkable. There were so many other ways to signal our resolve, to further pressure North Korea to the negotiating table. He went on to call Kim Jong-un 'Rocket Man,'—in front of the United Nations, schoolyard name-calling. Then, further undermining the dignity of the Office of the Presidency, he continued those threats and name-calling in Tweets.

Surprise. Tensions have ratcheted up, Kim Jong-un responding with new threats, including testing a hydrogen bomb over the Pacific. Unlikely, but to even utter that is giving as good as one gets.

There has been much criticism levied at Trump for worsening an already incendiary environment between the two countries, so what does he do?—He turns on the NFL. He has a reptilian instinct for survival. In so doing, he wrapped himself in the flag, the one that belongs to us all. "Fire the sons of bitches" referring to NFL players who went to one knee during the playing of the National Anthem.

I come from a generation which would never do that, but I would defend another person's right to protest that way over such weighty issues as "Black Lives Matter." Of course all lives matter in this country and to be born black should not be an impediment, but look where Trump brought President Obama—to the point of producing his birth certificate to prove his legitimacy as the President. If Obama was white, no such argument would have been made.

Now, if anyone is an illegitimate President, it is Trump. And he knows it—how he got to be President, by his actions and Russia's and astonishingly by those of the head of the FBI. Even his ignorance of American history, and his divisiveness seemed to work in his favor. He did not win by popular vote and although some of his marginal supporters say they would not vote for him now, he still has a solid 30 -35% base enamored by his strong-arm tactics, convinced he can do no wrong. And it is HE who is holding the rest of America hostage.

He knows his tenure as President is precarious, with the possibility of impeachment or the invocation of the 25th amendment, which provides for the removal of the President if "disabled" and unable to perform the duties of the office. One could argue that we are already there, but it is a high bar to achieve and it has to be set in motion by the Vice President and ultimately have the backing of 2/3 of Congress if the President objects.

With his pathetic response to the Charlottesville show of power by white supremacist groups and his attack on NFL players, mostly black (although he disavows that as being an issue), he dog whistles to his hard-core followers, many probably NRA diehards, and thereby creates a hostage situation. I can see clearly, now, the "strategy:" "remove me as your President and suffer the consequences of a new Civil War. " He has his army, he has the means of communication, he exhibits sociopathic thinking, and his politics of divisiveness have created such an environment. He would even risk nuclear war.

So, North Korea holds the world hostage, China holds us hostage, and Trump holds the majority of the American people hostage. Never has there been such a President who disrespects the very ideals which makes the American flag so sacred. He has done more than take a metaphoric knee to fortify his fragile ego.

Monday, October 2, 2017
Our Gun Culture
We are addicted to guns.

Now this horror in Las Vegas.

Other developed countries have more sensible laws. "The United States' gun homicide rate is 25 times higher than other high-income countries"—*The Guardian*: So, America, this is how other countries do gun control.

It's not only the laws, it's the culture. In what country, other than the U.S. would you see a politician brandishing a gun, like Alabama's Roy Moore proudly did, and then get endorsed by its leader?

After the terrorist attacks in Paris Trump said that it "would've been a much different situation if the city had looser gun laws" meaning if everyone had a gun the shooter might have been taken down earlier. Makes a lot of sense, arm everyone and that will lead to less shooting.

I wonder how Roy Moore's cap gun would have stood up in the Las Vegas shooting, or anyone's hand gun for that matter pitted against someone with a military grade automatic weapon firing from far away, and way above.

Senseless to repeat everything I've written about this self-inflicted plague, our love of guns. It starts with more sensible laws, better education, and a change in our thinking that having a gun somehow symbolizes freedom and machismo.

The key word index to this blog says it's 19th time I've written about the topic. With each outrage I feel the urge to say my piece.

Perhaps we will finally have the wisdom to approach this problem sensibly as have other developed nations. What politician has the courage and is willing to lead? Although he's taken contributions from the NRA, I nominate John McCain for the role. It is time to stand up for what is right. He's respected on both aisles, and an about-face would be a fitting legacy. "Our nation turns its lonely eyes to you."

Monday, October 9, 2017
To Tax or Not To Tax, A Question Again
It's interesting what issues home-town papers latch onto. The headline of today's *Palm Beach Post* chose to focus on Trump's tax cut "plan." Write a blog such as this long enough and like a leitmotif in a novel the same issues seem to recycle. Here we go again, trickle-down economics in the form of tax cuts that will benefit, mostly, the rich and the uber–rich.

I've touched upon economic inequality some two dozen times, including the impact of removing the so called "death tax," notwithstanding Trump's disingenuous "not good for me, believe me." Removing this tax entirely encourages family dynasties, which in this competitive world leaves those who have to begin their journey at the starting line way behind. An argument that is made for removing the tax is it is a disincentive for working hard. Warren Buffett doesn't think so and neither do the entrepreneurs of the world, people whose creativity and ideas drive their lives. Did Steve Jobs do what he did with the hope there would be no estate tax? The other argument is that some farmers who have vast land holdings upon death owe taxes on the appraised value. So, perhaps working farms should be exempt up to a certain amount. There are so many, sensible solutions other than trickle down.

Wednesday, October 25, 2017
Las Vegas Forgotten Already
Buy guns, kill people, console the victims' families, talk about legislation, forget and move on to the next news cycle, then repeat.

Less than a month ago the Las Vegas massacre dominated the news, followed by talk of gun control regulation, an immediate increase in gun sales fearing the latter, and promises of at least regulating bump stocks that convert semi automatic weapons into machine guns . Now it seems like it never happened, 58 people killed, hundreds injured. This is the pattern of the past. The NRA has puppet politicians well under control.

Imagine if the automobile was just invented and people went out and bought them, no license or testing required, few traffic laws, and who needs stop signs and lights? Autos still kill more people than guns, but those deaths now are nearly neck and neck. We choose to regulate automobiles, testing and licenses required, registration so we can track who owns what and if someone buys or sells more than a certain number of autos each year, he/she is considered a dealer and another level of regulation is reached.

Today, crazy people like Stephen Paddock can amass a war arsenal without any tracking information. Regretfully this means giving up some privacy, but we give it up to drive a car, why not owning a gun?

Tuesday, November 7, 2017
Over and Over Again
I'm sick of watching what has become of our country. Mass slaughtering reduced to biblical rhetoric of good vs. evil, with responses of tougher immigration laws if the murderer is anyone of middle eastern descent and "thoughts and prayers"

for the victims and their families if the assault is committed by a Caucasian nut job.

Good vs. evil. "May God be with you," offered to the Texas town of the church shootings. In a church of worship! Where was God at that moment? How can these incidents be reduced to the simplistic good vs. evil?

It plays into our psyche of "good guys" coming to the rescue, the rationalization that MORE guns are needed by the "good guys" to offset those carried by the "bad guys." Where is the Lone Ranger when you need him? Even better, Superman! The Texas Attorney General suggested that churches should consider armed worshipers. This is a solution?

Let's get serious about gun control once and for all. If we had more restrictive gun ownership legislation after the University of Texas tower shooting in 1966, where would we be today? It has to start sometime, and the moment has arrived to ban assault weapons. Go a step further and require registration of weapons as we do motor vehicles. Provide a government cash bounty for anyone turning in an assault weapon for a period of time, no questions asked. Anyone in possession of such a weapon after the bounty period is breaking the law.

This does not nullify the 2nd amendment, but it brings it more into alignment with today's weapon technology which the founding fathers could have never imagined. If the NRA doesn't like it, let them own muskets, the weapon of choice when the amendment was enacted.

Our gun violence and lax gun laws are the worst of developed countries. Many other countries just ban gun ownership and their lack of gun violence verses ours reflect that and cultural values as well.

And, please, the false equivalency argument of they'll use trucks instead, so why shouldn't we ban trucks is specious (as those who make the argument know). Any politician who can say that with a straight face ought to be run out of office. But as the Texas massacre takes place on the heels of the horrid truck terrorist attack in Manhattan, NRA apologists are quick to make that facetious case.

Trump responded to the Texas massacre saying "I think that mental health is your problem here. We have a lot of mental health problems in our country, as do other countries. But this isn't a guns situation." Yes, mental health problems need to be simultaneously addressed, but it IS a guns "situation" as well. And why did he genuflect to the NRA, rescinding a regulation that makes it harder for people with mental illness histories to purchase guns?

Our "leaders" must offer more than condolences and prayers to the thousands and thousands of families who have been impacted by gun violence and those who will be victims in the future.

At the beginning of 2018 my family and I were on a cruise, away from it all, and then we got back and I was writing theatre reviews. But then the horrible Parkland tragedy brought home, once again, what our priorities should be, completely unheeded, aided and abetted by the NRA.

Thursday, February 15, 2018
Over and Over, Again and Again
The terrible shooting at a school in Parkland, FL makes one stop and wonder how our nation can stand by and watch the 2nd amendment metastasize into a form of a rationalized killing field. One feels so helpless with a bunch of politicians calling it "evil" and offering prayers to the victims and their families and then do absolutely nothing. It should be THEIR children in those classrooms. How would they feel then? I've taken to twitter to express my knee-jerk response, but in this blog I've written nearly two dozen articles on the topic of gun control.

How in the world can we sanction military style weaponry as being a "right," in spite of the 2nd amendment? Even better than only banning them, we should require the registration of any weapon as we do automobiles. Something has to be done now.

So here are my knee-jerk Tweets, good for blowing off steam, but useless to create change. I just could not go about a "normal" day in my life without first expressing my outrage and disgust, at our politicians and our lack of moral leadership

Marco Rubio @thehill 6:16 PM - 14 Feb 2018 "We shouldn't "jump to conclusions" that gun control laws would've prevented Florida school shooting"
My Reply @lucanaemusing 7:11 PM - 14 Feb 2018
"Banning the sale of automatic weapons such as the AR-15 is part of a long term solution. No one is naive enough to contend it would immediately prevent such tragedies. Do your job Rubio to protect schoolchildren not the NRA. Such a ban does not violate the 2nd amendment."

@NPR 12:33 PM - 14 Feb 2018
"The President has been made aware of the school shooting in Florida. We are monitoring the situation. Our thoughts and prayers are with those affected," says Deputy Press Secretary Lindsay Walters in a statement.
My Reply @lucanaemusing 5:09 PM - Feb 14, 2018
"Prayers and thoughts and condolences, our President's action plan for gun control."

Joyce Carol Oates @JoyceCarolOates 1:00 PM - 14 Feb 2018
"Before a school shooting is over, it is too soon to talk about gun control; but when it is over, it is too late to talk about gun control unless it is also too early, since the next school shooting hasn't even begun (yet)."

My Reply @lucanaemusing 5:04 PM - Feb 14, 2018
"T***p took credit for no commercial airline deaths last year.
How about the thousands of gun deaths each year? When
do our elected representatives take action? Any action at all?
They are all culpable."

Friday, April 6, 2018
The Big Bad Wolf Comes for Little Red Riding Hood
Totalitarianism feeds on propaganda and the control of information. My former college psychology professor, Gustave
Gilbert, the author of *The Nuremberg Diary* said that Joseph
Goebbels, who had been an unsuccessful writer, "devoted his
considerable talents for propaganda to the task of winning over
Berlin's leftists to the cause of Hilterian fascism." (*The Psychology of Dictatorship*, 1950). Ultimately Goebbels served as
Reich Minister of Propaganda of Nazi Germany from 1933 to
1945. Per Wikipedia, "Goebbels' Propaganda Ministry quickly
gained and exerted controlling supervision over the news media,
arts, and information in Germany. He was particularly adept at
using the relatively new media of radio and film for propaganda
purposes."
Imagine if he had the Internet at his disposal.
Now we have Moscow born, former Trump special assistant,
and presently Sinclair Broadcasting's senior political analyst,
Boris Epshteyn, vying for the position of the "Ministry of Truth &
Public Enlightenment." Sinclair Broadcasting has been quietly
buying up local television stations, mostly in Trump country, to
spread its conservative propaganda. By now everyone knows of
the coordinated "Newspeak" perpetrated by Sinclair's stations
where local "news" anchors were required to read the same
statement: The sharing of biased and false news has become all
too common in the media. More alarming is that national media
outlets are publishing these same fake stories without checking

the facts first. Unfortunately, some members of the national media are using their platforms to push their own personal bias and agenda to control "exactly what people think."

Word for word, all Sinclair stations with local news broadcasters many of whom we have followed through their years, thinking of them as, well, just regular people like ourselves. Old friends.

One such station happens to be in our viewing area, a CBS affiliate. They too parroted this statement, as if they were speaking to us, although it was really Boris Epshteyn. These are friendly faces we've seen on air before our morning commutes or once we get home. A *Palm Beach Post* staff writer, Frank Cerabino, wrote a funny but profound parody of what these local news anchors "really said."

John Oliver eviscerated Sinclair's Newspeak in his last show.

A list of all the Sinclair stations, by State, shows the concentration in "flyover" States, with most major cities not represented. Think of their territory as mirroring the Electoral College.

Ironically, on the surface, the statement IS essentially true, and that is where the danger lies, voiced by an organization which indeed has "an agenda." The unsuspecting public is but a little Red Riding Hood being toyed with by a big bad Wolf, one who knows exactly what it's doing. After all, this is the organization which has pushed the "deep state" conspiracy theory.

One of the favorite techniques in propaganda is to say it over and over again. Fox News has been doing it for years. Now your local news broadcaster may be coming for your mind. "Oh Granny, what big teeth you've got!

Tuesday, May 1, 2018
Sense of Impotency in the Age of Trump
Gaslighting will do that to you. The endless stream of invectives and distortions coming from our own President and his

administration, ignored by many of our elected representatives, leaves one feeling a sense of helplessness, hopelessness, and even sickness. The easy way out is to get dragged into the melee, and engage with extremists from both ends of the political spectrum, taking our tribal positions. I've done it and still do, but there may be another way. Join RDI, the Renew Democracy Initiative. Here is a place for non extremists from both sides of the political divide to find solace and work together to preserve our Democracy, like-minded folk who believe in their Manifesto, particularly #13: "There is still a center in Western politics, and it needs to be revitalized— intellectually, culturally, and politically. The center right and center left are still joined by a broad set of common values, including respect for free speech and dissent, a belief in the benefits of international trade and immigration, respect for law and procedural legitimacy, a suspicion of cults of personality, and an understanding that free societies require protection from authoritarians promising easy fixes to complex problems."

Think about it. We live in an age where a porn star is suing a sitting President for defamation of character. Not that I don't think she has a right, particularly as we elected a man who boasted about grabbing women by their "pussy." A reality TV star has turned politics into a reality TV show. We elected him. The Office of the Presidency is demeaned every day and in so doing the moral compass of America's leadership disintegrates in a haze of gaslighting, jeopardizing the democratic principles we have built for more than 200 years. We've made such progress, and shame on us all to let it be undermined with catchy simplistic slogans like "Make America Great Again," or the endless stream of consciousness impulse tweets, mass-market entertainment passing as Presidential proclamations.

From RDI's site: "The world is in the midst of a modern political crisis fueled by fear, distrust, and confusion. Disturbing global trends, such as populism and authoritarianism, are imperiling the basic tenets of liberal democracy. The Renew Democracy Initiative ("RDI") came into existence as an effort to reinvigorate democracy and combat the extremism that deforms public debate. Our goal is to remind, to educate, to advocate for liberty."

Saturday, May 26, 2018
Memorial Day and Gun Violence
I conflate the two now.

In the past, I've written about Memorial Day and our soldiers who have died defending our country, although lamenting about how we've turned it into a sales "holiday" for mattresses and cars.

That should be the worst of it. Now we should also remember our teachers and students who have "fallen in battle" thanks to the NRA and our so called leadership acting as a facilitator.

The most recent shooting at a Santa Fe, TX school was not with an automatic weapon but an equally deadly hand gun and shotgun.

These guns were taken from the shooter's father.

It brings up the obvious question of responsibility. Should the father be held liable? Or society? Both of course.

Just so I get statistics right, I turn to Fact Check: In general, the overall number of people (31) and the number of students (26) killed in school shootings through 18 May 2018 was greater than the number of military personnel killed in combat zones (13). If all military deaths (including accidental training deaths) are counted, then that number (42) exceeds the total number of school shooting deaths (31).

But the precise numbers are irrelevant. Gun violence, now prevalent in our schools, is intolerable in a civilized society. Any society. All these weapons were "born to kill."

I've now written dozens of times about gun control and in particular the need to outlaw military type weapons, institute stringent background checks, age limits, etc., all the usual ideas and have seen the usual push backs to the same.

I've also (not uniquely) suggested that firearms be regulated in the same way automobiles are, requiring registration and tracking when one is sold.

I go back to this argument as it is more of a total solution than any others.

There are of course persuasive arguments against the bureaucracy of establishing a Federal or State system of a "Bureau of Firearms Control." Expensive. Loss of freedom, Big brother watching, etc. etc. But we tolerate those for automobiles, which also includes testing, insurance, inspection, etc. We do so for the greater good of society. We establish laws governing their use and prosecute when those laws are broken, even by generally "law abiding citizens." Gun ownership advocates make virtual talking robot arguments that gun laws only hurt the "good" people while "evil" ones ignore them and thus, we should have fewer gun laws. Talk about circular logic.

We take off our shoes at airports because someone tried to blow up a plane with a shoe. My constitutional rights allow me to wear shoes!

Annual gun deaths are now approaching those caused by motor vehicle incidents (the latter declining and the former steadily increasing).

Getting to the difficult part, implementation.

First, indeed institute stringent background checks, age limit laws, and ban the use of military style weapons.

Secondly, as Congress now sees fit to increase our national debt, go further and institute a Federal program for buying back weapons voluntarily surrendered, with higher premiums for military style weapons. Pay fair price. Return them no questions asked for a specified grace period.

Those choosing to keep their weapons, and those buying new ones, must register them with renewals required. If the registered weapon is given or sold to another, forms have to be completed, the item identified, with the new owner's name and address. Then the new owner has 30 days to register them. Registration fees will support the process.

Gradually a data base will be developed and ones who have a collection of weapons, an arsenal, would be identified and flagged as dealers, subject to another level of scrutiny and regulatory control.

This is complicated stuff and the devil is in the details.

Indeed, some (especially the "bad guys") will ignore all of this, but they will be subject to prosecution if found with unregistered weapons, or if someone is found with an unregistered weapon purchased or given by them. It will take time, maybe decades, to work through this group. It has to start sometime.

And while more regulatory control and knowledge of our lives is abhorrent to me, something has to be started NOW and a more comprehensive solution needs to be sought by our lawmakers. No more Sandy Hooks, Parklands, Santa Fes. Now. Please.

We don't even hear much anymore about thoughts and prayers regarding the latest incident. It's as if we've all become inured to them. That strategy never did work. We have heard enhanced rhetoric about turning our schools into heavily armed prisons. Is that really preferable to a "Bureau of Firearms Control?"

Yes, we must always remember those who died to defend our nation on Memorial Day, but think of our teachers and students who now face a war zone in schools. We need to defend them from NRA's agenda, cloaked in the sacred shroud of the 2nd amendment. None of this takes away one's right to bear arms, only military style weapons and makes other weapons subject to registration in the same way we regulate motor vehicles.

Tuesday, June 26, 2018
A Gathering Storm
We seem to be watching the slow motion creation of a dystopian plutocracy. Obfuscated by the administration's contrived crisis of dealing with undocumented immigrants and horrific scenes of families being separated, is an alt-right agenda of dismantling the so called social net. Stories such as a recent one in the *New York Times* are hidden by other events of Trump's creation.

Highlighted here are some salient points from the *New York Times* article of a few days ago, "Behind Trump's Plan to Overhaul the Government: Scaling Back the Safety Net".

I have depended on the *Times* for the Truth all my life and I see no reason to disbelieve any of this about "a small army of conservatives [who] have produced dozens of initiatives like the cabinet reshuffle proposal, with the goal of dismantling the social welfare system."

"Among the most consequential ideas is a proposal to shift the Supplemental Nutrition Assistance Program, a subsistence benefit that provides aid to 42 million poor and working Americans, from the Agriculture Department to a new mega-agency that would have 'welfare' in its title—a term Mr. Trump uses as a pejorative catchall for most government benefit programs. Mr. Trump, for his part, joked on Thursday that the plan was 'extraordinarily boring' before TV cameras in the Cabinet Room. But being boring in an all-too-exciting White House has provided cover for a small army of conservatives and think tank veterans who have been quietly churning out dozens of initiatives like the proposal to reshuffle the cabinet, with the ultimate goal of dismantling the American social welfare system from the inside out."

The first part of the plan, cutting taxes for the upper 1%, has already been implemented. What remains to be seen is the long term impact of those cuts on the deficit; most economists agree that GPD growth will not offset those cuts. This leaves an ever growing national debt, something the Republicans staunchly opposed before and now seem to be content with. When cries of deficit spending reach a crescendo in the future, their "Trump card" may be to throw the neediest 42 million Americans under the bus in the name of fiscal responsibility.

Monday, July 2, 2018
Congress shall make no law ... abridging the freedom of speech, or of the press
How about by Presidential Executive Order? Or just behavior?

I'm still recoiling from the murders of five employees of the *Capital Gazette* in Annapolis including a feature reporter, Rob Hiaasen. Hiaasen's career began at the *Palm Beach Post*, our local paper. We all feel a personal connection. Writers there remember him and one, Howard Goodman, has written the definitive article on the incident: "The targeting of journalists has to end."

As Representative Gerry Connolly, D-Va., said on CNN "This president plays with fire. He has deliberately demonized the press and journalists. To call them the enemy of the people is a remarkable statement from the head of our government. And that puts every journalist at risk. Now, he didn't do what happened yesterday in Annapolis, but he certainly helped create a climate ... where it's fair game to go after the press. And where does that end? And that's what I worry about, that sooner or later it leads to this kind of tragedy."

This is essentially reiterated in Goodman's article: "No one has inflamed the present atmosphere more than he, this man who occupies the highest office in our land. He has set a tone which he feeds at every rally and almost every day on Twitter."

I am not blaming him for Thursday's tragedy in Annapolis. But I do charge him with injecting a sense of hatred into the soul of this nation that journalists do not deserve and which—in a country with more guns than people—may all too easily turn into bloodshed."

However, is it no wonder? As Kellyanne Conway said: "You [the press] always want to go by what's come out of his mouth rather than look at what's in his heart."

We have looked and found the heart of darkness.

This is where the lines converge, a 2nd amendment run amuck and the perpetual debasing of the 1st amendment, lambasting the press. Until we can get our priorities straight, expect more gun violence and subsequent "thoughts and prayers."

Journalists must be protected.

Bills have been introduced in the House and Senate, one in February and the other in May. The Journalist Protection Act would make it a federal crime of certain attacks on those reporting the news. They've merely been "referred to committees on the Judiciary":

"Sponsor: Rep. Swalwell, Eric [D-CA-15] (Introduced 02/05/2018)

Committees: House - Judiciary

Latest Action: House - 02/05/2018 Referred to the House Committee on the Judiciary.

Sponsor: Sen. Blumenthal, Richard [D-CT] (Introduced 05/24/2018)

Committees: Senate - Judiciary

Latest Action: Senate - 05/24/2018 Read twice and referred to the Committee on the Judiciary."

Which will pass first, this Act or a Trump appointment to the Supreme Court? As our 1st amendment is undermined, and any action on the banning assault weapons unlikely, what kind of a nation are we becoming?

Monday, August 13, 2018
Random Thoughts, Rainy Day
I call them random thoughts as they are unconnected, except by a rainy day. While the pitter patter of the rain can be soothing when living on our boat in the summer, torrential downpours, thunder and lightning are not. Our dock is halfway into the Norwalk River, a long walk in wind driven rain, so while there are things to be done outside on the boat, and shopping to be addressed, today we are trapped inside a space which is a quarter of the size of my smallest NYC studio apartment when I was a young adult. Reading and writing are the best choices for today leaving the necessary errands and work for fairer weather.

Even writing has its challenges. No Wi-Fi here so cellular is our only means of communication. I'm accustomed to writing with things running in the background, particularly to look up facts, but on the boat I'm floating in space untethered.

In a way I'm glad to have this opportunity as the next week will be almost entirely devoted to preparations for, and then the wedding of our son, Jonathan, to our soon-to-be daughter in law, Tracie. Respecting their privacy I'm not going to say much about this eagerly anticipated affair, them, or their plans, but suffice it to say Ann and I are delighted, not only about the event, but they seem like perfect soul mates.

On to a completely unrelated subject. Random thoughts indeed. Nothing like falling asleep on a boat with a good book in one's hands. I'm generally into fiction but I like well written history as well, so for the past several weeks my night time reading has been Jon Meacham's *Franklin and Winston: An Intimate Portrait of an Epic Friendship.*

Meacham is not only a great historian, but a skilled writer at the same time. I've written about WW II in this blog, mostly from my father's perspective, and of course I've read a number of histories, especially from the FDR viewpoint. Meacham carefully, painstakingly brings out the great statesmanship of these two men, their developing friendship, FDR's crafting the Lend Lease program to deal with Britain's needs and yet at the same time balancing Congress' anti-intervention inclination before Pearl Harbor, even having to deal with some pro fascist feelings stoked by the likes of Lindbergh.

But Churchill won over FDR and a bond of friendship developed, although both men had their own egos and insecurities to be served. Thus, like all human beings, they were flawed but their trust in one another and their leadership truly saved democracy. When Stalin became more of a factor, they grew somewhat apart, but Churchill warned FDR about Stalin's own agenda, and was proven right, bringing them back together again.

Meacham makes copious use of original correspondence to underscore what these two men accomplished. The book was written some fifteen years ago. When read today one cannot help but think of those men and what, now, passes for "leadership" in our government. To every inspirational letter written or eloquent quote of these two titanic leaders, juxtapose one of the endless uninformed, despoiled tweets of our current leadership. Where would we be if our "transactional" President had faced the likes of Hitler and the needs of the British people in 1940? The book really needs to be read in that light now. I could quote galore to make this point, having turned down the corners of more than 50 pages for that very purpose, but now, with little time, on my old laptop, in the pouring rain, to what end? Simply read Meacham's brilliant work, and consider that question. Roosevelt and Churchill made history. History did not make them. They were the right leaders for terrible times.

Do we have the right leaders for our times? If you read *Franklin and Winston*, you may be asking (and answering) that question with every page.

Monday, October 29, 2018
Not a Time for only Thoughts and Prayers
Las Vegas slaughtering, shootings in schools, houses of worship
(let's not forget Sutherland Springs, Texas and the Charleston,
SC shootings) and now eleven people killed and six injured
when a gunman attacked the Tree of Life synagogue in Pittsburgh on Saturday. We're told (by our President) that the
greatest threat to our homeland security is immigrants and
foreign born terrorists. Meanwhile, what do all these horrific
events have in common? Most are by hate-filled home-grown
white nationalists, with large gun collections, frequently
brandishing automatic weapons for maximum slaughtering
effect.

Is it a surprise that the Pittsburgh killer blames Jews for
helping migrant caravan 'invaders'? Who first pointed out the
so called caravans had some "bad hombres and people of middle
eastern descent?"

Apparently the gunman used an assault rifle and three handguns, among his collection of 21 registered guns. But he was not
a big fan of Trump as he felt the President did not go far enough
and he was surrounded by Jews. On the other hand, pipe
bomber Cesar Sayoc felt that Trump's rhetoric was just right.
Our system fails to ring a bell when one person owns 21 guns?

No matter, it's pretty clear that the political discourse in
which Trump has been engaged, particularly at his Nuremberg
style rallies, foments division, violence and is intended to feed
the fragile ego of a demagogue.

Instead of building walls at the border, we need to build
legislative walls around gun access. Will it eradicate such shootings, no, but over time it is one of the building blocks of making
such incidents less likely.

Win the Midterms and begin to challenge the NRA. Haven't
we had enough of this?

Thursday, November 8, 2018
Post Midterm Thoughts
So broken: our political system and our way of life. And still another mass shooting, this one in a CA bar. We've become inured to them by lack of any action, the NRA's tentacles wrapped around Congress. There are solutions. It only takes the will.

Anyone who caught Trump's news conference yesterday, his firing of Sessions and replacing him with a Yes Man, should understand the fragility of our democratic system. Demagogues play the Press to their propagandist advantage. Demagogues demand obedience.

I had only one wish for the Midterms: gain the House, although like most moderate progressives, I was rooting for Beto, Gillum, et al. Still, I sleepily emailed ebullient messages to a few friends at 3.00 AM declaring "victory" with the subject heading "bring on the subpoenas."

But I am no Pollyanna, thinking that having control of the House will ameliorate the deep dark political divide in this country. It might exacerbate it, but as with an operation, the aftermath therapy can be more painful than the procedure.

We focus on Trump, which is the way he wants it but there are so many systemic issues. Our Constitution is the best political document ever drafted, but it was by 18th century thinkers.

The 2nd Amendment needs updating. Muskets are no longer the only "arms" that we have the right to bear.

The Electoral College needs fixing or abandonment, allowing the direct popular vote to determine the outcome of Presidential elections. Slavery and concern that the average person might not be best suited to make those decisions led to the Electoral College. We need to question its legitimacy in today's world where information is readily available to everyone.

Similarly, another consequence of the great Constitutional compromise was the one giving each State the same number of Senators, irrespective of population. I quote what Alexander Hamilton had to say about that in The Federalist below. Who could have seen what now exists, with thinly populated states such as North Dakota, about the population size of an El Paso, Texas, having the same Senate representation as the entire State of Texas itself, giving the people of ND nearly 40 times the political clout to have their say over Supreme Court Justices, etc.? Even a greater multiple when it comes to states like NY or CA.

Another bête noir of mine, and thankfully we now have a brief reprieve, is political advertising. Super PACs representing special interests, as well as extremist political party advertising, are a form of government approved brainwashing, appealing primarily to emotional issues. We've successfully removed cigarette advertising from our airwaves. Time has come to remove political advertising and endless robo calls (spend the $$ on our decaying infrastructure, or healthcare, etc. instead!). Make all political discourse over the airways subject to universally recognized debate rules. If a candidate has something to say, write an opinion piece for local and/or national publication, maintain a Web site expressing plans and opinions. Aren't we sick of the political advertising which portrays the opposition as being sent from hell?

Easier said than done, I know, but we have to do something to separate the democratic process from mass persuasion dollars. The next couple of months before our new House representatives are sworn in are going to be critical. May we survive those days to get democracy back on track.

The Federalist No. 22 by Alexander Hamilton

"Every idea of proportion and every rule of fair representation conspire to condemn a principle, which gives to Rhode Island an equal weight in the scale of power with Massachusetts, or Connecticut, or New York; and to Delaware an equal voice in the national deliberations with Pennsylvania, or Virginia, or North Carolina. Its operation contradicts the fundamental maxim of republican government, which requires that the sense of the majority should prevail. Sophistry may reply, that sovereigns are equal, and that a majority of the votes of the States will be a majority of confederated America. But this kind of logical legerdemain will never counteract the plain suggestions of justice and common-sense. It may happen that this majority of States is a small minority of the people of America; and two thirds of the people of America could not long be persuaded, upon the credit of artificial distinctions and syllogistic subtleties, to submit their interests to the management and disposal of one third."

Wednesday, December 12, 2018
"Only I can save you!"
During my publishing career I reprinted Gustav Gilbert's *Psychology of Dictatorship*. He was my professor in 1962, teaching a course of the same rubric during my brief tenure as a psychology major. He was all business in the classroom, nary a smile, but no wonder what he witnessed. Gilbert was the American Military Chief Psychologist at the Nuremberg trials, writing the *Nuremberg Diary* shortly thereafter and later his more academic *Psychology of Dictatorship*.

I'm reminded of this by yesterday's bluster of our president, threatening to shut down the government to "save" us from "criminals pouring into the U.S." and those who are not criminals, at the very least, carry "deadly diseases." "It's my wall or the highway." Scares the bejezzes out of his faithful followers.

At Nuremberg Gilbert interviewed some of the head Nazis, including Herman Goering, who confided the following to Gilbert: "... people can always be brought to the bidding of the leaders. That is easy. All you have to do is tell them they are being attacked and denounce the pacifists for lack of patriotism and exposing the country to danger. It works the same way in any country."

How prophetic.

APPENDIX

The last entry of 2018 is about the very issues that propel us into 2019: Government shutdown threats, Nuremberg style rallies, and the fear mongering over "caravans" "invading" our country in order to build the wall Mexico was going to finance. Meanwhile, middle class taxpayers are beginning to wake up to the fact that the" cuts" are not benefitting them much, while the upper one percent, no, actually, the upper 10% of the 1% are reaping windfall benefits. Our deficit soars as the inappropriate tax cuts were not needed as the economy was expanding before Trump took office. The NRA continues to rule. The Democratic primaries are now just beginning and one would hope that a reasonable (by reasonable, I mean non-extremist) candidate emerges to challenge Trump, if he is still around, or even runs. Only time will tell.

And I'm glad to end my collection here, before Robert Muller's report becomes public or partially public. That will shift everything but once again leading to places one can only conjecture. The recent public testimony of Michael Cohen, Trump's long time fix it man, speaks volumes about where we are headed.

I said at the onset that this is an overview—a chronology—of political and economic observations from my blog.

Yet those are but a fraction of what I've written. There are many personal entries and I've decided to include three in this appendix that cover the greatest influences on my life. These are my wife, Ann, my going to Long Island University for the education I was crying out for, and my father, whose influence deeply shaped my working ethic. Without these influences I would have never become the person I am and therefore these three entries constitute an important part of my biography.

I conclude with a fourth entry, which is a short story I wrote from one of my blog entries. I've written other short stories, but this one is very personal as it is part memoir, part fiction. It speaks to my sensibilities.

Although there are remarks in these entries that illuminate my life, I provide a brief idiosyncratic biography for a better understanding:

About the Author

My life story is essentially unremarkable. I was born in 1942 and my father went off to war in 1943. We moved into my mother's parents' house in Richmond Hill, Queens, when my father left. I vaguely remember my grandparents and my great grandmother who also lived there and my earliest recollection is being in a stroller with my mother or grandmother on Jamaica Avenue shopping at a vegetable market, my being given raw peas from a pod as a special treat. I have no idea why that image stuck with me all these years, but it was pleasurable. They say earliest recollections are meaningful.

Once my father came back home after the war, he returned to his family's commercial photography business which had been in the family since 1866. My mother thought she was marrying into what would become a wealthy family, but the commercial photography business was configured to provide prints for salesman sample catalogues. Advertising methods were changing and the business never kept up with the times.

This disappointment planted the seed for significant marital discord. I was rebellious in high school and took some pride in doing minimal work and hanging out with the wrong crowd. It wasn't until it was almost too late that I began to take high school seriously, with the thought of college.

My father, with whom I worked during summers in high school, and college, had a "plan B" for me (actually, his "plan A") which was to send me off to the Army Signal Corps school to learn photography and then go into the business with him.

So I had a number of factors working against me as I struggled to find myself, somehow knowing that I could do more than settling into a dying business. Those headwinds not only included my past poor academic performance, family turbulence, but a sterile cultural environment as well. I was never exposed to theatre or good music and literature at home.

When it finally became time to either go into the army or off to college, I took the initiative to apply to three schools, Kent State (which was my first choice as it would get me away from my family), New York University and Long Island University (the two which my parents preferred if I was to go to college, as I could commute, thus saving them the $$ for room and board. My poor HS performance resulted in outright rejections from Kent State and NYU, and acceptance "on probation" from LIU in Brooklyn.

The only way I could convince my father to go to LIU was to live at home and major in business (after all, I could learn more about photography from him), and so the die was cast. The pieces I wrote about my father, and my LIU years which appear in this Appendix, speak volumes about the consequences of this direction I chose for my life. Once in college my grades improved substantially, and I gradually cycled through majors, from general business, to advertising, to psychology, and finally English. I also inveigled my parents to accepting a move into the dormitory after the first semester by working and by getting a student loan.

In college I was introduced to the world of theatre, which fit like a glove with my interest in literature, becoming a life-long love, along with the piano, something I picked up with minimal and inadequate lessons. These past 10 years I've enjoyed performing piano programs at local retirement communities, particularly music from the Great American Songbook.

I also have to credit my wife of the last 48 years, Ann, for her enduring passion for the theatre. While we lived in Westport, she was off to the Wednesday Broadway matinees while I worked, but we frequented the Westport Country Playhouse and the Long Wharf theatre in New Haven together. My blog has become a platform for reviewing plays in the area and I now also act as a theatre critic for a local newspaper. I've reviewed scores of productions of our favorite regional theatre, Palm Beach Dramaworks, as well as other local theatres and still write an occasional review of productions at the Westport Country Playhouse or Broadway productions when we're in Connecticut and New York.

We also found we shared a love of boating and to this day still live on a boat part of the summers in Connecticut, albeit with diminishing time as aging and boating do not mix well. A number of entries in this book were written on a laptop on our galley dining table.

In addition to going to college as a fork-in-the-road decision for me (sounds silly nowadays, but this is at the end of the 1950's), the other was forsaking my father's business and starting in publishing from the ground up, beginning as a production assistant in 1964 at a subsidiary of Academic Press, Johnson Reprint.

From those two major decisions, the next 50 years flowed, including running a publishing company, Greenwood Publishing Group for nearly 30 years, publishing more than 10,000 titles during my tenure. I always considered my time in publishing to be a continuous post graduate education, dealing with scholars from every discipline, learning to work for my employees as much as it was the other way around, and learning the fundamentals of business, planning, and investment.

These formed my cultural values, work ethic, political perspectives, and, most importantly, my family and friends, and here I am to now look back and write about my time on this planet.

Sunday, May 22, 2011
A Special Day, A Special Woman
Ann, my wife and best friend, is turning 70. Incredible. When we met in our mid 20's, I remember listening to the words of the Paul Simon song of our youth, Old Friends, "Can you imagine us years from today, sharing a park bench quietly? / How terribly strange to be 70." Indeed, how terribly strange it seemed to us then, really unthinkable, but that is the curse of youth, a presumed eternity of life.

We were both working then for the same publishing company in New York City, but at the end of the 1960's I accepted a career opportunity in Westport, CT, and worked at that same job until retirement. Meanwhile, we raised a family: our son, and my son from a prior marriage.

Before taking on the responsibility of child-rearing, Ann continued to work in NYC even after we relocated to Westport, my dropping her off at the Westport train station early in the morning on my way to the office and picking her up on the way home. When Ann was pregnant she stopped working and we did what countless couples did, worked on the house, moved to a larger house, raised our family, worked and played hard (particularly on our boat), and did extensive personal and business overseas travel. Suddenly, the kids were gone and my working days were concluding. The 70's, 80's 90's, and, now, the first decade of 21st century flew by almost stealthily, but with gathering speed.

How does a marriage survive such a long period of time? By being best friends I think. Simply put, we're simpatico. I've watched the birthday milestones, now, of most of Ann's life and and sometimes threw large parties for her.

My favorite was her 50th as it was a surprise party, and it was not the first time I had successfully pulled one off for her. For Ann's 40th she thought she was going to a wedding. Friends of ours who had been living together had agreed to serve as the bait and I printed one wedding invitation, which was of course sent to us. So Ann was dressed to the nines and we had to drop off our young son at another friend's house on the way for babysitting, thinking she was going to a big "wedding." But at our friend's house everyone from Ann's past had gathered, including her mother and relatives from California. Her knees buckled when the door was opened.

So it was with much pleasure I was able to engineer another surprise party exactly ten years later. That afternoon we were out on our boat 'Swept Away' at our favorite Crow Island anchorage, the tiniest island in the Norwalk chain, where we literally lived during summer weekends, year in and year out. Many of our friends were there too on their boats but gradually they left and I had persuaded Ann to stay to enjoy the waning hours of the languid Sunday late afternoon. That should have been her first hint something was up, as I was the one who usually left first, to clean up the boat, and then return home to get ready for the workweek.

Unknown to her, our friends and many relatives were waiting at a restaurant at our marina where I had reserved a private room. Upon our return to the slip I suggested we go out for dinner, something I knew she would jump at after a weekend on the boat. I said I preferred the restaurant at the marina, that I was too tired to go off someplace else, and so she was ambushed by another surprise birthday celebration, this for her 50th.

Here is my toast to her at the gathering. While some specifics might make sense to those who have been close to Ann over the years, the gestalt paints a picture of a special person, without whom birthdays would be meaningless to me. [For the purposes of brevity and relevancy, this has been truncated and edited as many of the personal references would be meaningless in these pages—while trying to maintain the sense of humor and capturing her personality which was the intent of the original speech]:

"Welcome, friends and relatives, to Ann's 50th birthday celebration. Thank you all for helping to make this a special day for a special person and thank you to Patti, who was my co-conspirator in arranging this celebration.

The relationships one forms weave the fabric of one's life; by this definition, Ann has a real reason to celebrate on this special day. And those relationships are as much built around many small detailed moments as they are around life's more momentous occasions.

How many languid afternoons have we been anchored at our beloved Crow Island in the Long Island Sound, with Ann and friends locked in mortal battle over a scrabble board? She has always been a fierce competitor and has a real love of reading and words.

Then, there were those times with Sue and Ray, their Donzi skimming over the Long Island Sound at high speed Ann in the rear seat screaming, 'Raymond, Raymond, RAYMOND!' Yet she loved every minute of it, but not as much, perhaps, as those quiet, harbor cruises as the sun was setting at the Great Salt Pond, Block Island.

Potluck suppers on our boats also stand out among these special moments. Watching Ann cook in a small galley gives new meaning to the word "hyperactive."

And her love of the theater, eating, and, let's not beat around the bush, fine things in general, are well known. Going to a restaurant or the theater with Ann is an experience, ranging from her crying out 'BRAVO, BRAVO, BRAVO!' at the end of a performance, to turning to a stranger in a restaurant to ask for a review of his meal, and often being offered a taste.

So, it is no wonder that Ann's friendship with Arlene began in a restaurant on 14th Street, La Bilbania, in 1964. Her love of travel led her to London on a solo trip at age 21, but together with Arlene, they braved the vicissitudes of Montezuma's revenge traveling all through Mexico and a couple years later left most of the men in Spain and Italy pining for their early return. Their antics at the Pensione in Spain have been written about in some of the world's most notable tabloids.

But being a friend of Ann's is not always like trying to follow a big brass band. Patti and Ann, while ostensibly taking their dogs for a walk, engage in secret 'girl talk.' In fact, if there is one single, attribute that makes Ann Ann, it is her capacity for intimacy, for understanding human nature, for giving and helping. She has touched many lives.

She bravely left Atlanta, Georgia when she turned 18 for New York City, to find her life. When you think about it that was an extraordinarily bold act. Ann was one of the original "women's libber" but did not even know it.

Her cousins Mimi and Sherman were nurturing to Ann in her early New York years and, in fact, she ultimately inherited their rent-controlled apartment at 33 West 63rd Street. This became our first apartment after we were married.

As a young, single woman she made a career for herself, first as a receptionist and ultimately as a Customer Service Manager at the publishing organization where we met in 1965. It was here where she also met and hired another lifelong friend, 17 year old Maria, to be her secretary. They became inseparable. Little did she know that Maria would return to her native Sicily years later, ultimately to marry and settle there permanently. Nothing has stopped their unbreakable attachment, as over the years, Ann has traveled to Palermo almost every year to be with her closest friend and travel all throughout Sicily with Maria and her husband Beny.

Favorite activities in New York were going to the Theatre, dining at exotic restaurants, dancing the Twist at The Peppermint Lounge, ballroom dancing at Roseland, bicycling around the Village and even taking Flamenco lessons! Simply put, Ann was a beatnik, a bohemian who chose the path most of her Atlanta high school classmates could hardly imagine.

She became an accomplished career women, and, of course, let's not kid ourselves, she married well.

But that strong nurturing, zest-for-life instinct is never more evident than in her role as Mother to our sons, Chris and Jonathan. She was, and is, always there for them.

Finally, the most incredulous thing about Ann is that she puts up with me. That qualifies her for Sainthood! So to my best friend, I raise my glass to say, 'Happy 50th Birthday, and here is to the next 50!'"

So, another twenty five years have gone by. Why does it feel like (to us both) we are still kids? Of course our bodies deny that fact as does the mirror, but the mind seems to rule. I still think of her as that youthful, beautiful woman I married, someone who was so very different than I on the one hand, but seemed to share many of my interests, particularly the blog which she has helped to edit over the past 10 years and supported fully with her constant encouragement.

Thursday, August 11, 2016
Visiting the Past to See the Future
I just finished reading Paula Fox's *Desperate Characters* which is set in Brooklyn in the late 1960s. More on that in another entry whenever I can get to it, but the novel unfolds not only in the Borough of my past, Brooklyn, but mostly bordering the downtown section which is my old home and haunt, beginning with my student days at Long Island University. For years my friend Bruce and I have talked about revisiting the university together as Alumni, but we've never been able to coordinate the days. He's not around the corner, living in Massachusetts so I

forgive him. But as I closed the Fox book last Monday the urge was strong to revisit and I was compelled to act on the urge as planning never seems to go right so I turned to Ann and asked her whether she wants to go with me the next day. Why not give me a little advance notice (she had an appointment) she asked, but she promptly cancelled that appointment, agreeing to join me on an impromptu adventure. I emailed my son Jonathan to ask whether he might want to meet us at Junior's in downtown Brooklyn that day for lunch (revisiting would not be complete without sitting in that landmark once again).

He was surprised by our plans and asked whether we'd be driving in. No, I said, Metro North to Grand Central and then the IRT #5 train to Nevins Street—needed to experience it all (after all I commuted to the school by subway from Queens for the first semester in 1960). We're crazy he said, too much to negotiate, too many stairs, the jostling crowds, etc. Crazy I am I guess but the trip to and from was as meaningful as the visit itself, and less stress than driving and quicker too. All part of the "fun."

So we emerged from the Nevins Street station and were greeted by a Brooklyn I hardly recognized. Looking east and west on Flatbush Avenue revealed a skyline of a different place although some of the same tired buildings were standing. I seem to remember a Bickford's (or was it a Horn & Hardart?) there, long gone. Walking west towards the Manhattan Bridge there was the LIU I remembered, the old Brooklyn Paramount building and adjacent Metcalf Hall where all of our class-rooms were.

The door to the Paramount was open, a guard manning the desk, so we went in and showed him my "student ID card"—the last one I carried during the 1963-64 semester year.

He looked at it in disbelief as if I was a Martian but good naturedly directed us to the Admissions Office. As a student I worked there part-time, processing applications and I worked in the library as well. The Admissions office is essentially in the same place, but the entrance is no longer on Flatbush, but inside the campus gates so we entered there and I presented my ID card to the receptionist. "Oh my God," was her response. "I have to show this to the Associate Director," which she did.

We were told there is a tour at 2 PM so before lunch we had some time on our own to visit my old dormitory. Again, my card was greeted by disbelief but that allowed me to look around at the cafeteria and the student lounge there, all changed of course. I told the guard at reception—pointing at the three elevators—that when I lived there they were segregated. "Segregated?" he was obviously surprised by the implication. Yes, I replied, two of the elevators went to the men's floors and one was for the women. "Huh" he said, "there were separate floors for men and women?" Yes, in the early 60s, that is how it was. Times have changed.

Then I couldn't resist getting a photo of myself in front of 175 Willoughby Street, that old apartment house being my second residence after graduating and the one I lived in with our young son, Chris, until I was divorced. The building has been refurbished and looks better than when I lived there some 50 years ago. Our apartment had a clear view of the New York City skyline, but that is now blocked by a new apartment house.

So after these two nostalgic visits, off to Junior's. Same as I remember it, and the same late 50s early 60s music playing, displays of Brooklyn landmarks, in particular the Brooklyn Dodgers, or "dem bums." There we met Jonathan who was born long after I left Brooklyn. As in the past, Junior's serves way too much food but even so we couldn't resist capping off our lunch with a shared piece of their famous cheesecake. Yum!

Jonathan returned to work and we walked back across the street, way too early for the 2pm tour, hoping for a brief private tour. They were waiting for me. "Here he is!"

They had already planned a private tour for an "old" alumnus, so were lucky enough that Tiarra, a student Admissions Assistant, the same position I once held, was available to take us around. The change and additions to the school were striking.

What impressed me most about the LIU of today is its forward-looking, and application-results-oriented strategy, intended to give its students the best opportunities for employment after graduation. It's the hands on direction the school has taken, with its life-sciences and entrepreneurship focus as well as the facilities that students now have to maintain their health (what a gym facility!) and their social lives (i.e. social media and the numerous cafés), that really overwhelmed me, facilities which were unimaginable in my time.

Nonetheless it was nice to see the humanities thriving there as well, including its own theatre (in my day the theatre department produced plays at the Brooklyn Academy of Music). It was quite a trip down memory lane seeing the old Metcalf building, the Paramount, and my dormitory, but so impressive to see the new campus and its flourishing multicultural student population getting ready for the real world. I think LIU is really in sync with the times and Brooklyn itself. It's reinvented itself many times during its nearly 100 years in the Borough, a resilient survivor and innovator in the competitive world of higher education.

The facilities as I noted are phenomenal. A new gym, Olympic size swimming pool and endless exercise machines beckon.

I was wondering about the need for a second gym but Tiarra said the old Paramount was going to be restored to its former splendor in conjunction with the Barclay's Center as a theatre for events, the students getting discounts. Smart strategy for income methinks, sort of functioning as an endowment for the university.

Still the past has not been forgotten as the gym pays tribute to athletes of years gone by. I liked the billboard sized poster of some of the basketball stars I saw play, including Ed "Corn-flakes" Johnson, Luther Green, and Albie Grant. Albie was a small center / power forward who I grew close to in my senior year. A wonderful person—a great optimistic personality—who died way too early in life. To watch him play was among the more significant moments in LIU athletic history.

After a couple hours of touring, we were beat, but happy, and headed back to the IRT just as the #5 train pulled in, nearly full but we managed a seat until Grand Central, and then back "home" to our boat. I'm proud to be a LIU graduate, a school which has managed to adapt to and change with the times, giving its students an opportunity to succeed in the 21st century world, as I like to think I did in the 20th.

I've written several pieces about my Brooklyn years in this blog, but the one which is most relevant to this entry is a piece I wrote for *Confrontation Magazine* about 10 years after graduating. It still says it all about my experience then:

L.I.U.-My World in the Early '60s

Downtown Brooklyn sandwiched between the placid decade of the 50s and the Vietnam War was not unlike other communities in having a sense of optimism about its future. A thriving commercial center for small merchants, it had major islands in the same sea: the New York Telephone Company headquarters, the Brooklyn Hospital, Abraham and Straus department store, the Fox and Paramount movie theatres, the Board of Education, Fort Greene Park, and Long Island University.

It was September 1960 when I emerged from the DeKalb Avenue subway stop and made my way for the first time to L.I.U. Standing at the corner of Flatbush Avenue Extension and DeKalb Avenue, waiting for the light to change, Junior's and the Dime Savings Bank behind me, I faced a drab office building rising above the ornate but faded Brooklyn Paramount movie palace.

Farther behind me was a middle-class Queens community, my universe until this moment: a community of hard-working people imbued with the conviction that all things were possible in this society if one tried hard enough; it was with this sense I was going to college to learn business. But this seeming past eternity of punch ball; the Bungalow Bar man; picture-card trading; piano and guitar lessons; grammar school report cards that included grades for penmanship, neatness and posture; the Bunny Hop, Elvis ("a-wop-bom-a-lu-bop ... "); Ike; and high school (" ... if you don't take Latin, you won't be able to get into college .. ") was possibly fading, for I stood on the border between two lives, two cultures: was my background going to be my future, could I emerge out of this bland and benign land-scape into myself? Brooklyn would have much to do with the answer.

Sitting in my first class on the 8th floor, becoming a regular occupant of that same seat, I could see the digital clock on top of the Dime Savings Bank blinking at me. This and another clock on top of the Williamsburg Savings Bank farther up Flatbush Avenue became lighthouses in my Brooklyn experience. When, the following year, I lived in the dormitory, returning late in the evening from a night in Manhattan in a blinding snowstorm, I sensed these silent timepieces watching me scurrying home.

In later years I lived in downtown Brooklyn, worked in Man-hattan for a publishing firm, and regularly flew to the mid-west. Coming into LaGuardia Airport, we would sweep over Brooklyn and see the downtown area reaching out to Prospect Park while the fingers of the Brooklyn, Manhattan and Williamsburg bridges bound Brooklyn to Manhattan. Below was the beacon of the Williamsburg Savings Bank clock. Then, as now, I am drawn to that unique community I once called home.

I remember the student union on the ground floor of the small building adjacent to the Paramount building. Smoke hung in the stagnant air, bodies slumped on worn lounge chairs and elbows rested on Formica tables. Nixon versus Kennedy was the subject of heated discussion. These students, mostly from Brooklyn, seemed confident in their belief that politics could remake society. Eventually I found myself caught up in political causes as my apathy of the past waned.

With John F. Kennedy our new President-elect, the campus had a new vibrancy. A professor, delayed by listening to Beethoven's Eighth Symphony in his office, entered the classroom gesticulating those glorious rhythms. One professor challenged us to an exam: think of a question and answer it, the grade being as dependent on the nature of the question as on the answer. Another accepted a twisted pretzel from a student on the school quadrangle and published a poem on the experience.

Meanwhile I moved into the dormitory, severing remaining ties with a prior somnambulistic life. My room faced the front of the campus, with the monolithic slab of a factory that would become the shell of the architecturally renowned Humanities Building to be constructed a short time later. Behind the factory stood downtown Brooklyn, my microcosm of the real world.

The lack of classroom space mandated that the university rent space at Brooklyn Polytechnic, a neighboring institution where some of my classes were held. We made our way there along Myrtle Avenue, the elevator line rumbling over our heads, past furniture stores and shells of buildings. Decay was evident, but it was defiant decay: people stubbornly made their homes and pursued their lives here.

The return trip was frequently along Fulton Street, connecting the City Hall area with Flatbush Avenue and downtown Brooklyn. There, the cacophony of tiny record stores blurted out" ... baby, baby, baby, baby don't you leave me ... " merging with" ... be-bop-a-lu-la, she's my baby ... " The Chinese restaurant on the second floor beckoned, but I moved on toward the Dime Savings Bank, past shoe, appliance, fabric and other stores.

Across from the Dime Savings Bank was McCrory's, which embodied most of the merchant's downtown Brooklyn expectations. Here I was greeted at the door by the aroma of newly manufactured goods mixed with those of different foods cooking in various sections of the store. In the basement was a grocery where we bought food to supplement the fare in the dormitory. Shoppers would scrutinize the merchandise with almost-total seriousness as the IND subway loudspeaker announced, through corridors connecting to McCrory's, a train's arrival.

Opposite Junior's restaurant, then as now the neighborhood's most famous food emporium was another restaurant, Soloway's, a luncheonette run by a Greek family. Hamburgers sizzled in grease while French fries were bathing in deep fat. Students gathered around most of the tables and at the counter while strains of "Run Around Sue" thumped from the jukebox.

Junior's itself was reserved for special occasions when only the most obscene dessert would suffice. Also, late at night, when we could study no more, some of us went across to Junior's bar to chat with Pete, the bartender, who offered a different education: would Maris hit 60 home runs? Mickey Mantle was the better ballplayer, Pete opined. Pete had a thick neck with a trim gray crew cut. He was a kindly father to us, probably not realizing the important role he played in our student lives.

Manhattan was a short shuttle over the Manhattan Bridge via the BMT, and occasionally we went there. Perhaps on a date, sitting at the back of St. Patrick's Cathedral until dawn to beat the curfew for female residents of the dorm; or to Greenwich Village for a Black Russian or to see a production at Cafe LaMama or on the second floor of Max's Kansas City restaurant, where the Theatre of the Absurd played; but Brooklyn seemed to be all the world we generally needed and that was where we usually stayed. We sat on the Promenade in Brooklyn Heights, and took in the vista of the Brooklyn Bridge, downtown Manhattan, the Statue of Liberty, and further up, the spire of the Empire State.

During club hours we crowded into the auditorium to hear Malcolm X speak. Or we listened to local political candidates, heated debate overflowing the classroom after the speaker left.

The Cuban Missile crisis brought us back to days when, as schoolchildren, shades were lowered, lights turned out, and we were instructed to get down on our knees below our desks and cover our heads. Our mortality and civilization's could be ended by design or by caprice. We frantically darted about the dormitory, discussing whether we might soon be drafted.

I remember other areas I did not know until those days in Brooklyn. Working as a receptionist at the Brooklyn Tuberculosis Center several evenings a week, I participated in a too-common side of Brooklyn life: poverty. Sick, helpless people came, seeking assistance. I processed forms and offered reassurance, but felt ineffectual.

As a dormitory counselor I sometimes had to accompany students to the emergency room at the Brooklyn Hospital behind the university. I spent a week there myself, with pleurisy, in a ward. The squalor and the human tragedy I witnessed are echoed in the works of Theodore Dreiser which I read in the hospital for a term paper, seeing Frank Cowperwood's lobster and squid locked in deadly combat as symbolic of our struggle with life in this land of Brooklyn.

Next to the hospital was a prison. There, from the upper floors of the dormitory, the prisoners could be seen endlessly marching in circles. The prison was later destroyed to make room for a bigger hospital, the demolition ball pounding the 19th-century slabs into rubble, crushing the infinitely trodden steps in the courtyard.

Walking past the Admissions Office one Friday afternoon, a friend came running toward me. "Did you hear, Kennedy was shot?" Incredulous, I rushed to my dorm to listen to the radio. It was true.

I had tickets for a concert at the Brooklyn Academy of Music that night, one of the few cultural events in New York City that was not cancelled. An unrehearsed version of Beethoven's Egmont Overture was performed rather than the regular program. We filed out, silent, stunned, weeping openly. In quick succession Oswald was apprehended, and while we watched it on TV, Jack Ruby assassinated him.

With the advent of these acts, in particular as the Vietnam War encroached on all our lives, I knew the life I had known in Brooklyn could not remain the same. What changed, some years later, was often for the better for me. But whatever the benefits and the sad moments, I shall remember Brooklyn most as the place that allowed me to change into myself.

Saturday, November 10, 2012
Thoughts on Veterans Day
Veterans Day brings thoughts of my Dad, who died of cancer almost thirty years ago. He was a veteran of WW II, but never liked to talk about it. I learned more about his service experiences from letters he left behind, and a WWII scrap book he kept.

He was the "accidental soldier" like so many other GIs, ones who were drafted away from their families and friends. He was a most unlikely candidate for warrior. Perhaps that is why he brought his profession, photographer, with him, becoming a member of the Signal Corps. But that doesn't mean he didn't risk his life at times. He expressed not only his fears in his letters, but his hope he was fighting a war to end all wars as well. At the war's conclusion he was delayed in Germany as part of the occupying force. I vaguely remember his return.

I have a deep respect for what he did, and for all veterans who answered the call. The war that lives in my mind was the senseless one in Vietnam. From a killing field then, to a top tourist attraction now. My draft status at the time was 3-A as I was married and had a child. By the time the draft lottery was instituted in 1969, I was exempt as I was born before the 1944 birth-date cut off. But good friends of mine were called, Bruce, Ray, and Ron, friends to this day. I salute their service.

Soon after my Dad's death I wrote a tribute to him, a recollection which tried to capture his essence and our relationship. I originally called it "An Ordinary Man" as his story is not exceptional, but one of a man who lived his life as best he could, trying to do the right thing. Of course to me he was anything but "ordinary."

Recently I felt that essay, written so many years before, needed work, and I revised and retitled it to make it more accurate (the passage of time actually helped recall details). It is really the story of how, or why, I did not go into business with him, but I think it is a good depiction of him as well. So, in loving memory of my Dad, a veteran:

An Unspoken Obligation
Up Park Avenue we speed to beat the lights from lower Manhattan in the small Ford station wagon with Hagelstein Bros., Commercial Photographers since 1866, 100 Fifth Avenue, NY, NY imprinted on its panels. The Queens Midtown Tunnel awaits us.

It is a summer in the late 1950s and, once again, I'm working for my father after another high school year. In the back of the wagon I share a small space with props, flood lamps, and background curtains. The hot, midtown air, washed by exhaust fumes and the smoke from my father's perpetual burning cigarette, surround me.

My father's brother and partner, my Uncle Phil, occupies the passenger's seat. They have made this round trip, day-in and day-out since my father returned from WWII. They speak of the city, its problems, the Russians, and politics disagreeing on most matters. Meanwhile I sleepily daydream about where my friends and I will cruise that evening in one of their cars, a 57' Merc, probably Queens Blvd., winding up at Jahn's next to the RKO on Lefferts Boulevard.

The family photography business was established right after the Civil War, soon after my great-great grandfather, Carl, emigrated from Cologne, Germany with his brother, settling in New York City. Their portrait photography business at 142 Bowery flourished in the 19th century. The 20th century brought a new focus: commercial photography which necessitated moving to a larger studio, better located, at 100 Fifth Avenue on the corner of 15th Street. There the business remained until the 1980's, occupying the top floor.

My father took it for granted that I was being groomed for the business, the next generation to carry it on. Uncle Phil was a bachelor and since I was the only one with the name to preserve the tradition, it would naturally fall to me.

This was such an understood, implicit obligation, that nothing of a formal nature such as a college education was needed to foster this direction. Simply, it was my job to learn the business from the bottom up, working first as a messenger on the NY City streets, delivering glossies to clients for salesmen's samples, or for catalog display at the annual Furniture Show. As a youngster, I roamed NYC by subway and taxi with my deliveries without incident—after all, this was the innocent, placid 50's. Eventually, I graduated to photographer's assistant, adjusting lamp shades under the hot flood lamps so the seams would not show, and, later, as an assistant in the color lab, making prints, dodging negatives of a clients' tables, lamps, and sofas to minimize any overexposures.

I see my father through the lens of his working life, revealing a personality normally invisible to me. At home he was a more contemplative, private person, crushed by a troubled marriage. My mother expected more, often reminding him of his failures. But strolling down the halls of his photography business he is a transformed person, smiling, extending his hand to a customer, kidding in his usual way. "How's Geschaft?" he would say.

His office overlooks the reception area and there he, my Uncle, and his two cousins preside over a sandwich and soda delivered from a luncheonette downstairs. I sit, listen, and devour my big greasy burger. They discuss the business among themselves. Osmosis was my mentor.

In spite of the filial duty that prompted me to continue learning the photography business, I inveigled his support to go to college—with the understanding I would major in business. By then I think I knew going to school would be the first step away from the family business, a step, once taken, would not be taken back. The question was how to reveal this to him.

However, as silently was the expectation that I would take over one day, my retreat was equally furtive. We both avoided the topic as I went to college and yet continued to work there during the summers. Once I switched majors from business to the humanities, we both knew the outcome of the change, but still, no discussion. This was territory neither he nor I wanted to visit at the time.

My reasons were instinctively clear to me, in spite of the guilt I often felt. In the studio he was larger than life, the consummate photographer, but he was also provincial in his business thinking. He had bet the future on producing those prints for salesmen, discounting the impact of the developing mass media. My opinion on the matter would mean little. After all, he was my Dad and I was his kid. So I kept my silence and progressively moved away.

Why he never brought up the subject I will, now, never know, although I suspect he understood I wanted to find my own way in life. Ultimately, I married and found a job in publishing with an office, ironically, only three blocks from his studio. I still occasionally joined him for that greasy burger at his office during those first few years of my publishing career, his greeting me with a smile when I arrived, "so, how's Geschaft?"

Monday, May 30, 2016
A Short Story
I've written a number of short stories, an art that so many of my most admired writers have perfected, Raymond Carver, John Updike, John Cheever, and William Trevor. I've read most of their stories and I wish osmosis was a better teacher. This has been a more difficult challenge than I had imagined, the revision process being a particular struggle. So while I still work on several, it is bringing them to completion that confounds.

There is a thin membrane between memoir and fiction. Some writers literally adopt personal experience, while for others it is more an imagined personal experience—yet inevitably based on the author's world in some way. The stories I've written are more of the latter nature, but getting the story "right" has been a battle. Thus, I chisel away at them occasionally, never seem to be fully satisfied. I've said somewhere in this blog that I'd publish them—when "finished."

There is one story that is an exception to the above as it is more memoir, the only story I've written in the first person, and in fact it is based on one of my blog entries from a couple of years ago. Once I started to work on it, infusing it with several imagined scenes, cutting out other details, I've never gone back to compare the two and I don't want to. I know it has changed a great deal, although parts are inevitably intact.

I post it on Memorial Day though as the story inexorably leads there at the conclusion. It is about things we take for granted and their disruption, about aging and loss and remembrance. As a short story, I hope tone and feeling transcend literal details. So, I'll call this story "finished."

ROUTINE

There is a morning routine I developed in retirement. In the past, there were many morning routines: helping my wife get the kids off to school; the monitoring of the morning's commute; financial news to assimilate and preparing for meetings yet to come. Routines were established of their own accord, some by a matter of necessity, others by the natural progression of men, like me, now retired from the Profession of Routine, some seventy odd years and counting.

One of my remaining routines is during the early mornings. I am summoned by the Florida sun, and get dressed for a brisk walk. After fastening my iPhone to my belt, and donning my Yankees cap, I'm ready to go. Most days I decide en route. Perhaps "the loop" circuit past the new houses or remodels in the neighborhood, guessing real estate values, or a walk near the river, peppered with dog-walkers, joggers and other morning enthusiasts, reviewing the emerging demographic.

Some people will reciprocate my "Good Morning!" greeting while others pretend not to have heard, averting their eyes. Over the years I have noted a direct correlation between age and "good morning" reciprocity, with younger walkers more likely to just pass by as if I am invisible or, worse, dead. Their loss I imagine. What else can I think in my self-defense?

But on Sunday mornings, my walk is to my local 7-Eleven where they carry the Sunday *New York Times*. This walk is longer, taking me through our local country club golf course, which always seems alive like the inside of a terrarium. The course had been recently redesigned, with the greens, small lakes, and undulations making it seem ethereal.

I speak as if I am a golfer. I am not but most of my acquaintances are now. This makes friendships somewhat tenuous as when we get together as couples, well, the ladies have much in common, but the men talk golf and exchange golf jokes, some of the same ones they've told for years, the manner of the telling trumping repetition.

I once said to them that I played golf while in high school and college—in fact was an ambidextrous golfer as one of my father's friends gave me some old left-handed woods he no longer needed (and I am left handed) and another of his friends gave me some right handed irons—and that is how I learned. My friends listened politely, but knowing I no longer play golf their discussion resumed about their day on the course, with the good natured jousting of men who are poor golfers but have this one thing in common besides their age and infirmaries. They have their own routines and those normally do not intersect with mine.

Today while walking through the country club grounds I saw that the often discussed dismantling of the multilevel diving board adjacent to an Olympic size pool had suddenly occurred. It was there last week (and for decades before). Insurance costs forced my municipality to tear down the iconic high diving platform. There is now a space in my memory of where it once stood.

I walked past the golf carts, humming in their electric charging stalls, early morning golfers gathering over coffee, and the water sprinklers timed to come on, one-by-one, the sole task of a less complicated machine. I headed over to Route 1, and then north to the 7-Eleven. The sun was hardly breaking above the palm trees.

A routine like this has trained my eyes, and I tend to notice things out of place. As I cross the parking lot in front of the driving range, an older white Ford Explorer is usually parked there, someone out practicing early. It wasn't today. I didn't think much of it, other than maybe the driver has left town for the approaching summer. I had never seen him, only having noticed the car, as if it was simply part of the golfing landscape.

Sitting back with the Sunday *New York Times* is a routine I developed since college; I couldn't imagine a Sunday morning without it. And my walk to the 7-Eleven made it seem that the Grey Lady herself waited especially for me. It is not easy to dismiss these thoughts.

When my wife and I moved to Florida, I had arranged for the *Times* to be delivered; but service was unreliable. There were issues too with placing temporary holds while on vacation. I remember the feeling of dismay upon discovering several papers, still soggy in their plastic bags, abandoned on my driveway after one such absence. I cancelled delivery that morning. Though one can read the *New York Times* online, I prefer holding those familiar pages in my hands. So naturally I was relieved to find the most generic convenience store stocked it, in walking distance away, a commonplace 7-Eleven across the golf course.

Upon walking into the store this particular morning, I immediately saw some things askance. Sales bins had replaced the stacks of local and national newspapers. It looked like a yard sale before home owners move on. I recognized the woman behind the counter. She always greeted her regular customers, and we both normally found ourselves in small talk, such as "how are you this beautiful morning?" "Can't complain, wouldn't do me any good," she would laughingly say. Sometimes I would tease her about having bought a quick pick lottery ticket the week before—when the prize was almost a half billion dollars—the level at which I could be induced to spend a couple of bucks on an impossible gamble. "Hey, you promised this was the winning ticket. I didn't even get a booby prize!" And she'd say, "You didn't pray enough!"

No such banter this morning. There were two other employees with her, seemingly serious in their efforts of recording outgoing merchandise and taking inventory, clipboards in hand. The newspaper rack—now in the back—was depleted but thankfully there was one copy of the Sunday *Times* left.

My 7- Eleven lady behind the counter detected my consternation and said "you got the last newspaper we will ever have delivered here—the store is closing in a couple of days." I was stunned. "I've been coming here for years, every Sunday, are you relocating?" No, but fortunately she was being transferred to another 7-Eleven some ten miles away. "I haven't lost my job at least" she smiled. I smiled for her.

I wished her the best, knowing I would never see her again. We both lingered there for a moment. I felt my head make an affirmative farewell. Then, I walked out—the ring above the door announcing my departure—with the copy of the store's last *New York Times* under my arm. In all those years I never thought to ask her name.

Crossing the parking lot in front of the golf driving range, I saw that white Explorer just arriving in its familiar parking place. An elderly gent emerged. "Good morning," I said to the man whose car I had noticed for so many years. He returned the good morning. I said "you're late today. By the time I see your car, you are already on the driving range."

"Got a late start today," he almost whispered.

Up close, he was slightly taller than I, thin, and seemed in fairly good shape, figured him for maybe ten years older. He was opening the SUV's cargo door for his clubs when he asked "Where are you from originally?" (He sized me up as not being a native Floridian; perhaps the *Times* under my arm was a clue).

"New York City, you?"

"Yeah, I lived there for several years after WW II."

He said he was in shipping logistics after serving as an infantryman during the War. He didn't look old enough to be in WW

II, so I asked. "I'm 92," I was shocked, and he seemed to be used to such surprises. I told him my father was a Signal Corps photographer in Europe during the War and he replied "I was first in the European theater and then shipped to the Pacific."

"My father was afraid that'd happen to him after Germany surrendered," I confessed.

He then hesitated and finally said "I'm eligible to be buried in Arlington Cemetery."

"Such an honor," I replied "but I think you have many good years before having to think of that. You're in great shape, still teeing off every Sunday!"

He chuckled. "The real honor is still being here," waving his arm across the golf course. And, indeed, in that moment, the sun had now fully risen above the palm trees. A warm breeze started to blow across the greenery on which our shadows lay as well.

Not knowing how to exactly reply, I said "Memorial Day is tomorrow and my father will be very much on my mind, but I'd like to say I'm grateful for your service too. Just wanted you to know that."

"Thanks," he said, "it's a sad day for me, remembering those guys, they were good buddies, some who died right next to me, no further away from where you're standing. Others I simply outlived and everyone in between."

He was still gathering his clubs from the SUV but stopped and turned to me and said, almost as if he were quoting someone he knew standing nearby "War is not where you die, but where you fight to live." He paused before suddenly hoisting his bag on his shoulder and said "Anyway, right-o, I'll see you around another Sunday—?"

"Bill," I replied, "name is Bill".

"John's mine, pleasure talking with you." We shook hands. Then he walked towards the driving range. His own routine was about to begin.

No sense calling back to John to tell him this was probably my last Sunday walk through the golf course, "Yes, see you around" I said loudly, almost as if saluting him, as he marched away. I stood there for a moment, watching him go off, and then turned and left for home.

www.ingramcontent.com/pod-product-compliance
Lightning Source LLC
Chambersburg PA
CBHW022002090426

42741CB00007B/857